Changing White Attitudes toward Black Political Leadership

Despite the hopes of the civil rights movement, researchers have found that the election of African Americans to office has not greatly improved the well-being of the black community. By shifting the focus to the white community, this book finds that black representation can have a profound impact. Utilizing national public opinion surveys, data on voting patterns in large American cities, and more in-depth studies of Los Angeles and Chicago, Zoltan L. Hajnal shows that under most black mayors there is real, positive change in the white vote and in the racial attitudes of white residents. This change occurs because black incumbency provides concrete information that disproves the fears and expectations of many white residents. These findings not only highlight the importance of black representation; they also demonstrate the critical role that information can play in racial politics and point to the ability of at least some whites to change their minds about blacks and black leadership.

Zoltan L. Hajnal is an assistant professor of political science at the University of California, San Diego. He received his Ph.D. in political science from the University of Chicago. He has published articles in numerous journals, including the *American Political Science Review*, the *Journal of Politics*, *Urban Affairs Review*, and *Social Science Quarterly*. He received the American Political Science Association's award for Best Paper on Urban Politics. His research has been funded by the Russell Sage Foundation and the Andrew W. Mellon Foundation.

W9-BUC-142

Changing White Attitudes toward Black Political Leadership

ZOLTAN L. HAJNAL, 1968 –
University of California, San Diego

CAMBRIDGE
UNIVERSITY PRESS

CAMBRIDGE UNIVERSITY PRESS
Cambridge, New York, Melbourne, Madrid, Cape Town, Singapore, São Paulo

Cambridge University Press
32 Avenue of the Americas, New York, NY 10013-2473, USA

www.cambridge.org
Information on this title: www.cambridge.org/9780521857475

First published 2007

Printed in the United States of America

A catalog record for this publication is available from the British Library.

Library of Congress Cataloging in Publication Data

Hajnal, Zoltan, 1968–
Changing White attitudes toward Black political leadership / Zoltan L. Hajnal.
    p.   cm.
Includes bibliographical references and index.
ISBN 0-521-85747-3 (hardback) – ISBN 0-521-67415-8 (pbk.)
    1. African Americans – Politics and government.   2. African American leadership –
Public opinion.   3. Whites – United States – Attitudes.   4. Voting research – United
States.   5. Public opinion – United States.   6. United States – Race relations – Political
aspects.   7. African American mayors – United States – Public opinion.   8. African
American mayors – United States – Case studies.   9. Chicago (Ill.) – Politics and
government – 1951–   10. Los Angeles (Calif.) – Politics and government.   I. Title.
E185.615.H26   2006
306.2089'96073–dc22   2006013120

ISBN-13   978-0-521-85747-5 hardback
ISBN-10   0-521-85747-3 hardback

ISBN-10   978-0-521-67415-7 paperback
ISBN-10   0-521-67415-8 paperback

Contents

Acknowledgments

As with most other academic endeavors, this book has been a long time coming. It started as an off-hand comment early in graduate school and has grown through graduation, fellowships, and my time as a faculty member at the University of California, San Diego. Over all those years I have incurred countless intellectual and emotional debts. If so many people had not taken the time and energy to help me along, this project would definitely have suffered in quality and it may never have been completed. I can never begin to repay all of the debts, but I would at least like to acknowledge those who helped make this book much better than it otherwise would have been, and perhaps even more importantly those who helped keep me sane through an often arduous process.

I want to first say thanks to my friends who labored with me in graduate school. John Baughman, Greg Bovitz, Pam Cook, Nancy Crowe, Robert Eisinger, Kevin Esterling, Anna Greenberg, Karen Hoffman, Thomas Kim, Roger Larocca, and Chris Parker all offered helpful advice and, on occasion, unwelcome but very necessary criticism. The rest of the University of Chicago American Politics Workshop, where I presented much of this research, also deserve thanks. Four of my partners in crime, Paul Frymer, Jamie Druckman, Andrew Grant-Thomas, and Taeku Lee, deserve special recognition. Each provided seemingly endless support; their comments and kindness have had a profound influence not only on the end product but also on me as a person.

I owe large and lasting debts to my dissertation committee, Michael Dawson, Don Green, William J. Wilson, and Lynn Sanders. Michael read every word of every draft and although I didn't always like to hear what he had to say, this would have been a much less worthwhile project without his assistance. Don Green, who was my first true mentor and who I still hold responsible for getting me mixed up in the business of political science, has been there all along. His enthusiasm and encouragement were invaluable and his scholarly advice equally indispensable. William J. Wilson's contributions were also numerous. Above and beyond his counsel, I benefited from his help in getting an Urban Poverty Fellowship, which not only provided me with a stimulating environment in which to work but also helped to pay for dinner.

After leaving Chicago, I had the good fortune to spend time at four different institutions, Brandeis University, the Public Policy Institute of Chicago, the University of California, San Diego, and Princeton University, each of which provided a stimulating intellectual home. Along the way, I met a number of close colleagues who generously gave of their time and advice. Sidney Milkis at Brandeis was instrumental in giving me the confidence to transition from student to scholar. Debbie Reed, Paul Lewis, and Mark Baldassare at PPIC gave me the time and resources to complete my *American Political Science Review* article – an important building step in the intellectual development of this project. My colleagues at UCSD, Amy Bridges, Steve Erie, Karen Ferree, Clark Gibson, Peter Gourevitch, Gary Jacobson, David Lake, Mat McCubbins, Phil Roeder, Sam Kernell, Thad Kousser, and Sam Popkin, helped me to formulate my ideas and work through the all-too-frequent problems. Their insights and advice have shaped the book in a range of important ways. Among my UCSD colleagues, Amy Bridges stands alone. Over the years here, she has been an incredible mentor and friend.

I am also very grateful to the numerous academics who gave of their time not because they had to but simply because they cared. Charles Bullock, Ira Katznelson, Arthur Lupia, Tony Marx, and Raphael Sonenshein all read and commented on different sections of the book. Paul Sniderman's sage advice was critical. He has left a profound mark on the final product. I also owe a special debt to Liz Gerber, who over the years has not just read my work but has encouraged my efforts and offered valuable assistance on both a professional and a personal level. Other scholars associated with the Center for Advanced Behavioral Studies at Stanford, the Institute for Governmental Studies at UC-Berkeley, and the American Politics Workshop at Harvard also gave their time and provided important feedback.

I am proud to be associated with Cambridge University Press. Dennis Chong and Jim Kuklinski paved the way for me at the Press and then handed off the project to Lew Bateman, who has done an excellent job of guiding this manuscript from rough draft to more polished product. I thank all three of them for believing in this book. Anonymous reviewers at the Press similarly deserve thanks for forcing me to present clearer and more compelling evidence.

I would be remiss not to mention the money that made it all happen. I was lucky enough to get support for this project from the University of Chicago, the Mellon Foundation, the National Science Foundation (in the form of an Urban Poverty Fellowship), the Center for the Study of Democratic Politics at Princeton University, and the Hellman Fellowship at UCSD. For all this support, care, and advice, I am amazed and grateful.

Anyone who knows me knows that my family is my rock. My parents, Vivian and Zoltan, and my sister, Catherine, were always there for me on the far too many days when I was down and defeated. They picked me up, pointed me forward, and gave me all the love I needed to continue. From my family, I have learned not only to endure but how to live. I offer them my deepest, warmest thanks. They will always be front and center in my heart.

In the middle of this project, a new little girl came into my life. And already by age four, Lina has been able to offer invaluable assistance. As a true native Californian, when times were tough, she simply told me, "Don't worry daddy. Relax. Breathe in, breathe out." It seemed to work. Lina is often a distraction from work but she is a distraction that I will cherish forever.

Last and clearly not least, I offer my thanks, my friendship, and my love to my wife, Barbara Walter. Over the past years she has played every imaginable role in my life and in my career. Without her I would not have begun this project. Without her I certainly would not have finished. Her words of advice, her love, and – yes – her thoughtful criticism helped me more than I can say. For that and much, much more I dedicate this book to her.

Introduction

One of the great hopes of the civil rights movement was that African Americans, by gaining the right to vote, would be able to elect representatives who could ultimately reduce or even eradicate racial inequality. To many in the community, black elected officials were "saviors who were going to uplift the people, eradicate police brutality, house the homeless, [and] find new jobs for everyone who was struggling."[1] In the 1960s, 1970s, and 1980s, as blacks began to win office and displace thousands of white incumbents, many in the African American community were understandably jubilant. As one voter who witnessed the transition put it, "It was almost like the feeling you have when you see your first-born – a sense of accomplishment, of utter elation" (quoted in Donze 1998).

Decades later, it is clear that black representation has made a difference. Many black leaders have tried valiantly to improve the lives of their black constituents, and black representation at different levels of office has been associated with concrete, positive change for the black community. It has led directly to increases in the numbers of African Americans in many city governments (Browning, Marshall, and Tabb 1984; Eisinger 1982; Levine 1974), to greater black political participation (Tate 2003; Gay 2001; Bobo and Gilliam 1990), to modest shifts in spending policies (Brown 1996; Karnig and Welch 1980), and to the implementation of reforms to police practices (Headley 1985; Lewis 1987).[2] But none of these

---

[1] Bill Campbell, former mayor of Atlanta, made this comment regarding the expectations surrounding the first black mayors (quoted in Fulwood 1995).

[2] Not everyone agrees that black leaders have made a difference. Some scholars have argued that black incumbents have done no more for the black community than white incumbents

changes has been dramatic. According to most studies, black political representation has not lived up to expectations (Smith 1996; Singh 1998; Reed 1988; Perry 1990; G. Peterson 1994; Browning, Marshall, and Tabb 1997; Marable 1992). Despite large gains in the number of black elected officials across the country, there has been only moderate change in basic indicators of African American well-being and, even more importantly, almost no change in various measures of racial inequality.[3] Though black officials have controlled the mayoralty in seven of the ten largest cities in the country and have achieved nearly proportionate representation in the House of Representatives, figures comparing black to white poverty, unemployment, and educational attainment remain largely unchanged. In 1967, when the first big-city black mayors were elected in Cleveland and Gary, blacks were three times more likely than whites to be poor, twice as likely to be unemployed, and one-third as likely to have completed college. Today, with more than 9,000 black elected officials across the country, those figures are nearly identical (Blank 2001; Dawson 1994). Richard Arrington, mayor of Birmingham for twenty years, summed up the situation when he was asked what blacks had to show economically for his tenure in office: "Quite frankly," he said, "we don't have very much" (quoted in Edds 1987).

But only part of the story of black political representation has been told. Studies have overlooked important gains associated with black

in similar cities and districts (Mladenka 1989, 1991). Swain (1995), for example, has argued that white Democrats have done as much for African American interests as black Congress members from the same types of districts (but see Tate 2003; Whitby 1998; Herring 1990).

3 The black community experienced undeniable gains in the early and mid-twentieth century (Thernstrom and Thernstrom 1997). The black middle class, for example, grew from just 12% of the black population in 1949 to 41% today (Farley 1996). But since the late 1960s, the story has grown more complicated. Blacks have made progress in absolute terms. High school graduation rates, for example, have improved considerably, and earnings have increased slightly (Farley 1996). But relative to whites, most indicators of black well-being reveal little change in the past several decades (Blank 2001; Klinkner and Smith 1999; Thernstrom and Thernstrom 1997). Despite the passage of civil rights legislation, increased social interaction between whites and blacks, and some claims that race has been diminishing in significance in recent decades, studies reveal only minimal decreases in residential segregation (Massey and Denton 1993; Massey 2001), fairly widespread racial discrimination in hiring and the housing industry (Kirschenman and Neckerman 1991; Bertrand and Mullainathan 2004; Massey and Denton 1993), persistent racial stereotyping (Bobo and Johnson 2000; Lee 2000), and strong racial undertones to many of the political choices whites make (Mendelberg 2001; Carmines and Stimson 1989; Gilens 2001). In short, there are few signs of major gains since 1970 and plenty of evidence that race retains much of its significance in American life (Dawson 1994).

officeholding because they have focused almost exclusively on the black community while essentially ignoring the *white* community. In this book, I explore how experience with black leadership affects the attitudes, actions, and political choices of white Americans. Examining white reactions to black leadership – looking specifically at changes in the racial attitudes, voting behavior, and policy preferences of white Americans – demonstrates that black representation has meaningful and positive effects that are rarely considered in evaluations of the performance of black leaders. Although the election of African Americans to public office has not yet improved the condition of blacks to the degree many people had hoped, it has had a significant impact on white attitudes and voting behavior, and these shifts, though small, could ultimately be the catalyst for the acceptance of more significant progress toward racial equality in American society.

THE INFORMATION EFFECTS OF BLACK LEADERSHIP

Experience with black incumbents has real consequences for many members of the white community because it imparts critical *information* about black preferences that reduces whites' uncertainty and fear about blacks and black leadership; this information essentially changes the way that many white Americans think about the black community and therefore subtly alters the nature of racial politics and race relations in this country. Prior to the election of a black candidate, most white voters have little or no experience with black leadership. For this reason, many rely on racial stereotypes and past patterns in race relations to assess the likely consequences of a black candidate's victory. The result is that many whites fear that a black leader will favor the black community over the white community. They expect a black leader to redistribute income, encourage integration, and generally channel resources toward the black community. In short, they imagine that black control will have negative consequences for themselves and their neighbors. Once a black candidate is elected, however, whites gain access to better information about the policy preferences of black leaders and the effects of black leadership. They become able to judge black candidates on their records. And because the white community rarely suffers under black incumbents, those records are, in almost every case, better than white stereotypes and fears suggested they would be. When blacks have the power (or are perceived as having the power) to inflict harm on the white community and they choose not to do so, many whites are forced to reevaluate their assumptions.

The idea that white behavior in biracial electoral contests is governed by uncertainty and information is a novel one. Existing explanations of the voting behavior and attitudes of whites tend to focus on two very different mechanisms: (1) prejudice and (2) white backlash against perceived racial threat. Taking these in order, it has been argued that black representation – no matter how positive its effect on the white community – should have little or no effect on white attitudes and political behavior because white Americans are basically prejudiced and unwilling or unable to change their views of blacks (Hurwitz and Peffley 1998; Kuklinski et al. 1997; Allport 1954; Adorno et al. 1950). If prejudice is indeed behind white opposition to black empowerment, then the words and actions of black incumbents cannot affect whites' views, because these views are too stable and too deeply ingrained to be easily altered (Fazio et al. 1995; Devine 1989; Fiske 1998; Rothbart and John 1993). And even when whites experience black leadership and gather information from the experience that runs counter to stereotypes and expectations, they will simply ignore or discount evidence that challenges their prejudices (Macrae, Hewstone, and Griffith 1993; Weber and Crocker 1983; D. Hamilton, 1981).[4] The second model suggests that black leadership spurs white backlash. At least one text (Sidanius, Devereux, and Pratto 1991) argues that whites have a strong incentive to protect America's racial hierarchy and their hegemonic position within it. Indeed, past patterns in race relations indicate that when white social status is threatened by black gains, members of the white community tend to react by mobilizing to reverse those gains (Olzak 1990; Stenner 1995). If past patterns prevail, the election of blacks to office might represent just another step in an ongoing racial battle.

UNDERSTANDING THE VARIATION IN REACTIONS

Certainly, neither of these two theories applies to all white Americans across all contexts. Why do whites in some cities learn to accept a black

---

[4] The fact that stereotypes of blacks are still widespread is taken by many as evidence that "blatantly prejudiced attitudes continue to pervade the white population" (Kuklinski et al. 1997). The specific terms that whites use to describe blacks may have changed but there is ample evidence that large segments of the white community continue to see blacks as less intelligent, less hardworking, more difficult to get along with, and more violent than whites (Bobo and Johnson 2000; Lee 2000; Devine and Elliot 1995; Schuman et al. 1997).

mayor, while in other cities whites' opposition remains constant or even grows? And why within a particular city do some white residents react more positively to black leadership than do others? In addition to assessing the general nature of white reactions to black leadership and testing my information model of those reactions against the existing prejudice and white backlash models, it is an important secondary goal of this study to explain variation in whites' reactions to black leadership.

Variations in white reactions follow predictable patterns. First, white reactions are affected by the actions of specific black leaders and the information that those actions provide. A black mayor who presides over a city where housing prices plummet and crime soars is likely to provide white residents with different information, for example, than a black mayor who aids in a city's renaissance. But the actions of particular leaders are not the central factor governing white reactions, because black representation almost always proves to be less detrimental to white interests than many whites fear. What accounts for most of the variation in white responses is not variation between individual black leaders, but rather white voters' judgment of the *credibility* of the information that they receive about black officeholders: the more power that whites believe black leaders have, the more they will credit and be influenced by the information they receive from those leaders' words and deeds. Practically speaking, this means that whites' reactions to black representatives are heavily dependent on racial demographics, which influence a representative's efficacy in office. In addition to variation among leaders and across locations, it is important to consider differences between individuals, focusing particularly on partisanship and exploring the question of whether Democrats or Republicans are more likely to learn from black leaders.

WHY BLACK REPRESENTATION AND WHITE LEARNING MATTER

Understanding the relationship between black leaders and white voters is important for a number of reasons, both substantive and theoretical. It is clear from the trends in the number of black elected officials that African American representation is an important and growing phenomenon. In 1960 only 280 blacks held office across the entire United States (Jaynes and Williams 1989). Today there are over 9,000 black elected officials in America (JCPS 2003). Blacks have won the mayoralty in most of the nation's big cities, there are roughly 600 African Americans in state legislatures nationwide, and blacks now hold about 10 percent of the seats in the U.S. Congress. African Americans are still underrepresented at most levels of government, but undeniably they play a role among America's political elite.

Moreover, white voters are becoming increasingly critical to black electoral victories. Each year more blacks win office in racially mixed and predominantly white areas (Bositis 2002). Already six of the ten largest plurality white cities have had black mayors. Douglas Wilder's term as governor of Virginia marked the first time a black politician had been elected governor of an American state. Notable black congressional representatives such as Julia Carson, Robert Scott, and Barbara Lee can also be added to this expanding list of successful cross-over candidates.

It is also clear that if black representation is to continue to expand, black candidates will have to win over more white voters. Black politicians already represent most of the majority black districts and cities around the country (Handley and Grofman 1994; Handley, Grofman, and Arden 1997). In addition, court decisions in the 1990s have made it more difficult to alter electoral lines to create additional majority-minority districts. If more blacks are to be elected, they will have to win in racially mixed districts.

Black representation, furthermore, may be setting the trend for an even bigger phenomenon: Latino and Asian American representation. The Latino population is expected to double in the next ten years. By mid-century, Latinos may represent as much as one-third of the U.S. population, while Asian Americans, currently the fastest-growing population in the country, could account for almost 10 percent (Bureau of the Census 2002b). Latino and Asian American representation still lags far behind African American representation, but these demographic projections suggest that the situation may change relatively quickly. Already, recent gains in Latino and Asian American officeholding have far outstripped black advances (NALEO 2002; APALC 2003). What all of this suggests is that minority representation is likely to become an increasingly central aspect of American politics. Whether white and non-white Americans follow a path toward mutual understanding and interracial cooperation or move instead toward distrust and escalating conflict may well depend upon today's minority leaders and their interactions with white constituents.

In addition to speaking to these substantive issues, this study provides insight into a number of important theoretical questions about the nature of race and politics in America. One of the most central debates in American politics today concerns how much race shapes political choices. On one side of the debate are scholars who insist that race and racial prejudice remain the primary factor in American politics in general and in white voting preferences in particular (Reeves 1997; Bell 1992; McCrary 1990; Huckfeldt and Kohfeld 1989). According to these scholars, "racism is an integral, permanent, indestructible component of this society" (Bell 1992: 217). Epitomizing this camp, Robert Starks maintains that "race is such an overriding factor in American life that to support its elimination or diffusion as a factor in elections through deracialization is folly" (1991: 217). On the other side of the debate stand those who believe that race has lost much of its significance in the electoral arena and that white voters are now willing to support black candidates in greater numbers (Swain 1995; Thernstrom and Thernstrom 1997). As Abigail Thernstrom notes, "Whites not only say they will vote for black candidates; they do so" (Thernstrom 1995). Some scholars even suggest that race is no more an issue in biracial elections than it is in other electoral contests (Highton 2004; Citrin Green, and Sears 1990; Thernstrom 1987). A black candidate is likely to lose, they argue, for many of the same reasons that a white candidate is likely to lose.

One of the central goals of this book is to show that this debate addresses the wrong issue. The key question is not *if* race is central in the minds of white voters, it is *when* race is central in the minds of white voters. By showing that the transition from white to black leadership frequently leads to notable shifts in white attitudes and behavior, I will demonstrate that race plays a much more dynamic role in American politics than we have understood. Though race and racial prejudice remain prevalent in American society, change is possible under the right circumstances. To really understand how race "works" in the American context, we have to find out when racist voting is more likely, when color-blind politics tend to emerge, and ultimately why these differences occur.

In this study, I also make important observations regarding the role that information plays in the minds and voting decisions of the American population. For decades, scholars have argued that Americans simply do not have enough information about politics to make reasoned, rational decisions (Campbell et al. 1960; Converse 1964; Delli Carpini and Keeter 1996). It is true, for example, that less than half of all Americans know both the name and the party affiliation of their representative in Congress (Jacobson and Kernell 1981). Many cannot even distinguish between the policy platforms of the Democratic and Republican parties (Bennett 1995). What political knowledge Americans do have is usually not molded into coherent, consistent reasoning about issues and events in the electoral arena (Converse 1964).[5] From this viewpoint, it would seem unrealistic to expect experiences under a relatively small number of black representatives to inspire real change in the views or actions of the public. But recent scholarship suggests that the average American does have enough information to make reasonable decisions about the political arena (Lupia 1994; Popkin 1991; Lupia and McCubbins 1998; Lau and Redlawsk 1997). If the job of evaluating leaders only requires individuals to know basic facts about their own well-being and trends in the welfare of their communities, then they may have enough information in their daily personal lives. Moreover, there is clear evidence that voters regularly incorporate current events in the making of political decisions (Popkin 1991; Alvarez 1997; Bowler and Donovan 1994; C. Franklin and Jackson 1983; Allsop and Weisberg 1988).

In keeping with this recent trend, one of my central contentions is that politics – even local politics – can be extremely informative and consequential. Under the right circumstances – for the purposes of this study, when race is involved – Americans *will* pay attention to the political arena and will assess local politicians by evaluating conditions in their own communities. Moreover, this evaluation can have real consequences. By showing that whites tend to oppose black challengers when they are uncertain about how black leadership will affect them, but that they become measurably more willing to support black incumbents when they have experienced black leadership and know more about its effects on their well-being, I hope to confirm the critical role that information plays in the arena of racial politics.

Finally, there are obvious implications for how we view descriptive representation and the degree to which we should try to expand minority representation. If the "politics as usual" that frequently occurs when black representatives are elected has a positive impact on white Americans and leads to a change in the white vote and in the racial sentiments expressed by a sizeable part of the white electorate, then there is at least one reason to try to expand descriptive representation. And if black leaders can help black constituents – even if only to a limited extent – while at the same time subtly changing white views and votes, this alone would seem to

---

[5] As a result, many claim that political decisions are predominantly shaped by long-term forces, such as party identification, which are acquired early in life and are not easily changed (Campbell et al. 1960; Beck and Jennings 1991; Green et al. 2002; Green and Palmquist 1990).

make it imperative to create a body of elected officials that more closely resembles the public.

THE EMPIRICAL STRATEGY

The empirical goals of this book are twofold. The first goal is to offer a broad account of how white Americans react to having African Americans as their leaders. Few researchers have even thought to ask about the impact of black leadership on the white community. Fewer still have tried to answer that question. And no one has answered it in a systematic way. Studies that have touched on the relationship between black leaders and their white constituents have been largely anecdotal in nature – focusing on one leader or city – and often limited in their scope – focusing on only one aspect of white behavior. The result is a range of contradictory conclusions. We simply do not know how white residents respond to black representation.

To assess how black leadership affects the white community, I will focus on two critical measures of white political behavior. The first is the vote. After experiencing black leadership, are white Americans more or less likely to support black candidates? The second is racial attitudes. After experiencing black leadership, are white Americans likely to view blacks and black leadership more positively, more negatively, or about the same way? If black leadership can bring about real, positive change on both of these measures, it is clear that the election of African Americans to office represents an important step in American race relations.

For each of these two measures, I will assess changes in white political behavior as systematically as possible. Rather than examining a single city or a single leader, I will examine an entire universe of cases of white reactions to black representation. In particular, throughout the book I will analyze white reactions across the full range of cases of black mayoral leadership. That analysis will include an examination of every black incumbent's reelection bid in the twentieth century, a comparison of a complete set of black challenger and black incumbent electoral bids, and a test of white views across a nationally representative sample of cities. Once all of these tests have been performed, we should have a complete and fairly compelling picture of the impact of black leadership on the politics of the white community.

The other important empirical contribution of this book is to test the three different theoretical accounts of the white community. Are most whites really governed by the information model or is social dominance or racial prejudice a more important determinant of white reactions to black leadership? Fortunately, since each of these theories offers different predictions about changes in the white vote and in white attitudes, by looking systematically at how black leadership affects the vote and racial attitudes, we should be able to determine which of these three models is at play.

THE CASE OF BLACK MAYORS

I focus on the implications of black leadership at the mayoral level for four reasons. First, in order for white residents to react in any way to black leadership, they must be aware that black leadership exists. Whereas the names of school board members or lower court justices are relatively unknown to the residents of most communities, people can usually identify their mayor. In cities with black mayors, in fact, available evidence suggests that the overwhelming majority of residents can identify the mayor (Cole 1976).

Second, to test the willingness of whites to support black leadership, the office to which a black person is elected must be viewed as important and powerful. Whites may support black candidates who seek offices that whites perceive as powerless and unimportant without fear of the consequences. The mayoral office, which is considered by most people to be a powerful and influential post, represents a truer test of white willingness to support black leadership than would a test of another, less powerful position.

Third, for white residents to be able to judge black leaders, they must be able to observe the actions of a black incumbent and connect them to changes in local conditions or policies. As the executive of a city, the mayor focuses on local issues and often acts unilaterally. State and national legislators, by contrast, often concentrate on regional or national issues and must generally obtain the support of their colleagues before acting. Even though the official powers of mayors are often quite limited, evidence strongly suggests that the public views them as responsible for local conditions. A poll undertaken in Washington, DC, where the mayor's power is limited, found that a clear majority of city residents believed the mayor "can control" or "exact influence" on almost every policy issue facing the city (Coleman and Sussman 1978: A1). Because residents feel that their mayor has the power to influence policy, they are quite willing to judge black leadership in general on the basis of a black mayor's performance.

Finally, on a more practical level, black mayors make an excellent choice simply because there are so many of them. In 2001, there were 451 black mayors in the United States, 49 of whom served in cities with a population of over 50,000 (JCPS 2002). Black mayors have held office in four of the five largest American cities, and, in fact, almost 10 percent of all big-city mayors are African American (JCPS 2002). There are enough cases of black mayors in cities with different racial demographics to allow for empirical analysis; the availability of data on city-level voting patterns, local government spending, campaign rhetoric, and economic and social conditions makes the mayoralty one of the only feasible choices for statistical study.

Differences between the mayoralty and other political offices mean that the results of this study cannot necessarily be applied to other types of black leadership. In fact, I believe that white learning is likely to be more pronounced under black mayors than under most other types of black leaders. As I suggested earlier, when black people are elected to serve as state or federal legislators, they are less likely than black mayors to be viewed as being responsible for local conditions or policies; thus, experience with black legislators should do less than experience with black mayors to change white views and votes. By the same token, there may be offices that foster more pronounced learning. A black president, for example, would surely be seen as much more powerful than a black mayor and would therefore present an interesting and important test case of the information model.

AN OVERVIEW

This study proceeds as follows: the first chapter explains the three different theories of black representation – the information model, the prejudice model, and the white backlash model – in greater detail and describes the predictions they make regarding the effect of black leadership on white political behavior, including the predictions the information model makes about variation across leaders, individuals, and cities. The chapter concludes with an overview of existing research and a description of my methods.

Chapter 2 analyzes changes in the white vote under incumbent black mayors to answer three questions about black candidates: (1) Are white voters more or less likely to support black challengers than they are to support the same black candidates when they run as incumbents? (2) Does black incumbency at the mayoral level lead to changes in the nature of the white vote? In particular, does experience with black leadership teach voters to pay increasing attention to nonracial factors such as endorsements, candidate quality, and the economy? (3) Does information from one black incumbent play a role when white voters consider other black candidates? In other words, is any learning that occurs transferable from one candidate to another?

Chapter 3 looks at changes in white racial attitudes under black mayors. What is it that whites do or do not learn from their experiences with black leadership? Do they simply learn not to fear a particular black incumbent, or do their attitudes toward the black community also change? Here, I utilize responses to the American National Election Study (ANES) surveys, which have over the past half-century polled a representative sample of Americans about a range of their political views, to compare white attitudes before and after the election of a black mayor and to assess changes in white attitudes as experience with black officeholding increases.

I examine variation in white reactions to black leadership from one city to another in Chapter 4. Because I contend that the credibility of the information that black incumbency provides is critically dependent on the amount of control that blacks are able to exercise once in office, I look at changes in white voting behavior between black challenger and black incumbent elections in twenty-five cities in terms of the racial makeup of these cities to determine whether demographic differences can explain why whites seem to learn from black leadership more readily in some places than in others.

In Chapter 5, I look more closely at the course of black mayoral leadership in a single city, Los Angeles. This case study is designed to provide more direct evidence of the *process* of racial learning and to demonstrate as clearly as possible how information from black incumbency slowly translates into changes in white attitudes and behavior. Throughout the chapter, I tie the thoughts and actions of white residents in the city to the actions of Tom Bradley during his twenty-year tenure as mayor. I then, in Chapter 6, follow white attitudes and actions in Chicago, a city where black leadership has had little to no positive effect on white political behavior, in an effort to understand and explain the lack of change. I show that ongoing white opposition to Harold Washington and subsequent black candidates in Chicago is at least in part a function of the inability of the city's black leaders to prove themselves. Because Washington's tenure led to political stalemate, white residents could not learn about the real consequences of his leadership, and widespread white concerns about blacks taking control of the local political arena remain.

Chapter 7 considers the generalizability of the information model beyond the mayoral office, beyond the African American race, and beyond race itself. I begin by considering the effects of black representation at the congressional level. After pausing to look at African Americans' reactions to black mayors, I offer a brief account of the history of Asian American and Latino elected officials and discuss some of the similarities and contrasts between race, religion, and gender in terms of the potential applicability of the information model. In my conclusion I review the major findings of the book and discuss a number of the substantive and theoretical implications of this research. I outline some lessons for policy makers interested in either expanding minority representation or structuring electoral districts to minimize racial conflict.

I

Black Leadership

The Possibilities

In a nation that has long been divided by race, the election of black leaders is of great historic importance. But it is in many ways an uncertain step with unknown consequences. Black leadership raises both meaningful possibilities and real risks, especially when African Americans are elected in racially mixed areas. After winning elections, black officials must lead communities that are racially diverse and often bitterly divided. How does white America respond to African American leadership? We have anecdotal evidence from various cases, but we know very little about the general pattern and ultimate consequences of black leadership: We don't know whether minority political leadership tends to exacerbate or reduce racial tension, whether black incumbents are more or less successful than their white counterparts in subsequent elections, or under what political, economic, and racial conditions white support can be maintained or increased over time.

In this chapter, I detail three different accounts of black-white relations that offer predictions about what might happen after the onset of black leadership. I begin by presenting in full my information model of white behavior, which focuses on the information that experience with black incumbents provides white voters. I then contrast this model with two conventional theories drawn from the existing literature on race relations and American politics: the prejudice model and the white backlash model. Finally, I review existing accounts of white responses to black leadership, note some of the deficiencies of these accounts, and suggest a more systematic approach to assessing the effects of black representation on white political behavior.

THE INFORMATION MODEL

The information model suggests that black leadership should significantly change the voting behavior of whites and the way white Americans think about black candidates because the candidates' terms impart critical information that greatly reduces uncertainty and dispels white fears about blacks and black leadership. The logic is fairly straightforward. When black challengers run for office, many white residents are uncertain about the consequences of black leadership and fear that black leaders will favor the black community over the white community, thereby reversing the racial status quo. To prevent this from happening, large segments of the white community are apt to mobilize to prevent a black electoral victory. But if a black challenger is able to overcome white opposition and win office, most white fears are not borne out. Black leadership may lead to marginal changes to a few aspects of black well-being, but for the vast majority of the white community, the world under black leaders is strikingly similar to the world under white leaders (Smith 1996; Singh 1998; Mladenka 1989, 1991; Eisinger 1982; Tate 2003; Browning, Marshall, and Tabb 1997; Marable 1992). Once black officeholders have the opportunity to prove that black leadership generally does not harm white interests, uncertainty should fade, whites' views of blacks and black leadership should improve, and more whites should be willing to consider voting for black candidates.[1] Black leadership therefore serves an important although difficult to observe informational role.

White Uncertainty and Fear in Black Challenger Elections

To understand the important informational role black leadership plays for the white community, one must first understand why white Americans fear black leadership in the first place. When blacks run for offices they have never held, most whites do not know what to expect. Normally, voters have less information about a challenger than they do about an

---

[1] My information model is akin in some ways to the interracial contact hypothesis developed by Allport (1954) and confirmed by others (Jackman and Crane 1986; Sigelman and Welch 1993). The interracial contact theory maintains that social contact or friendship with minorities of the same socioeconomic status should have a positive effect because it places individuals from two groups in a cooperative setting where their similarities become evident. In this way, social contact and friendship differ fundamentally from most interracial interactions, which are often competitive in nature. I believe that the act of experiencing black leadership may represent a different type of interracial contact that also generally leads to a positive learning experience.

incumbent. When that challenger is black, information is even sparser: most whites have not lived under a black mayor, a black representative, a black senator, or a black president. They simply do not know what the consequences of black leadership are likely to be.[2] Whites express concern about racial integration, school busing, and the flight of white businesses, to name just a few of their fears. A truck driver in Chicago described his concern about a black mayoral victory in this way: "I don't know how to say this but I am afraid [Harold Washington] is going to exert all of his powers for the black community and the white community is going to get nothing. My fear is that he is going to try to push racial integration, which is fine as long as I don't lose money on my house . . . because I just can't take the loss" (quoted in Coleman 1983a).[3]

Having little or no personal experience with black leadership, many white voters rely on heuristics, or shortcuts, to try to gauge how black leaders are likely to behave once elected (Conover and Feldman 1989; Rahn 1993; McDermott 1997). When the candidates under consideration are black, the chosen heuristic is usually race (Reeves 1997; Terkildsen 1993; Williams 1990). Given the fraught history of race in this country, persistent economic differences between white and black America, ongoing racial conflict in many cities and states, and sharp disagreement between whites and blacks over government policy, white voters have some logical reasons to assume that black leaders will try to serve black interests, however wrong that assumption usually turns out to be (Kinder and Sanders 1996; Schuman et al. 1997).

Black challengers can and usually do try to counter the uncertainty surrounding their candidacies by running "deracialized" or pro-white campaigns, but white voters tend to ignore these candidates' campaign statements, which they perceive as having little credibility (Lupia and McCubbins 1998). Moreover, black candidates' efforts to deracialize their campaigns are often overcome by their white opponents, who attempt to garner white support by playing on white fears. The media also sometimes heighten uncertainty by continuously noting the racial nature of black-white contests and reminding voters in certain contests that a black victory would put an African American in control of a particular office

---

[2] Underlying this account is the belief that uncertainty, rather than ambivalence, is at the heart of white views toward black challengers (Alvarez and Brehm 2002).

[3] As Bartels (1986) has shown, uncertainty in and of itself is likely to hurt a candidate's chances of winning an election, so the extraordinary uncertainty surrounding black challengers puts them at a severe disadvantage with white voters.

for the first time (Mendelberg 2001; Reeves 1997; Graber 1984). In the end, the limited information that whites generally have, the inflammatory campaigns that white opponents frequently run, and the racial heuristics that whites rely on all tend to fuel negative projections about the impact of a black victory. Heightened uncertainty in black challenger elections leads most whites to believe they are facing an anti-white candidate and to vote to prevent a black takeover.[4]

Why Does Black Incumbency Make a Difference?

Incumbency gives any officeholder a critical advantage (King and Gelman 1991). Often, we think of that advantage in terms of an incumbent's access to resources or endorsements, but incumbency also plays a vital informational role. As Popkin has noted, "The incumbent is, to a certain extent, a known commodity. In contrast, a challenger is often a great unknown" (Popkin 1995: 33). As residents become more and more familiar with an incumbent and his or her actions, their uncertainty and fear about what he or she might do slowly fades away. Because uncertainty surrounding black candidacy is usually much greater and misperceptions about the consequences of black leadership are more widespread, this process is all the more important for black representatives.

The key is that whites believe the information they get from their experiences with black leadership is *credible*. It is not simply cheap talk (Lupia and McCubins 1998, Alvarez 1997). Experiments in social psychology have increasingly found that one of the few times whites really change their attitudes about blacks is when they know that blacks are free to choose their actions. Wilder, Simon, and Faith (1996), for example, maintain that whites' stereotypes of blacks change only when whites witness African Americans who act anti-stereotypically *and* when they view that behavior as internally caused. In short, only when blacks can wield authority are their actions likely to be seen by whites as truly informative. Thus, black political leadership is especially important in the minds of white residents because it marks one of the first times that blacks have authority

---

4 This pattern of white mobilization in the face of a new challenge from blacks has been demonstrated in a range of political interactions between blacks and whites. Research has shown that as black voter registration increases, whites also increase their registration rates (Alt 1994; Loewen 1990). Racial bloc voting, already prevalent throughout the country, increases in areas and districts where blacks become active voters (Mayer 1996; Murray and Vedlitz 1978).

to enact policies or make changes that could harm the white community. Once black representatives have had a chance to govern, and thus an opportunity to assist the black community at the expense of the white community, whites obtain important information about the interests and preferences of black representatives. If black officeholders are perceived to have *voluntarily* pursued an agenda that helped both the black and white communities, then whites who feared a black takeover may reevaluate their opinions of black leadership: when white residents do not lose their jobs, when blacks do not move into white neighborhoods in large numbers, and when crime does not proliferate under a black mayor, white voters learn that they have less to fear from black leadership than they originally thought.[5] If they choose to, these voters can begin to base their assessments of black leadership on black incumbents' track records rather than on stereotypes, exaggerated fears, or the incendiary predictions of white candidates, leading to a more limited focus on racial considerations in subsequent biracial elections.

If this information model is valid, we should see a distinct pattern in elections in which black and white candidates oppose each other. In black challenger elections, because most whites' decisions about whether to support the black candidate will be based on racial fear, few should choose to support the black candidate. In black incumbent elections, on the other hand, racial fears should play a diminished role, and a greater number of white voters should cast ballots based on the track record of the incumbent and the specifics of the campaign. As more blacks are elected to leadership positions over the years, uncertainty regarding black leadership should decline in American society as a whole, and whites should become increasingly inclined to consider supporting black challengers.

An important assumption behind this model is that whites have information about black leadership. This may be a difficult assumption for some to accept. As I mentioned in the introduction, existing studies suggest that the average American knows very little about politics (Berelson, Lazarsfeld, and McPhee 1954; Bennett 1995; Campbell et al. 1960;

---

[5] Survey experiments have shown that when given information about blacks that clearly contradicts stereotypes, whites' political views do change (Peffley, Hurwitz, and Sniderman 1997). Pettigrew (1976) and Eisinger (1980) were among the first to notice the impact of black incumbency on white fears. More recently, Swain has argued that information may be a key variable for black candidates: "It is instructive that the black candidates who have been most successful in winning white support typically have provided the voters with plenty of information about themselves" (1995: 209).

Converse 1964; Delli Carpini and Keeter 1996).[6] There is ample evidence, however, that information levels vary across contexts. Numerous studies show that the public is especially well informed about the select issues that they care about (Hutchings 2003; Iyengar 1990). Thus, if the election of a black candidate to office is something that many white Americans perceive as an especially important or especially threatening event, these individuals are likely to have or to acquire information on the subject. It is clear, furthermore, that many white Americans *do* care who their mayor is. As Thomas Pettigrew (1976) has noted, "Running for captain of the ship" is the ultimate test of how averse whites are to black control. Even in cities with weak mayors, the mayor is seen as the symbolic leader of the city and the main person responsible for local conditions (Coleman and Sussman 1978). If the city falls apart, the mayor is likely to be the first one blamed (Holli and Green 1989; Stokes 1993). And as we will see, the typical white-black contest sparks extraordinary attention from the electorate. For white Americans who care about race, then, the election of a black mayor is an important step worth paying attention to.

Moreover, white voters do not need a lot of information to assess black leadership.[7] They need only know two things: 1) that an African American is in office, and 2) that their own well-being or the well-being of friends has not been negatively affected.[8] More sophisticated voters may learn specifics about the policies and actions of black leaders and acquire data on the economic and social well-being of the black and white communities at different points in time, but such detailed information is far from necessary for an individual white resident to update his or her

---

[6] Page and Shapiro remark that "it is undeniable that most Americans are, at best, fuzzy about the details of government structure and policy" (1992: 13). The incoherence of individual public opinion may, however, be overstated by these studies. Other accounts have suggested that much of the instability of individual opinion is due to measurement error (Achen 1975) and real ambivalence about issues (Hochschild 1981; Alvarez and Brehm 2002).

[7] An emerging trend in the recent literature on information is to argue that individuals do not need a lot of information to make reasonable choices. Individuals can use a variety of "cognitive heuristics" or shortcuts to simplify the political environment and help make rational decisions (Tversky and Kahneman 1974; Simon 1945; Lupia 1994; Popkin 1991; Iyengar 1990). Some have even found that because political choices are often simple, those with limited cognitive ability tend to make decisions in a very similar fashion to those with the highest levels of cognitive ability (Rahn et al. 1990).

[8] Such information is not usually difficult to obtain: as I have mentioned, media coverage of white-black political transitions is usually extensive and often highlights the significance of new black leadership (Graber 1984).

view of black leadership. In other words, the information hurdles to white learning are not high.

Fortunately, for the information model, the available evidence suggests that most white residents do have both critical pieces of information. First, white residents are very likely to know about the existence of black leadership. Surveys indicate that most residents generally know who their mayor is and that, when the mayor is black, almost all residents are aware of the race of the mayor. Cole (1976), in particular, in a study of twenty-five cities in New Jersey found that roughly 80 percent of city residents could identify their mayor. Even more importantly, having a black mayor increased knowledge and interest. In cities with black mayors, roughly 90 percent of respondents could identify the mayor. Other polls in other states and cities have partially corroborated these results.[9] Second, there is evidence to suggest that most white Americans do get enough information to evaluate black leadership. As we will see in the two case studies, and at various points throughout the book, when asked, the vast majority of white residents are willing to evaluate local economic conditions and the performance of their local (black) leaders. Moreover, these evaluations have a substantial impact on voting preferences in subsequent elections.[10] This is evident both in the case studies presented later in this book and in several recent studies of mayoral approval, which show a close link between evaluations of a range of specific city services and mayoral approval under black and white mayors (Stein, Ulbig, and Post 2005; Howell and Perry 2004; Howell and McLean 2001). In short, most white residents of cities with black mayors seem to have enough

---

[9] A May 2000 Kaiser poll found, for example, that, nationwide, 58 of every 100 respondents knew their mayor. When that mayor was a big city black mayor, knowledge levels seemed to be even higher. A May 1992 Gallup poll indicated that 92% of respondents nationwide had heard of and had an opinion on Tom Bradley. The figure for David Dinkins was 72%. The same survey indicated that even Richard Arrington was known by some 46% of the national population. Other surveys likewise demonstrate that mayors tend to be more well known than Congressmen or state representatives (Lewis, Taylor, and Kleppner 1997).

[10] We also know that in other contexts, e.g., national politics, there is ample research indicating that individual Americans can accurately gauge trends in economic circumstances. As Conover and her colleagues note, "the public is remarkably accurate in their assessments" of national economic trends (Conover, Feldman, and Knight 1986: 574). Moreover, data from a variety of elections suggest that individual voters can and do use these assessments to help determine their vote choice (Nadeau and Lewis-Beck 2001; Kiewiet 1983). Incumbents who preside over expanding economies are likely to garner more votes than incumbents whose tenure coincides with dips in real income or increases in unemployment (Erikson 1989; Tufte 1978).

information to at least consider changing their views of blacks and black leadership.[11]

ENDURING RACIAL STEREOTYPES

Believing that white residents will respond rationally to new information and will be open to change on matters of race may very well be naïve; the availability of credible, positive information about black leadership does not guarantee that whites will assimilate it and change their views.[12] Traditional accounts, in fact, seldom suggest that the white population is receptive to change where race is concerned (Key 1949; Allport 1954; Tajfel 1981; Dovidio and Gaertner 1986; Kinder 1986; Jackman 1977). Instead, scholars are more apt to argue that because the bulk of the white community is guided by racial animosity and racial prejudice, there is little reason to suspect that white attitudes or behavior will change in response to black leadership (Allport 1954; Hurwitz and Peffley 1998). Prejudice, "an emotional, rigid attitude" that is "irrationally based," is likely to be too deeply embedded to be easily discarded (Pettigrew 1972; Fazio et al. 1995; Rothbart and John 1993). As Allport notes, "A prejudice, unlike a simple misconception, is actively resistant to all evidence that would unseat it" (1954: 9). Even if the words and actions of black incumbents do not fit whites' racial stereotypes, a prejudice model predicts that whites will use an array of tactics to try to maintain those stereotypes and create cognitive consistency (D. Hamilton 1981). They will ignore events that do not square with their views of blacks and discount contradictory evidence as an exception to the rule (Kunda and Oleson 1997;

---

[11] It is worth making one last comment about information levels: much of the recent literature on political information notes that aggregate opinion is much more rational and coherent than individual opinion. By aggregating preferences, we can often cancel out measurement error and individual mistakes to obtain views that are more responsive to real-world events (Page and Shapiro 1992; Erickson and Wright 1989; Bowler and Donovan 1998; but see Althaus 2003; Bartels 1996). As Hutchings notes, "Collective opinion is often remarkably informed and influential" (2003: 6). Thus, when we focus on the aggregate white vote or average white views, we stand a good chance of seeing opinion change that is directly related to changes in local conditions.

[12] Of course, a critical assumption behind this information model is that white residents use this new information and change their minds as a result of learning that black leadership does not harm the white community. Sniderman and Piazza (1993) have been able to demonstrate marked changes of opinion on matters of race when respondents are exposed to new information and arguments, but ultimately the only way to test the assumption that information leads to white learning is to look for changes in whites' views and votes before, during, and after the election of a black leader.

Rothbart and John 1993; Macrae, Hewstone, and Griffith 1993; Weber and Crocker 1983).

But is this a realistic picture of white America today? Race relations have been fundamentally transformed in the last century (Klinkner and Smith 1999; Schuman et al. 1997; Thernstrom and Thernstrom 1997). Expressions of biological racism have declined precipitously. As Kinder and Sanders comment, "Remarks, once thoroughly representative of a particular time and place, are unimaginable today" (1996: 92). White Americans offer almost unanimous support for the principle of racial equality (Schuman et al. 1997). And there are those who believe that whites are no longer fundamentally driven by racial animosity (Sniderman and Carmines 1997; Thernstrom and Thernstrom 1997). Still, there is ample evidence that racial stereotypes and racial prejudice continue to play a central role in American politics. Surveys indicate that much of the white community stereotypes blacks and believes that blacks as a group are not as intelligent, not as hard working, more violent, and more disagreeable than whites (Bobo and Johnson 2000; Lee 2000). Longitudinal studies of stereotypes, in fact, find that whites' views of blacks have changed little in recent decades (Devine and Elliot 1995; McConahay, Hardee, and Batts 1981; Schuman et al. 1997). Moreover, a range of research indicates that these racial considerations play a critical role in white political decision making. Racial considerations influence many of the policy choices whites make (Gilens 2001), strongly shape white partisanship and white voting patterns (Mendelberg 2001; Carmines and Stimson 1989; Peffley, Hurwitz, and Sniderman 1997; Edsall and Edsall 1991), and, most importantly for the purposes of this study, affect white willingness to support black candidates (Terkildsen 1993; Reeves 1997; Colleau et al. 1990). In one study, white respondents who knew little about candidates besides their race rated black candidates as worse than white candidates on 19 out of 20 leadership and personality characteristics, viewing black candidates as less trustworthy, less able to "get things done," and less intelligent (Williams 1990). And in many real-world contests, such stereotypes clearly prevent whites from voting for black candidates (Kinder and Sears 1981; Pettigrew 1972; but see Citrin, Green, and Sears 1990; Highton 2004). As one scholar put it, "Black political aspirants cannot compete equally or effectively in electoral jurisdictions comprised overwhelmingly of white voters because of the continued vigor of racial prejudice and discrimination" (Reeves 1997: 9).

Thus, the prejudice model predicts that no matter how well the white community does under black leadership, black incumbency will ultimately have no effect on whites' attitudes toward blacks or on whites' behavior toward black incumbents. Because racial prejudice is widespread, this model argues, there is little reason to believe that black officeholders can change the way white Americans think about race or the way they vote in black incumbent elections. In the end, no matter what black leaders do or do not do in office, few whites are likely to be significantly affected by their experiences with black leadership.

WHITE BACKLASH

Another view in the literature on racial politics proposes that white actions and attitudes, rather than stemming primarily from prejudice and racial animus, instead reflect concerns about racial hierarchies or social status (Sidanius, Devereux, and Pratto 1991). According to this view, whites may dislike blacks and hold a range of stereotypes about them, but what they care most about is maintaining their hegemonic position in society. As Sidanius and his co-authors note in their outline of social dominance theory, there is "a very general and basic human desire to perceive one's group as superior to and possessing greater social status than the generalized other" (Sidanius, Pena, and Sawyer 2001: 380). To the extent that this is true, having African Americans in positions of leadership poses a real threat to whites. When blacks attain positions of power over the white community, the pre-existing racial order is turned upside down, regardless of what black leaders do in office. Since the stability of the racial order is critical to the white community, there is every reason to believe that whites will respond to black electoral victory with counter-mobilization. As Piven and Cloward predicted in the late 1960s before the election of the nation's first big-city black mayors, "Negro control can only deepen racial cleavages in the urban area" (1977: 17).

The backlash model of behavior is supported by the historical record. Most infamously, Southern whites responded to the significant expansion of black political representation during Reconstruction with massive resistance, instituting a program of unprecedented violence, poll taxes, new residency and registration requirements, and at-large elections (Parker 1990; Foner 1984; Holt 1979). In Louisiana, for example, in less than one year, Democrats killed over one thousand people in their effort to regain control of the political process (Kousser 1974). Over a thirty-year time span, white Southerners virtually wiped out all of the gains made by black voters: in 1872, there were 324 blacks elected to state legislatures and Congress in the former Confederate states, but by 1900 only

5 black officials were in power (Kousser 1992). More recently, the actions of many whites during the civil rights movement reaffirmed the backlash hypothesis, as white violence spiked in response to the passage of various civil rights initiatives and numerous other encroachments on white privilege (Stenner 1995). Olzak (1990, 1992) found that in subsequent years, white racial violence was particularly pronounced during periods of uncertainty or instability in race relations. Specifically, rates of racial violence rose in response to black migration to formerly white-dominated urban areas, black entry into formerly white professions, and political challenges to white supremacy in the South. Green and his colleagues (Green, Strolovitch, and Wong 1998) have demonstrated that racial migration was a key determinant of hate crimes against blacks in the late twentieth century. As Klinkner and Smith (1999) have astutely noted, moreover, progress toward racial equality has been uneven. Episodes of progress and black gains have almost inevitably been followed by retrenchment. The historical record is clear: at many points in American history, white Americans have not welcomed blacks' gains in the political arena. If past patterns of white behavior in the face of black empowerment are any indication of how whites will respond to a modern-day transition from white to black political leadership, we should expect black electoral victories to be followed by heated white backlash.

VARIATION ACROSS CONTEXTS, INDIVIDUALS, AND LEADERS

Although these three theories are implicitly set up in opposition to one another, no single model can explain the outcome of every biracial election in American politics or the thinking of every white voter in those elections. The intention of this study is merely to see which theory best accounts for underlying trends or changes on the margin.

In addition, given that white responses to black leadership do vary from one case to another, a second important aim of this study is to understand why white responses differ across leaders, contexts, and individuals. Variations in the style and substance of black leadership, different local demographic contexts, and differences in individual characteristics may all affect how whites respond to their experiences under black leaders.

I use the logic of the information model to make predictions about where we should see the most pronounced and positive changes in white attitudes and behavior and where we should find ongoing white resistance to black empowerment. It suggests that variation in white reactions to black leadership should be directly related to variation in the level and type of information that whites receive from black leaders. In particular, three factors should shape the information environment and ultimately determine how large segments of the white community react to black leadership: the impact of particular black leaders, individual attitudes, and demographic context.

Learning Across Leaders

Since the information model argues that experience with black incumbency changes white views by demonstrating to whites that black leadership does not appreciably hurt white interests, white reactions should be dependent, at least in part, on the words and actions of black leaders and the ongoing well-being of the local white community. In particular, efforts on behalf of the black incumbent to redistribute substantial resources from the white community to the black community may increase white fears about the likely long-term consequences of black leadership. Similarly, regardless of the stated intentions and policy actions of black leaders, economic downturns that affect whites should eliminate gains in white support. Cities or districts where housing prices plummet or crime rates soar – two primary white fears – should see little or no change in white willingness to support black candidates.

At the same time, as I have mentioned, the hurdle for black leadership is not high: black leaders need only prove to be better than the exaggerated fears of many white residents. Coleman Young, for example, was arguably one of the most radical black mayors of his generation. He vigorously pursued affirmative action and often put the black community first, but by the end of his tenure in Detroit, only a tiny fraction of white residents had lost their jobs or their homes because of his actions. Because his policies were less radical than many whites expected, even his tenure seemed to allay white fears (Eisinger 1980).[13] In fact, even if black mayors wanted to radically redistribute resources toward the black community, the reality is that in most cases they probably could not. Even in cities where they have a great deal of power, mayors generally cannot unilaterally redistribute wealth or reform the macroeconomy. State and federal constraints, competition from other cities, and rival politicians all serve as

---

[13] For many white Detroit residents, the defining moment of Coleman Young's tenure was probably his efforts to prevent a race riot by intervening with black protesters in 1975 rather than his actions to enact liberal policies on affirmative action or police reform.

more or less binding constraints on local political leaders (Eisinger 1983; Peterson 1981). It seems clear, then, that a black incumbent can serve the black community in important ways while still allaying white fears. In the majority of cases, there should be at least some reason for many whites who live under a black mayor to learn that their fears about black leadership are not warranted.[14]

In the end, while most cases of black leadership should lead to greater acceptance by whites, the extent of that change in any given case will be contingent both on local conditions and on black leaders themselves. As such, it will be important to consider local policy initiatives, campaign rhetoric, and changes in the social or economic well-being of the white community when assessing white reactions to black leadership.

Learning Across Individuals

The political views and biases of individual white people also factor into the process of white learning. The same information can be interpreted in different ways by different individuals. In this study, I examine partisanship as a mitigating factor on individuals' views. White Democrats often largely agree with the political views of liberal black challengers, and thus they are the voters whose views and votes are most likely to be transformed by information garnered from black leadership. With little reason other than racial fears to oppose liberal black challengers, white Democrat voters may be especially sensitive to information that reduces those fears. Conservative white Republicans, by contrast, may have multiple reasons, in addition to race, for opposing liberal black candidates. Also, given what many argue is a clear link between conservatism and anti-black attitudes (Kinder and Sanders 1996; Kinder and Sears 1981), we might predict that white Republicans will be more resistant to the information that black representation provides.

Individual characteristics other than partisanship may also influence whites' reactions to black incumbents. Those who know more about the policies and actions of black leaders and their effects on local conditions might more readily learn from and accept black leadership. Individuals who are educated and well informed, however, are also less likely to hold

[14] At the same time, there are likely to be some exceptional cases in which the information provided by a black incumbent confirms white fears. Marion Barry's tenure in Washington, DC, for example, probably did little to improve whites' views of black leadership.

exaggerated expectations about black leadership in the first place. Thus, it is not clear whether their behavior will change more or less than the behavior of those who are relatively uninformed. One could also argue that learning under black incumbents should be related to an individual's initial level of racial prejudice – that the least prejudiced whites will respond most openly to new information about blacks. But again, because the least prejudiced individuals are among those least likely to have opposed black leadership initially, it is not clear whether we should really expect more change among this group, and, in practice, it is extremely difficult to assess change in either group. It is almost impossible to evaluate change among the least prejudiced without panel data, because without it we do not know if those individuals who are least prejudiced before the election of a black leader are the same individuals who are least prejudiced afterward. Likewise, given that surveys rarely include questions about respondents' knowledge of local politics, we cannot know who is more informed about local events under black leaders.[15]

Learning Across Cities

According to the information model, in order for whites to change their minds about blacks and black leadership, they need credible information. They must be able to observe the power of a black leader and connect that power to local conditions. In other words, whites must believe that blacks have some measure of control over local events. If, for example, whites are unsure whether the continued well-being of the white community is due to the newly elected black mayor or to an obstructionist white city council, they gain little information from the tenure of their mayor, and their views and votes are unlikely to change.

The degree of control exercised by a black incumbent should vary systematically with the racial demographics of the city in which that incumbent holds office. I will explain how black control and hence informational effects should vary predictably across three types of cities: minority white cities, majority white cities, and racially balanced cities.

---

[15] One could substitute educational attainment or knowledge of national politics as proxy for information about local racial politics, but it is not clear how closely either measure is associated with local knowledge. I did attempt to see if changes in attitudes were more pronounced among whites with more education or higher levels of political knowledge. The analysis, which was similar in form to the analysis of partisan differences that is presented in Chapter 4, revealed no clear or consistent patterns.

The most credible information regarding the interest and intentions of black leaders is likely to be found in white minority cities, such as Oakland and Newark, and thus it is in such cities that we should find the greatest amount of change in white attitudes and voting behavior. In white minority cities, the perceived threat from black leaders should be extremely high because whites are outnumbered and a black mayoral victory is likely to signal a real transfer of political power. If elected, a black mayor would likely have the support of a large black constituency as well as the support of other black elected officials. Blacks might not have control of the city's economic and business interests, but they would very likely have some control over most of the city's major political offices (Grofman and Davidson 1994). If a black leader wanted to pursue radical changes in policy, that leader would likely have the means to do so and white voters would know this. The possibility of such radical change and the fear that this evokes should convince most whites to vote against any black challenger. After a black challenger wins the mayoralty, the black community seemingly gains the power to advance its agenda. Although this initially increases many whites' fears of radical social and economic change, it also allows black leaders to provide clear evidence of their policy preferences and true intentions. When blacks enact agendas that do not hurt whites, whites' fears should abate. Thus, it is in white minority cities more than anywhere else that white voters can draw lessons from black leadership.

In contrast, black leadership in majority white cities, such as Minneapolis and Seattle, should provide less information about the underlying preferences of black leaders, because black officeholders in these cities have little opportunity to take over the policy-making process, and whites are aware of that fact. The prospect of a black mayor's election should spark little fear in majority white cities, because whether or not the black challenger wins the mayoralty, whites will continue to dominate the political landscape, and any successful politician will have to cater to white interests. Since the threat most whites perceive from such a candidate is low, many liberal whites should ignore race and vote for the black challenger based on his or her nonracial qualifications. This seems like good news for the black community, but because whites control the local political arena even after a black mayor enters office, the information white voters receive about the black leader's true preferences is clouded. They cannot know whether the actions of the black incumbent are designed to serve black interests or simply to placate the larger white community. The absence of any real change in white well-being under a black mayor may convince some white residents that they have little to fear from this black leader, but other white voters will dismiss the mayor's record on the ground that whites remained largely in control of the city. Such skeptical white voters will continue to fear the onset of "real" black political control and to oppose black candidates, while the white voters who supported the black challenger in the first place will continue to support black leaders. In majority white cities, then, the information model predicts that changes in white beliefs and behavior will be moderate.

Racially balanced cities, such as Chicago and New York, represent a third distinct racial environment. What sets racially balanced cities apart from other cities is their proximity to a racial tipping point. In cities where blacks have about half of all registered voters, a significant number of important political offices, and other resources, the election of a black mayor may be all it takes for the black community to gain political control.[16] This has important implications for the information whites receive from black leadership, the level of white uncertainty regarding future elections, and consequently the behavior of white elites. First, proximity to a racial tipping point should spark intensified opposition from white elites, who believe that losing control of local politics will mean losing access to their jobs and livelihoods. Thus, in racially balanced cities, black mayors should have a particularly difficult time getting their agendas enacted due to resistance from the officeholding white elite. Each action by a black mayor is likely to be followed by a counter action by members of the white elite. As a result, few of the policies advocated by a black mayor are likely to be enacted. Since black mayors are blocked from achieving their goals, white voters receive little new information from these mayors' tenure in office, and learning is limited. Proximity to the racial tipping point also leads to considerable uncertainty among white residents about the future course of local politics. If blacks can gain control of the local political arena at any point, every election could determine whether a black-led coalition or a white-led coalition will control the local political arena. With limited learning from the first term of a black mayor and with blacks that much closer to actually taking over, whites who originally feared black leadership should be even more

---

[16] Black city council representation is closely correlated with the percentage of blacks in a city. In the racially balanced cities examined in this book, blacks held, on average, a third of the council seats at the time of the transition to a black mayoralty. This means that with some support from white liberals (or in some cases Latinos and Asian Americans), the black-led coalition probably controlled close to half of the city's major political offices.

pronounced in their opposition and white voters should continue to vote against the black incumbent in large numbers. In these racially balanced cities, white opposition should not decline and elections should continue to be racially charged and competitive affairs. In sum, then, the information model forecasts that the most pronounced and positive change in white attitudes and votes should occur in minority white cities, with more moderate positive change in majority white cities and little positive change – or even negative change – in racially balanced cities.

EXISTING RESEARCH

Unfortunately, at this point we know very little about white reactions to minority representation across the United States. The evidence to date is sparse, anecdotal, and often inconsistent. One can find cases to support each of the three different theoretical claims described here.

The earliest reports on black mayors and perhaps the bulk of reports on all black leaders point to the positive effects of black leadership on white residents and fit closely with an information model of white behavior. In one of the first assessments of white reactions to black incumbents, Peter Eisinger found, for example, that white elites in Atlanta and Detroit "responded initially to the prospect of transition with fear, but living under black government brought gradual and widespread acceptance" (1980: 75). Another study considered white voting in two mayoral elections each in eight cities and found that white support for black candidates jumped markedly after blacks became incumbents (Watson 1984). In perhaps the starkest case, in Los Angeles, Tom Bradley, began his tenure with 62 percent of whites opposing his candidacy amidst widespread concerns that the black mayor would hurt the white community. He ended his career twenty years later, after winning reelection five times – each time with the majority of LA's white voters offering him their support (Sonenshein 1993). A number of other accounts of a single black incumbent or of voting patterns in a series of local elections in one city have also concluded that incumbency increases white crossover voting for black candidates (Vanderleeuw 1991; Stein and Kohfeld 1991; Bullock and Campbell 1984; Pettigrew 1976; J. Franklin 1989; Persons 1993). Surveying these findings, Colburn recently claimed that "the more often blacks served in prominent political positions and as mayors, the more acceptable they were to whites" (Colburn and Adler 2003: 40). This positive turnaround in the white vote across these cases seems to offer support for an information model of white political behavior.

There are, however, important exceptions to this pattern of growing white support for black incumbents. Reports from the late 1980s and early 1990s tended to be much less sanguine about white acceptance of black leadership. Accounts of politics in several cities seemed to affirm a white backlash model more than an information model (Rivlin 1992; Abney and Hutcheson 1981; Grimshaw 1992; Pinderhughes 1994). In Chicago, for example, Harold Washington's election as the first black mayor of the city seemed to lead to more rather than less racial conflict (Rivlin 1992). The *Wall Street Journal* noted that Chicago had been transformed during Washington's tenure from "the city that works" to "Beirut on the lake." Public opinion data in Atlanta similarly suggest that the election of a black mayor led to increased rather than decreased distrust among whites (Abney and Hutcheson 1981). When, amid severe racial tensions, black incumbents lost a series of reelection bids in the nation's largest cities, many thought "the end of the rainbow" had occurred (Sleeper 1993). Observers saw these incumbent defeats as a sign that whites ultimately would not accept black leadership (Rivlin 1992; Holli and Green 1989; Browning, Marshall, and Tabb 1997).

Still other studies, particularly those that focus on congressional elections, appear to demonstrate little or no reaction to black incumbents (Bullock and Dunn 1999; Gilliam 1996; Bobo and Gilliam 1990; Gay 1999; Parent and Shrum 1986, Voss and Lublin 2001). Studies that have followed a number of black congressional candidates as they move from competing as challengers to running as incumbents have found that their white support has remained relatively stable (Bullock and Dunn 1999; Gay 1999). The same type of nonreaction has been repeated in several cities, for example, New Orleans, where the presence of a black mayor appears to have had little impact on either race relations or white voting patterns (Gilliam 1996; Bobo and Gilliam 1990; Parent and Shrum 1986). This white nonresponse offers at least some support for a racial prejudice view of white Americans. Thus, while it looks like white Americans are usually responding positively to black leadership, the evidence is somewhat inconsistent.

The main problem is that most of this evidence is anecdotal. Studies have tended to focus on a particular individual or city and to generalize from these single cases. We have few quantitative estimates of black incumbent success rates across a range of cases. As that is the case, it is difficult to make claims about the "average" white reaction to experience with black leadership. Another real problem is that most existing studies have failed to distinguish between black challengers and black incumbents. Since all black candidates are simply lumped together, there is no way to tell whether black incumbents do better than similar black challengers. As a result, we really do not know whether race declines in importance after blacks are elected to office.

IMPROVING ON EXISTING RESEARCH

There are two main goals to the empirical analysis that follows. The first is simply to offer a broader, more representative account of how white Americans respond to black representation. Given the anecdotal nature of previous studies, it is imperative that we get an overall picture of how whites respond to their experiences with black leadership. The second empirical goal is to test the information model. Is information the key to understanding the impact of black representation, or is some other mechanism such as social dominance or racial prejudice at play when African Americans enter office?

Fortunately, these two empirical goals can be achieved by focusing on the same set of empirical tests. First, to provide a broad picture of how black leadership affects white political behavior, I need to assess change not on one measure as past studies have tended to do but instead on an array of key indicators. Therefore, I focus on change across two sets of important measures: white voting patterns and white racial attitudes. These two measures assess critical but different features of the white response to black leadership. The vote, because it determines election outcomes and the distribution of a wide array of public resources, is the most direct and telling measure of white willingness to support black leadership. Racial attitudes, because they provide us with a glimpse into what white Americans are thinking about blacks and black leadership, are the most direct and telling measure of the underlying motivations of the white community. Change on one measure alone could be viewed by some observers as ambiguous, but change on both measures is clear. If black representation leads to a positive change both in white voting behavior and in white racial attitudes, then we know that black leadership has led to a positive and meaningful transformation of the white community.

To address the second goal of testing the information model, I need to test a prediction that it uniquely and necessarily makes. Fortunately, the predictions made by the information model contrast with the predictions made by any other mainstream theories. If the information model is true and white residents do learn from black representation, then two changes in white behavior must logically follow. Whites will become more willing to vote for black leadership and white attitudes toward blacks will improve. No other theory predicts this pattern of white reactions. If prejudice is the main force driving white behavior, then one would predict little or no change on either the white vote or white attitudes. A social dominance perspective predicts that whites should react negatively to any challenge to the racial status quo. And if we were to make predictions based on previous instances of black leadership (e.g. in the late nineteenth century), we would expect whites to mobilize to try to oust black leadership.[17] Thus, to see if the information model explains white reactions to black leadership, I can look at the same two measures: white voting patterns and white racial attitudes. If black representation leads to positive change on both measures, then we have compelling evidence in favor of the information model.

To accomplish both of these tasks and to systematically assess changes in white political behavior under black representation, I examine three different data sets related to black mayoral leadership. In each case, I do not examine a handful of black representatives in one or two cities – as past studies have generally done – but instead I examine an entire universe of cases of white reactions to black representation. The primary tool to assess change in the white vote is a series of fifty-two black challenger and black incumbent elections. Since I want to look at how experience with a black incumbent changes the white vote, I compare and contrast the white vote in two elections in each city – the election in which a city elects its first black mayor and the election immediately following, in which the same black candidate runs for reelection. Also, since I want cases where white voters were forced to choose between black and white leadership, I exclude cities where the black candidate ran against a black opponent in either election. Finally, since I want to be as comprehensive as possible I include all cases in cities with over 100,000 people that fit this criterion. The two key questions that I try to address with this first data set are: (1) Are white voters more or less likely to support black challengers than they are to support the same black candidates when they run as incumbents? (2) Does black incumbency at the mayoral level lead to changes in the nature of the white vote? In particular, as time goes by under black leadership, is the white vote less governed by racial aspects of the election and more focused on nonracial factors such as endorsements, candidate

---

[17] Even a pure realistic group conflict model, which might predict a positive change in white voting behavior – given that black leadership proved ineffective – would still not predict a positive change in white attitudes.

quality, and the economy? In addition, to see how voters behaved across a larger array of cases and over a longer time period, I examine the outcome of every reelection bid of every black mayor in cities with over 50,000 residents in the twentieth century. The goal here is to show that, across the range of cases, white voters regularly support black incumbents.

The main tool to assess change in white racial attitudes is a series of nationally representative public opinion surveys conducted by the American National Election Study (ANES). With an array of questions on racial attitudes, a sufficiently large sample of white respondents, enough geographic dispersion, and a long time period, the ANES is the only survey that can be used to assess the effects of black representation on white attitudes. Two questions are critical to gauging the impact of black leadership. First, controlling for selection effects, do whites who live under black mayors express less racial fear and less negative views toward black leadership and the black community than do whites who live in other cities? Second, in cities that have elected a black mayor, is there an appreciable change in white attitudes over time? In particular, do white attitudes toward blacks and black leadership improve as experience with black officeholding increases? These main data sets, coupled with other secondary data, should provide a fairly complete picture of white reactions to black mayoral representation and a fairly discerning test of the information model.

There are, of course, some limitations to the analysis. Although I am able to measure the white vote and white views at key points before, during, and after the transition from white to black leadership, I offer less in the way of direct evidence of the specific information that whites residents have about black leaders. Exactly what is it that white residents do or do not know about local black leadership at different points in time? Strictly speaking, this kind of evidence is not required to test the information model but this kind of data might help to give us a more detailed understanding of the learning process. Unfortunately, survey data asking whites what they did or did not know about different aspects of black leadership at different points in time is quite limited and exists in only a few cities. Nevertheless, in the book I do utilize the data that are available. As I detailed earlier in this chapter, survey data not only strongly suggest that most white residents know if they have a black mayor but also that they are quite willing to offer evaluations of local conditions and mayoral performance. As Chapters 5 and 6 will demonstrate, these evaluations have a substantial impact on mayoral approval (see also Stein, Ulbig, and Post 2005; Howell and Perry 2004; and Howell and McLean

2001). In addition to data from larger surveys, I also present data from a range of interviews with a number of white residents in a variety of cities. These interviews do not emerge out of a random sample design but they nevertheless indicate what it is that many whites fear before black leaders are elected and more importantly how those fears decline as the years under black leadership go by. Finally, I also attempt to tie the political behavior of white residents more directly to the actions of black leadership by matching changes in local conditions under black mayoral leadership to changes in the views of white residents over time in two in-depth case studies of Los Angeles and Chicago.

The other main limitation of the analysis is that I could not follow a representative set of individuals as they experienced the transition from white to black leadership. As beneficial as such panel data would be to assess change over time, they are simply not available. Instead, I use two alternate types of analyses to assess change over time. To measure changes in the white vote, I focus on aggregate rather than individual data. Using this aggregate data I can easily compare the white vote at different points over the course of black leadership and note any changes that occur over time. To measure changes in white attitudes using pooled individual data, I develop a set of more complex methodological tests that attempt to isolate the effects of black leadership. Specifically, I develop a two-stage least-squares model that controls for selection of individuals into a particular city and I incorporate in that model a range of factors other than black leadership that might influence white attitudes. In addition, to assess changes over time in white views, I not only compare white attitudes in black-led cities to white attitudes in white-led cities, I also compare white attitudes early in a black mayor's tenure to white attitudes in the latter years of a city's experience with black mayoral leadership – a comparison that allows me to get reasonably close to measuring change over time. Finally, in the analysis of both the white vote and white racial attitudes, I explicitly control for changes in voter turnout and out-migration to help ensure that the changes we see under black leadership are real. No data in social science, short of experiments, can prove a temporal or causal connection with absolute certainty, but the tools that I employ should provide a fairly accurate assessment of the changes that occur over time under black representation.

Another potential concern is selection bias. If the cities that elect black mayors are cities where white residents are especially tolerant or cities where whites are on the cusp of accepting black leadership, it is possible that the positive change we see under black representation is the result of selection and not a sign of a real change in white political behavior. There are a number of factors that indicate that selection bias is not a significant problem in this case. Many of these are discussed in Chapters 2 and 3 but several are worth highlighting here. The most obvious reason to discount this selection hypothesis is the strongly negative reactions of the vast majority of white residents to the candidacies of black mayoral challengers. Some 70 percent of all whites voted against the successful black challenger in the cities that I examine. Many of these white voters were quite willing to express their animosity toward black leadership and their fears about what would happen if blacks gained control. In about half of these cities, whites turned out at record or near record rates to try to prevent a black victory. Moreover, as Chapter 2 will show, when whites voted in these elections, racial concerns all but determined the white vote in these cities. Clearly, in the cities that did elect black mayors, most white residents were far from ready to support black leadership. Another reason to doubt the selection hypothesis is the fact that an examination of surveys by the ANES shows that the racial attitudes of white residents in cities prior to the election of a black mayor were not appreciably different from the racial attitudes of whites in cities that were not about to elect a black mayor. Put another way, whites in cities that elect black mayors for the first time are similar to whites in cities that do not elect black mayors. Third, the available evidence suggests that a particularly racially tolerant white population is generally not the main reason for the election of a black mayor (Karnig and Welch 1980). In fact, the presence of a black mayor has much more to do with the size and resources of the local black community than with the nature of the local white community (Karnig and Welch 1980). Finally, when I do assess changes in white racial attitudes, I undertake a series of tests to help ensure that changes in white views are not due to selection bias. The first and most important tool is the use of a two-stage least-squares model that directly controls for selection into cities with black mayoral leadership. In addition, I look to see if the change in white views under black mayors is evident even when I only include whites from cities that have elected a black mayor at some point in their history. By confining the analysis to whites who live in cities that have or will elect black mayors, any change in white attitudes that is evident during the years when a black incumbent is in power cannot be due to especially racially tolerant cities electing a black mayor since all of the cities in the analysis elect black mayors. Also, as previously noted, when assessing changes in white views, I compare white views early in the tenure of a black mayor to white views later in the tenure of a black mayor. This additional test indicates that even when the analysis is confined to whites who currently live under a black mayor, there is a marked improvement in white views over the tenure of the black mayor – a change that is not likely to be due to especially racially tolerant cities electing black mayors. Combined, these points strongly suggest that the changes we see under black mayors are real.

2

The Transformation of the White Vote

In this chapter, I begin to assess how experience with black leadership affects whites' political behavior. The goal of the first part of the chapter is to offer a test of the three competing explanations of white voter behavior developed in Chapter 1. If the information model is accurate, white Americans should be more supportive of black incumbents than of black challengers. If the predictions of the white backlash model are correct, whites' opposition to black incumbents should increase with time. And if the racial prejudice model is accurate, the white vote should be relatively unaffected by black leaders' incumbency. The results of this first test are fairly clear: white voters are significantly more willing to support the same black candidate when he or she runs as an incumbent. Regardless of who they face or where they run, black incumbents usually win reelection.

This first test cannot tell us why white voters change their minds about black candidates, of course. This is an important omission, because there are a number of reasons why black incumbents might get more white support than black challengers. After all, most candidates, black or white, are able to garner more votes when they run as incumbents. To address this issue and, more importantly, to see if racial learning plays a role in increasing white support for black incumbents, I will look more deeply at the nature of the white vote in black challenger and black incumbent elections in the second part of the chapter. If the information model is correct, we should find black incumbent contests to be somewhat less racialized: threat should play a diminished role in the vote of a significant portion of white voters, and conventional nonracial factors should re-emerge as critical considerations. The results of this second test show that in black incumbent elections, white voting patterns more closely resemble the norm than they do in black challenger elections: turnout declines to average levels, racial considerations seem to diminish, and traditionally important electoral influences such as endorsements and candidate quality re-emerge as central factors in the white vote.

The results of both of these tests support the information model. But if the model is accurate, some of the positive information that whites obtain from watching black incumbents around the country should be relevant when new black challengers enter the political arena. Over time, whites should grow less fearful of new black challengers, and they should be more willing to vote for these candidates. Since black leadership is certainly not the only new element affecting white votes over time, my test of this hypothesis is at best suggestive. Nevertheless, the results of this test, too, support the information model, as the information whites acquire about blacks in one place does appear to affect outcomes in other contests in other locations. Combined, these three tests would seem to indicate that black leadership does provide many white Americans with critical information that allays their fears and reduces the significance of race in subsequent local elections. Before turning to the tests and analysis of their results, I want to first provide a brief review of the existing literature on white voting in biracial contests.

WILL WHITES VOTE BLACK?

Scholars, activists, and judges have all given enormous attention to the simple question "Will whites vote black?" For many, it is *the* central question in discussions of minority rights in this country. Despite the attention that has been given to this question – or perhaps because of it – existing scholarship has provided no clear answer. Some scholars are now convinced that whites will vote black. They cite public opinion surveys in which white respondents overwhelmingly report that they are willing to support black candidates, and they point out that the list of African Americans who have won office in primarily white states, districts, and cities is impressive.[1] They also emphasize exit poll data from a range of congressional and gubernatorial elections that suggest race is no more an issue in biracial elections than it is in other electoral contests in America (Highton 2004; Citrin, Green, and Sears 1990). Several scholars have gone so far as

---

[1] When asked if they would vote for a "qualified black candidate for president," over 90% of white respondents answer yes (Schuman et al. 1997). The number of whites who say they would vote black are even higher for other political offices (Williams 1990).

to interpret these results as a sign that race is largely irrelevant in biracial contests (Thernstrom and Thernstrom 1997; Thernstrom 1987; Swain 1995). As Abigail and Stephen Thernstrom claimed in 1997, "whites are voting black – in increasing numbers – to a degree that was unimaginable 30 years ago" (Thernstrom and Thernstrom 1997: 295).

But others have reached a very different conclusion. When given the choice between a white candidate and a black candidate, these scholars maintain, the vast majority of white voters will embrace the candidate of their own race. There is considerable evidence to support this view. Studies that have examined electoral outcomes in hundreds of contests suggest that in a typical biracial contest one can expect an average of 70 to 90 percent of white voters to vote white (McCrary 1990; Bullock and Dunn 1999; Henry 1987; Stein and Kohfeld 1991; Loewen 1990; Bullock 1984; O'Loughlin 1979; Murray and Vedlitz 1978; Black and Black 1973; Lieske and Hillard 1984; Sheffield and Hadley 1984).[2] More-over, these and similar studies find that the more important the office, the fewer whites are willing to vote for a black candidate to fill it (Stein and Kohfeld 1991; Williams 1990; Bullock 1984). The geographic distribu-tion of black elected officials also strongly hints at an ongoing aversion to black candidates on the part of white voters. Today, roughly 80 per-cent of all black elected officials are elected by majority black electorates (Canon 1999; Handley and Grofman 1994; Hedge, Button, and Spear 1992; Campbell and Feagin 1984). Even though 70 percent of all blacks live in state and federal districts that are majority white, only about 1 percent of all majority white districts have ever elected a black official (Handley and Grofman 1994). The clear implication is that whites will not vote black and that race remains central in the minds of white voters. Accordingly, many scholars believe that race and racial prejudice remain the primary factor in American politics (Reeves 1997; McCrary 1990; Huckfeldt and Kohfeld 1989).

How can scholars reach such starkly different conclusions about the role of race in American politics? The answer is that all black candidates are not equal in the minds of white voters. A sharp distinction should be made between black challengers on one hand and black incumbents on

[2] Findings in experimental studies are slightly more mixed. Some studies have found that whites support a black candidate as much or more often than an equivalent white can-didate (Sigelman et al. 1995; Colleau et al. 1990), but others have found that race, skin color, and individual racial prejudice all affect voting (Terkildsen 1993). There are also signs that whites appear to be hiding their intentions. In one experiment, the proportion of whites stating that they were undecided doubled in biracial contests (Reeves 1997).

the other. For white voters, black challengers represent uncertainty, fear, and, often, a racial threat; if whites do not know how black leadership will affect them, they will generally choose to vote white. Black incumbents, by contrast, are likely to be relatively well-known commodities – they have a record, and in all but a few cases that record allays fears about the consequences of black leadership. With this new, reassuring information, whites become much more willing to support black incumbents. Thus, it would not be surprising to find that those studies that reach positive conclusions about white willingness to support black candidates often do so because they tend to focus almost exclusively on black incumbents. Similarly, those that offer more pessimistic accounts of American race relations and white willingness to vote for African American candidates do so, perhaps, because they tend to focus on black challengers. Unfortunately, since almost all of the existing research on racial politics has failed to take into account the important distinction between challengers and incumbents in data analysis, we do not yet know whether this assumption is correct.

If this information model is accurate, the critical question is not whether whites will vote for blacks but *under what circumstances* they will vote for blacks. And, more specifically, what difference does black incumbency make? Does experience under black incumbents change the way whites think about black candidates, make them more willing to support black incumbents, and reduce the role of race in biracial electoral contests?

DOES INCUMBENCY MATTER?

To begin to answer these questions, I collected data on white voting patterns in a representative sample of mayoral elections involving black candidates. I collected these data with two goals in mind. My first goal was to provide as direct an assessment as possible of the impact of incumbency on the white vote. To do so, I amassed data on white voting patterns in sets of two mayoral elections in cities that have experienced a transition to black leadership. For each case, I contrast the white vote in the first election, in which a black challenger ran successfully against a white incumbent to become the first black mayor of the city, with the white vote in the election immediately following, in which the black mayor ran for reelection against a white opponent.[3] By comparing sets of two

---

[3] Including cases in which two black candidates run against each other would, obviously, reveal little about white acceptance of black leadership.

elections that involve the same black candidates, I am able to assess the effects of incumbency on the white vote directly. I confine my analysis to general or run-off elections rather than primaries to avoid complications introduced by multiple candidacies and voter disinterest. To analyze other aspects of the electoral outcome, I also collected data on overall turnout and the margin of victory in each election. A detailed account of each of the variables and its sources is described in the statistical Appendix to Chapter 2.

My second goal was to be as comprehensive as possible in order to ensure that the results of the data analysis are representative. Since all previous studies had considered only a small number of cases, I decided to create a complete data set that included all relevant cases across the country. To do this, I compiled a set of the entire universe of cases for cities with populations of over 100,000 that fit the criteria just outlined. In total, there were fifty-two elections in twenty-six cities. While this is admittedly a small number, it represents two-thirds of the cases of white-black transition in large American cities. What is happening in this set of cases, then, should be more or less what happens generally when a white mayor is replaced by a black mayor in a large American city.

It is also important to note that my selection criteria do not appear to have created a set of cities with exceptionally liberal or especially racially tolerant white populations. Although some of the cities, such as San Francisco, Minneapolis, and Seattle, are generally seen as liberal, others, including Memphis, Birmingham, and Houston, would be much more likely to be labeled conservative, and still others, Durham and Hartford, for example, fall somewhere in the middle. As we will see, most whites in these cities were not ready for black leadership and not particularly racially tolerant when black candidates were trying to win the mayoralty for the first time. On the contrary, black challengers in many of these cities faced nearly unanimous opposition. And, in many cases, whites turned out in record numbers to try to prevent a black victory. In fact, a comparison of the racial attitudes of white residents in these cities prior to the election of a black mayor with the racial attitudes of white residents in other cities using the survey data from the ANES (presented in Chapter 3) found no consistent or substantial differences in white views. For these cities, the key to black victory was the black vote, not white support. This comports with existing research that suggests that the size of the black community and the resources of the black community are much more important in determining the success of black candidates than the nature of the white community (Karnig and Welch 1980).

TABLE 2.1 *Voting Patterns in Black Challenger and Black Incumbent Elections*

	Black Challenger	Black Incumbent
White Voters for Black Candidate (%)	30	36
Margin of Victory (%)	12	21
Turnout of Registered Voters (%)	59	52

To illustrate how white voters respond to black mayoral leadership, Table 2.1 presents a comparison of black challenger and black incumbent elections. The numbers tell a fairly clear story: when the same black candidate runs for reelection for the first time as an incumbent, the proportion of white voters who support that candidate grows by an average of 6 percentage points, from 30 to 36 percent of all white voters. A six-point shift in the vote is certainly not unheard of in American elections, and one could argue that this change represents relatively little movement on the part of white voters. Yet this relatively small change is clearly important, for if whites were reacting to incumbent black mayors as they have responded to other forms of black empowerment in the past, we would have seen the opposite: a white backlash characterized by heightened mobilization and resistance. Similarly, if prejudice were the main factor behind white opposition to black candidates, we would most likely see no change at all. The fact that white support grew, even if by a small amount, is very informative.[4]

The growth in white support is more impressive when one considers that whites in these cities had only two or four years (depending on the length of a mayoral term) to experience black leadership. In cities like Los Angeles and Newark, where the same black mayor ran repeatedly for reelection, white support grew with each election. According to

[4] It is also worth noting that the increased white willingness to support the same black candidate suggests that a fairly large portion of white voters who were motivated by race in the challenger contest had a change of heart in the incumbent contest. If most of the white support in the black challenger contests and most of the increase in white support in the incumbent contests comes from Democrats – a reasonable assumption given that all but one of the black candidates are self-described Democrats and most advocated at least a marginally liberal agenda – a shorthand calculation (estimating that half of all white voters in these cities are Democrats) indicates that one-quarter of the white Democrats who voted "race" instead of party in the black challenger election reverted to voting along partisan lines in the black incumbent election. In other words, a substantial proportion of all racially motivated white voters change their minds after just a few years of black leadership.

Sonenshein (1993), Tom Bradley's white support in Los Angeles grew in each of his first four elections. All told, his white support almost doubled from 32 percent in 1969 to 62 percent in 1985. Thus, the six-point shift may represent only the first step in growing white acceptance of black leadership. In addition, this analysis in some ways understates the exceptional nature of the white support that these black incumbents won. I do not compare the average challenger to the average incumbent but instead focus only on the most successful black challengers. Most black challengers lose their electoral bids. Thus, if I had included a cross-section of all black challengers, the contrast between support for challengers and support for incumbents would be much greater. The limited data that are available attest to this point. In an analysis of a series of city council and mayoral elections in Atlanta, Bullock (1984) found that incumbency more than doubled white crossover voting. His findings were echoed in an analysis of the vote in mayoral and council elections in New Orleans (Vanderleeuw 1991).

It is worth noting that the black candidates in the sample gained substantial white support as incumbents *despite the fact* that they did not get the boost in electoral resources that most incumbents receive. For most white candidates, incumbency has enormous benefits: it usually means more endorsements, more money, and weaker opponents. This is much less true for the black candidates in my sample.[5] Largely because they needed tremendous resources to be elected in the first place, the majority of these twenty-six black candidates garnered few new electoral resources as incumbents. In 81 percent of the cases, they received no new Democratic Party endorsement when they ran as incumbents. In 62 percent of the cases, they gained no new endorsements from local newspapers. These black incumbents also tended to face strong white challengers. Specifically, 62 percent of the incumbents faced opponents who had the same or a higher level of experience than their opponents in the challenger election. The candidates were able to muster only marginally greater financial resources as incumbents, and one-third actually raised less money than they had as challengers. It would make little sense, then, to attribute the growing white support for these candidates to the conventional resources of incumbency.

The six-point increase in the percentage of white residents who voted black was not the only significant change from the challenger to the

---

[5] Data sources for these comparisons are described in the appendix.

incumbent elections. There was an even sharper decline in the absolute number of white voters who opposed the black candidates.[6] Across all twenty-six cities, the number of white votes for the white candidate declined by 19 percent on average between the challenger and the incumbent elections. This result suggests that as many as one-fifth of all white voters who opposed black leadership may have changed their minds sufficiently either to support the black candidate or to choose not to vote at all. As a consequence of both the drop in voter turnout and the higher level of support for the black incumbents, the incumbents' average margin of victory jumped from 12 percent in the challenger elections to 21 percent in the incumbent elections, leading to victory for the black incumbents in all but three cities.

The final factor to consider is voter turnout. Table 2.1 reveals that turnout decreased substantially in the black incumbent elections. In a little over half of the challenger elections, turnout had reached or exceeded record levels.[7] On average, it exceeded the national average by over 10 percentage points (Hampton and Tate 1996). But this mobilization quickly faded away when blacks ran as incumbents: across the twenty-six cities, turnout dropped from almost 59 percent in challenger elections to 52 percent in incumbent elections, falling in many cases to average or below average levels. In Charlotte, for example, where Harvey Gantt faced well-known white Republican city council members in both of his elections, voter turnout fell by over 15 percentage points from 50 percent in Gantt's challenger run to 34 percent, near the historic norm, in his reelection bid. From this data, it seems that black incumbency at the mayoral level transforms extraordinary black challenger elections into more ordinary contests for reelection.

The opposition that the black challengers faced was by no means totally erased when they ran as incumbents, of course. The data in Table 2.1

---

[6] This assumes that the decrease in support for the white candidate comes from white voters. Two facts make this assumption reasonable. First, there was almost no black support for the white candidate in any of these elections. Exit polls and precinct analysis of the black vote indicate that on average 95% of black voters supported the challenger and 93% supported the incumbent. Also, across the cities, there are few voters who are neither black nor white. Blacks and whites combined make up 92% of the population in these twenty-six cities.

[7] Although Table 2.1 only presents aggregate turnout rates, it is clear that white turnout rates follow the same pattern. In cities where turnout figures are available for whites and African Americans separately, the numbers suggest that both groups turn out in large numbers in challenger elections and in considerably smaller numbers in incumbent elections.

indicate that large numbers of white voters continued to oppose the black incumbents. But in the average case, after a few years of black incumbency, white Americans became more accepting of black leadership. Again, the most remarkable aspect of this shift was not its size but the fact that there was any positive change at all. Peter Eisinger noted, in his study of Atlanta and Detroit, how sharply the elections of black representatives in those cities contrasted with expectations: "What has occurred is particularly noteworthy when it is set against the history of race relations in those two cities themselves, against the habits of racial oppression in American society in general, and indeed against a virtually worldwide tendency to deal with ethno-racial political competition by violent means" (Eisinger 1980: xxi). In many cities, even city residents themselves seemed surprised at their mayoral election's outcome. As one reporter in Birmingham put it, "This city, once branded by the Rev. Martin Luther King Jr. as 'the most thoroughly segregated in America,' accomplished something Tuesday that many of its residents consider remarkable: it reelected its first black mayor with a biracial coalition and the largest victory margin in city history" (Russakoff 1983). The fact that whites' anti-black mobilization declined after only a few years and significantly more whites became willing to support black leadership was not only a positive sign for race relations in these cities – it was a positive change that many did not foresee.

A Broader Phenomenon: All Incumbent Black Mayors

The changes in white voter behavior noted above may be unique to the twenty-six cities in the data set or limited to the first few years of black leadership. To assess black incumbency more broadly, I collected data on the reelection bids that took place in the twentieth century of every black incumbent mayor in every city with a population over 50,000.[8] In each case, in addition to the outcome of the contest, I obtained information on the racial makeup of the city, the race of the opponent, the number of terms the incumbent had been in office, and the number of black mayors who had previously served in the city.

[8] This data set was compiled using the National Roster of Black Elected Officials, local newspaper reports in each city, and a data set of mayoral names (Wolman, Strate, and Melchior 1996), and it includes the race of the mayor, the challenger, and the winner. As in the first data set, I focus on general or run-off elections rather than primaries, where factors such as multiple candidacies, lack of interest, and limited availability of empirical data complicate empirical analysis.

The findings from my analysis of this larger set of cases echo the results for the twenty-six cities. First, black incumbents won in the vast majority of the cases. Since 1965, black mayors have won 78 percent of their reelection bids (98 out of 126 cases). In fact, depending on the exact comparison, black incumbents do almost as well as or even better than white incumbents. Between 1970 and 1985, the only period for which I was able to obtain equivalent data for both black and white mayoral incumbents, black mayors were reelected 89 percent of the time (31 out of 35 cases), a slightly higher rate than white mayors, who were reelected 84 percent of the time (359 out of 429 cases). From these data, it would seem that black and white incumbents are treated almost equally by the American electorate.

Second, there was no sharp decline in black reelection rates over time, and thus little indication that the information provided by black incumbents was losing efficacy over time. Although the first African Americans to serve as mayors of their cities were particularly successful when they ran as incumbents for the first time (winning 83 percent of these reelection bids), they also did well in subsequent electoral bids, winning 74 percent of the time. Equally important, there does not appear to be a major distinction in success rates between the first black mayor of a city and others who follow. The overall reelection rate of cities' first black mayors (80 percent) by no means dwarfs the reelection rate of subsequent black mayors (73 percent).

But does the success of black incumbents have anything to do with white voters? After all, the majority of black mayors represent minority white cities. Given the fact that black voters tend to favor black candidates over white candidates, the success of black incumbents could merely be an artifact of black unity and voting strength and not the result of increasing white support (McCrary 1990). But this appears not to be the case: if we confine the analysis to minority black cities, where white voters presumably have a good chance of controlling the outcome of the contests, black incumbents still do well. Black mayoral incumbents in minority black cities won reelection over 80 percent of the time, only marginally below the overall white incumbent reelection rate. Moreover, black incumbents did not win these contests simply because white voters were forced to choose between two black candidates. Even in minority black cities in elections in which black incumbents faced a white challenger, black mayoral incumbents won reelection 73 percent of the time (19 of 26 cases). In fact, black incumbents actually did better against white candidates then they did against black candidates.

It is also worth noting that the pattern of declining turnout that was evident in the twenty-six black challenger/black incumbent elections can be found across the wider range of cases. In an analysis of a broad sample of mayoral elections in large American cities, Hampton and Tate (1996) found that the mere presence of an African American candidate in the contest raised turnout by 10 points over the national average. But this changed when blacks ran as incumbents. The same data show that having a black incumbent in the contest actually lowered turnout by 4 percent (Lublin and Tate 1995). Black challengers spark extraordinary mobilization, while black incumbents seem to spark only average interest.

THE SHIFTING CALCULUS OF THE WHITE VOTE

Across a wide range of cases and on a number of different measures, black mayoral leadership appears to lead to positive changes in white political behavior. These positive changes seem to favor the information model over both the backlash and the prejudice hypotheses, but they do not themselves demonstrate racial learning on the part of white voters. There are a number of possible reasons why black incumbents might be successful and why white voters might change their minds about black leadership. Most officeholders, whether they are white or black, get more support when they run as incumbents. To see if race and racial learning are behind the changes in the white vote observed in the data, more tests are required. In this section, I begin to examine the nature of the white vote more closely to see if the change in the vote can be linked to information. If the information model is accurate, we should see a distinct pattern emerge: in black challenger elections, the white vote should be largely based on racial fears; in black incumbent elections, fear should play a diminished role, and white voters should begin to base their votes on the track record of the incumbent and the specifics of the campaign.

I collected an array of data on the campaigns and candidates for each of the fifty-two elections in the original set of twenty-six cities. To assess the role of race and fear in each contest, I included two different kinds of measures. First, I used a measure of the black population size as a proxy for racial threat. The size of the black population is regularly employed as a measure of racial threat, and in a wide range of cases white political choices have been shown to be shaped by the local racial context (Giles and Hertz 1994; Key 1949). If fears about the consequences of black leadership are in fact driving the white vote in black challenger elections, we should find that white voters' preferences are closely tied to the size of the black community. The larger the black population and the more likely it is that blacks could actually gain control of the local political arena, the more we should see whites fearing black leadership and voting against black candidates.

Second, I included a measure of the racialization of each black candidate's campaign. If fear about racial change is behind white opposition, then what black candidates do or say regarding racial policy should also affect the white vote. The less black candidates talk about serving the black community and the more they run deracialized campaigns that promise a race-neutral administration, the less fear there should be in the minds of white voters and the more likely it should be that white voters will support black candidates.[9] To measure the racialization of a given campaign, I coded the extent to which the black candidates' speeches, policy platforms, and mobilization efforts were targeted at blacks, whites, or both. This is admittedly a subjective measure, but in practice it was fairly easy to divide campaigns into three categories: campaigns that had any sort of explicit, pro-black focus; campaigns that addressed the black community implicitly through a generally pro-black policy agenda or by actively mobilizing black voters and speaking before black audiences; and campaigns that never mentioned black interests and were fairly race neutral.[10] A comparison of the racialization measure employed in this study with a similar measure used in Lublin and Tate (1995) suggests that the coding is

---

[9] This type of deracialization hypothesis has been the subject of a lengthy debate, with some believing that deracialization is a critical strategy for black candidates and others maintaining that it is impossible for black candidates to effectively downplay the significance of race (C. Hamilton 1977; Henry 1992; Perry 1996; but see Starks 1991; Wright 1996).

[10] In practice, most black candidates ran dual campaigns, using different tactics and addressing different issues depending on the racial makeup of their audiences. Few campaigns were overtly racial. Fewer still were clearly race neutral. In the end, the range of campaigns was not that wide. Tom Bradley, who is seen as having the quintessential deracialized campaign, talked about affirmative action and the problems of the black community. On the opposite end of the spectrum, Harold Washington did make the famous "It's our turn" comment, but the vast majority of the time he avoided mentioning black interests and instead talked repeatedly about white interests, about serving the whole city, and about such issues as reform that primarily interested white liberals. Very few campaigns were coded as explicitly racially focused. In black challenger campaigns, there was an even split between implicitly pro-black and race-neutral campaigns. In black incumbent elections, race-neutral campaigns were a slight majority.

valid.[11] If the information model is accurate, this measure should have a bigger effect on the white vote in black challenger elections than in black incumbent elections.

If whites cease to fear the consequences of a black takeover, conventional nonracial factors that are normally important determinants of electoral outcomes should begin to play a more significant role in black incumbent elections. To see if this is the case, I examine the extent to which three basic factors of the electoral context affect the white vote in black challenger and black incumbent elections: candidate quality, political endorsements, and campaign spending. In contests at almost every level of politics, each of these factors has proven to be critical to electoral outcomes. More-qualified candidates – with quality generally measured in terms of political experience – surpass the electoral fortunes of less-experienced candidates at both the congressional and local levels (Jacobson and Kernell 1981; Krasno and Green 1988; Lieske 1989; Krebs 1998).[12] Similarly, major endorsements have been shown to play a primary role in most local contests. In particular, both political party endorsements and city news-paper endorsements affect voting in local elections (Bullock 1984; Lieske 1989; Krebs 1998). Finally, campaign spending has been closely linked to the electoral fortunes of candidates from presidents all the way down to city council members (Arrington and Ingalls 1984; Krebs 1998; Green and Krasno 1988; Jacobson 1980; Cox and Munger 1989; Gierzynski 1998). Candidates who are able to outspend their opponents by wide margins seem to be much more likely to win at the polls.[13] Measures of each of these factors are fairly straightforward and are detailed in Appendix A.

---

[11] Coding from the current data set was compared to the coding of a similar variable from the Race and Urban Politics Data set (RUPD), a data set covering 315 mayoral elections in twenty-six large cities. The RUPD variable, which purportedly measured the racial character of a candidate's campaign, correlated at 0.97 with the racialization measure used here (see Lublin and Tate 1995 for a detailed description of the data set).

[12] The exact causal relationship between candidate quality and electoral outcomes is, however, likely to be somewhat complex. Strong incumbents often deter quality challengers from entering the contest in the first place, which makes an assessment of the causal ties difficult (Bond, Covingten, and Fleisher 1985; Jacobson and Kernell 1981).

[13] The relationship between money and outcomes is also somewhat complex. Some feel that challengers can benefit more from spending than can incumbents (Jacobson and Kernell 1981). Others see reciprocal causation: how well a candidate is expected to do affects the candidate's fundraising ability (Goidel and Gross 1994). In light of this first claim, I look at the spending of each individual candidate separately and not just at the spending advantage of one candidate over another.

TABLE 2.2 *Determinants of the White Vote in Black Challenger Elections*

	White Support for the Black Candidate
RACIAL FEAR	
Percentage Black of City Population	−0.72 (0.13)***
Racialization of Black Candidate's Campaign	−0.58 (0.26)*
CONVENTIONAL POLITICS	
Candidate Quality	
Quality of White Opponent	0.01 (0.08)
White Incumbent Running	−0.09 (0.07)
Quality of Black Challenger	−0.05 (0.08)
Endorsements	
Democratic Party Endorsement	0.02 (0.05)
Local Newspaper Endorsement	0.01 (0.05)
Constant	0.64 (0.11)***
Adj. R^2	0.67
N	25

Note: OLS regression. Figures in parentheses are standard errors.
***$p < 0.01$
**$p < 0.05$
*$p < 0.10$

The Importance of Race in Black Challenger Elections

In Table 2.2, I begin to test these propositions by analyzing the aggregate white vote in black challenger elections. Although the number of cases is relatively small and is not necessarily representative of all American cities, the table does reveal a stark, clear pattern. As predicted by the information model, when black candidates challenged for the mayoralty for the first time, the aggregate white vote was tied almost exclusively to racial fears.

The first measure of racial fear indicates that the larger the black population in the cities in the sample – and hence the greater the perceived threat that blacks would gain some measure of control over the local political arena – the less willing whites were to support a black challenger. The size of the black population accounts for the bulk of the variation in aggregate white behavior; by itself, it accounts for 60 percent of the variation in white vote choice. Even considering the selection bias inherent in these cases, it is impressive how closely the white vote was tied to the size of a city's black population. In the five cities with the highest proportion of African Americans, Baltimore, Birmingham, New Orleans, Memphis, and Newark, on average only 16.9 percent of whites supported the black challenger. In contrast, in the five cities where blacks represented the smallest proportion of the population and thus the smallest threat, a slim majority of white voters (on average 50.4 percent) supported the black candidate. Overall, the regression results indicate that a 10 percentage point increase in the proportion of a city's residents who were black led to a 7.2 percentage point drop in white support for the black mayoral candidate.

The importance of racial threat seems to suggest that these challenger elections were less about the candidates or the specifics of the election than they were about the size of the threat of a black takeover – a conclusion that is echoed over and over again in accounts of the elections. One of the most well-known accounts of Birmingham's election, for example, concluded that "whites worried not so much about Richard Arrington Jr. [the black challenger], but about blacks, the group they believed he represented. Had that day now come when 'the last shall be first, and the first shall be last?'" (J. Franklin 1989: 172). The transition was viewed very similarly in Atlanta, where Peter Eisinger found that "the change was understood not in terms of a turnover in the personnel of city hall but as a loss by one race to the other" (1980: 154). Wilbur Rich's account of Detroit reached the same conclusion: "Many white residents of Detroit responded to the 1973 election of Coleman Young with intense apprehensions and fear. . . . Many whites saw the race as the last stand before the takeover by the onrushing black majority" (1987: 208).

The role played by the black candidate's campaign, and in particular white voters' aversion to racially focused campaigns, also serves to confirm the critical importance of racial fears in these black challenger elections. What black candidates did or did not say about the interests of blacks apparently influenced the white vote in these contests. All else being equal, black challengers who ran essentially race-neutral campaigns garnered almost 60 percent more of the white vote than challengers who ran racially explicit campaigns. Even though all of the twenty-six black challengers tried in some way to assure white residents that they would not be ignored, white voters seemingly keyed in on small differences between campaigns. Thus, a candidate like Harold Washington probably lost substantial white support as a result of telling a black audience "It's our turn," even though most of his campaign was race neutral. And, at the other end of the spectrum, candidates like Thirman Milner, who emphatically told white voters that "there is no such thing as black legislation" and who often repeated his desire to be "mayor of all of Hartford," seem to have been rewarded with additional white votes. Candidate Charles Box recalled that "The key ... was to take the fear of the unknown out of the equation" (quoted in Colburn and Adler 2003). Box was so concerned about racial fears that he centered his campaign in Rockford on having personal interactions with as many white voters as possible.[14]

In addition to supporting the information model, these findings also contribute evidence toward the resolution of two ongoing debates in the literature on American racial politics. First, the clear negative relationship between white voting behavior and the size of the local black population in these mayoral elections reaffirms the important role that racial context plays in American race relations. Existing studies have reached very different conclusions about how the increasing presence of racial and ethnic minorities affects the white population. Although most studies have found that a larger black population is associated with greater racial antagonism (Key 1949; Murray and Vedlitz 1978; Giles and Hertz 1994; Alt 1994; Taylor M. 1998; Fossett and Kiecolt 1989), several recent works have concluded either that there is no relationship at all or that the relationship is positive (Welch et al. 2001; Kinder and Mendelberg 1995; Bledsoe et al. 1995; Carsey 1995). The results reported here support the position that a proportionately larger black population *does* represent a racial threat to white voters.

In addition, the relationship between the racial focus of a campaign and the white vote seems to suggest that deracialization can lead to increased white support. Again, there has been considerable debate on this point. Though many have maintained that black candidates can garner white support by deracializing their campaigns (Perry 1991; Nichols 1990; C. Hamilton 1977), others disagree. In one of the most extensive studies, Wright found that "black [mayoral challengers] in Memphis were unable to garner significant white crossover support regardless of their use of deracialized strategies" (1996: 151). Similarly, Starks contends that "There is no way in which a contemporary American campaign can utilize a deracialization electoral strategy and hope to eliminate race as a

---

[14] This phenomenon does not seem to be confined to mayoral candidates. Gubernatorial candidate Douglas Wilder proclaimed, "I have never been a civil rights activist of any kind" (quoted in Jeffries 1999). Harvey Gantt tried hard to run a nonthreatening, deracialized contest in his senatorial bid against Jesse Helms (Wilson 1993). Alan Wheat, one of the most successful black crossover candidates, was also well aware of white fears during his Senate campaign. His campaign coordinator stated, "We knew and they knew that there is just enough racial discomfort among whites that just showing his face was enough of a message" (quoted in Sniderman, Swain, and Elms 1995: 10).

factor in that campaign" (1991: 217). But the documented results seem to indicate that whites can be quite sensitive to the kinds of campaigns black candidates run. When black candidates move from a racially explicit campaign to a less racially focused campaign, they are able to attract greater white support. This might lead some to recommend deracializing black campaigns as an effective strategy to increase white support and expand black representation. It is important to consider, however, whether any gains in white support are large enough to offset a possible erosion of black support and black turnout – to say nothing of the restraints on policy changes – that most likely accompany deracialized campaigns.[15]

The Irrelevance of Conventional Political Factors in Black Challenger Elections

Up to this point, I have detailed the factors that *do* matter in black challenger elections to show that the uncertainty and racial concerns highlighted by the information model appear to govern white reactions to black challengers. An account of the factors that *do not* matter in these contests is, however, just as telling. Looking back at Table 2.2, it is apparent that none of the factors generally viewed as being critical to local electoral outcomes substantially affects the outcome of elections in which blacks challenge for control of a city's mayoralty for the first time.

The first of the normally critical electoral variables tested is candidate quality. The evidence presented here suggests that candidates' experience did not play a significant role in these black challenger elections: whether black challengers faced an unknown and untested white opponent or someone who was well known and had held a prior office seems not to have significantly affected their prospects of winning white support. Chicago provides one of the starkest examples: even though Harold Washington faced an unknown Republican, Bernard Epton, who began his bid with limited campaign experience, no campaign funds, and no

---

[15] Supplementary analysis suggests that the kinds of campaigns black candidates run may also be related to the policies that black mayors enact and the voting behavior of the black community. Among the elections that I looked at, black candidates who deemphasized race were also less apt to enact such policies as affirmative action and redistributive spending that might benefit the black community. Deracialized campaigns also appeared to be linked to lower black turnout. Neither of these relationships is particularly robust but it may be that by shying away from race in their campaigns, black candidates lose black votes and limit the kinds of policies that they ultimately can enact. In short, black candidates may have to walk a fine line between trying to get elected and trying to serve the black community.

organization, 80 percent of white Chicagoans voted for Epton; presumably this means that many of them were simply voting *against* Washington. The election in Newark also appears to illustrate how little white voters cared about the qualifications of the white candidate. In that city, 90 percent of white voters supported the white candidate, Hugh Addonizio, even though he had recently been indicted on multiple counts for having ties to organized crime and was on trial the day of the election. Perhaps even more extraordinary is the fact that the white vote in these biracial elections was unrelated to whether or not the black challenger faced an incumbent. In the nineteen cases in which black challengers ran in an open-seat contest, they did not do significantly better than in the other six cases, where they faced a white incumbent.[16]

Just as white voters were not deterred by the poor qualifications of white candidates, they seemed not to have been positively influenced by the qualifications of the black challengers. Having held prior office as a state legislator or city council member did little to improve black challengers' prospects of success. Despite the fact that Ernest Morial had been a state legislator in New Orleans for years and Wilson Goode had been city manager in Philadelphia in the three years prior to his mayoral bid, both failed to garner more than a quarter of the white vote in their cities. At the opposite end of the spectrum, black challengers such as James Sharp in Flint and James Usry in Atlantic City, both of whom had held no previous elected office, did only marginally worse with white voters than their more qualified peers.[17]

Political endorsements – the second traditionally important factor tested in Table 2.2 – also do not appear to be significantly tied to the white vote in these black challenger elections. Despite the fact that past research has found that newspaper endorsement and party endorsements greatly influence the outcomes of local elections, neither had much impact on the white vote when white voters were faced with the prospect of a perceived black takeover (Bullock 1984; Lieske 1989; Stein and Fleischmann

---

[16] Other tests also indicate that open-seat contests were in most respects no different from elections in which the black challenger faced a white incumbent. Racial factors were equally important in both types of contests, and nonracial factors were equally unimportant.

[17] Thus, Niemi and Weisberg may be right about most elections in America when they echo the wisdom of political science and claim "It makes a difference who the candidates are" (1993: 217), but when one candidate is black and vying to take over a position previously held by whites, the only thing that seems to matter about the two candidates is the color of their skin and the fear that it invokes.

1987; Krebs 1998). Both Kenneth Gibson in Newark and Wilson Goode in Philadelphia won the endorsement of their city's Democratic Party organization and its major newspapers, usually a sure sign of widespread white support in these strongly Democratic cities, but in each case the endorsements were followed by strong white opposition. The same pattern held in Detroit. As one reporter described the campaign, the focus was not on endorsements or campaigns but on race: "The unions were for [Coleman Young]. The business and political establishments were for him. The liberal, money-laden suburbs were for him. But when they tallied the votes, none of that mattered. The only issue that counted when Coleman Young became Detroit's first black mayor in 1973 was race" (Cantor 1989).

Alternate tests suggest that even the policy platform of the black candidate's campaign was not as important as it is normally.[18] The liberalism of the black candidate's campaign, as measured by statements about overall policy direction and specific policy initiatives in newspaper reports and the candidate's speeches, had no clear effect on white support. Whether policy liberalism was included in the model in Table 2.2 or examined alone, it appeared to have no impact on the decisions of white voters in these challenger elections.[19]

The impact of conventional factors is not simply masked by the inclusion of other variables: even when both of the racial fear variables are omitted from the regression, none of the remaining independent variables is significantly related to white voter behavior in black challenger elections. Even simple bivariate tests reveal no clear link between any of the

[18] Due to the collinearity between campaign liberalism and the racialization of the black candidate's campaign, the liberalism measure was not included in the final model.

[19] Chicago and Philadelphia provide perhaps the starkest example of the irrelevance of what one might call conventional politics in the face of a black mayoral challenge. Even though the tone and content of the campaigns in the two cities were almost polar opposites, the outcome in both cases was almost exactly the same. In Chicago in 1983, in what has been described as "one of the most racist campaigns outside of the Southern states" (Alkalimat 1986: 7), Harold Washington's white opponent, Bernard Epton, ran a highly charged campaign that centered on the slogan, "Epton Now, Before It's Too Late." In sharp contrast, in Philadelphia in the same year the general election had few explicit racial references. Wilson Goode's white opponent didn't mention race. Throughout the campaign, "Philadelphians congratulated themselves, while accepting the plaudits of the national media, because their contest was free of the open anger that marked Chicago's" (Kleppner 1985: 250). Yet, despite the contrasting tones, the end result was almost identical. Exit polls indicated that white support for the two black challengers differed by only 3 percentage points. The vast majority of white voters in both cities chose not to vote for the black candidate.

conventional nonracial factors and the white vote.[20] With the possible exception of campaign spending, where there is some evidence that white voting is related to the white opponent's spending, the data suggest that when a black candidate challenges to become the first black mayor of a city, all that seems to matter is race and the fear that accompanies a perceived black takeover.[21]

These black challenger elections stand out not only because they are different from the typical urban contest but also because they are very different from previous elections in the same cities. A comparison of these challenger elections with previous contests in the same cities indicates that in many of these cities voting patterns that had held firm for decades were shattered when the possibility of an African American winning the mayor's office became real. Cities with apathetic electorates suddenly witnessed record-high turnout levels. In Birmingham, turnout jumped from 48 percent to 68 percent when Richard Arrington ran for mayor. Similarly, in Seattle, the proportion of registered voters going to the polls rose from 41 percent to 60 percent when Norm Rice sought the mayoralty. In Charlotte, when Harvey Gantt ran to become the city's first black mayor, turnout more than tripled from the previous election, growing from 14 percent to just over 50 percent. Amazingly, in roughly half of the cities in the sample, including Birmingham, Chicago, Charlotte, Cleveland, Gary, New Orleans, Newark, Memphis, and New Haven, turnout exceeded or came very close to passing the previous highest level in the city.

Perhaps even more unusual is the way that party allegiances were ignored when white voters faced the possibility of black leadership. In many cases, vast numbers of white residents ended decades of support for the Democratic Party to support a white Republican (Nelson and Meranto 1977). In Chicago – a city that had not elected a Republican for fifty-six years and had given white Republican nominees on average less than 5 percent of the vote in previous decades – white voters gave Bernard Epton, Harold Washington's white Republican opponent, 80 percent of their votes (Lewis, Taylor, and Kleppner 1997). In Cleveland, 70 percent

---

[20] As this implies, collinearity between the independent variables is not a problem here. Although the number of cases is small, ordinary least-squares regression still represents the best way to analyze the impact of each of these factors on the vote.

[21] Neither spending by the black candidate nor the relative spending advantage of the white opponent over the black challenger was significantly related to white vote choice but in some specifications, spending by the white opponent was negatively related to white support for the black challenger. Since campaign spending data are available in only two-thirds of the cases, spending was not included in the final model.

of all white Democrats switched over to the white Republican candidate rather than support the black challenger (Cho 1974). The fact that 70 percent of all white voters in the twenty-six black challenger elections in the data set opposed the black candidate and voted white, even though most of the black challengers were Democrats running in overwhelmingly Democratic cities, strongly suggests that party was less important than race in these contests.[22]

Overall, the story that these aggregate electoral data tell is clear. As predicted by the information model, when blacks challenge to take over offices they have never held, uncertainty and racial concerns end up dominating the white vote while other more conventional, nonracial factors play at best a secondary role. In almost every way – from the central role played by the size of the black community to the wholesale abandonment of the Democratic Party by white Democratic voters – the perceived threat of a black challenger leads to an exceptional kind of election.

Individual Voices

The regression results in Table 2.2 are important in that they help substantiate the role that race and racial fears played in the challenger contests. They do not, however, allow us to get into the minds of white residents. If we focus on the vote and the actions of white residents, we can only infer what they are thinking when faced with the prospect of black electoral victory. To know more about what whites are feeling and exactly what it is they fear, we need to listen to the voices of individual white residents. These voices echo my analysis of the aggregate white vote.

Although whites in the cities under consideration expressed an array of feelings about the prospect of black mayoral leadership, and although some did end up supporting black challengers, newspaper coverage suggests that many white residents were intensely concerned about the possibility of a black takeover. In Chicago, a white voter expressed his fears

---

[22] Although cities do not report voter registration data by race and party, one can very roughly calculate the proportion of whites who are Democrats by assuming that nearly all African Americans in a city are Democrats and that Latinos and Asian Americans (who are generally a very small proportion of the population during these elections) are evenly divided between Democrats and Republicans. When an estimate of the proportion of whites in each city who are Democrats is added to the regression in Table 2.2, it is significantly related to white support for the black challenger, suggesting that white Democrats are more likely to vote for black challengers. Thus, although there is little doubt that white Democrats abandoned their party at high rates in these elections, white Democrats were probably more likely than white Republicans to support black challengers.

about a black victory this way: "There will be turmoil in this city. What are the blacks trying to do, win the whole United States from us? I'm scared" (Peterson 1983b). The fears of many whites are, in retrospect, quite fantastic. In Los Angeles, one resident viewed a black victory this way: "If we have a colored mayor we'll have colored people pushing us out of the city. The whole city will be black if Bradley wins – all those people will be moving up from the South" (Reich 1973a). An elderly parishioner was quoted in the *Chicago Tribune* as saying "if that black man gets elected, no white woman would be safe on the streets" (Coleman 1983a). One possibility – neighborhood integration – was foremost in many whites' minds. Democratic Committee member Aloysius Majerczyk explained that his constituents were "afraid of scattered-site housing" and "concerned about the stability of [the city's] neighborhoods" (quoted in Rivlin 1992: 185–6).

The importance of these racial concerns also came through in analyses of exit poll data. In the few cities where whites were polled about both their racial concerns and their preferences in the mayoral election, white individuals' support for the black challenger was closely tied to whether or not they indicated that they had strong racial concerns (Kaufman 1998; 2004; Kinder and Sanders 1981; Pettigrew 1972; Jeffries and Ransford 1972; Sears and Kinder 1971). Moreover, these same studies found that demographic factors, such as political ideology, partisan identification, or socioeconomic status – normally powerful predictors of individual voting preferences – played unusually limited roles (Kaufman 1998; Halley, Acock, and Greene 1976).

Black candidates themselves were all too well aware of the enormous uncertainty surrounding their candidacies. In addition to running largely deracialized campaigns – almost half ran totally race-neutral campaigns, and only two explicitly talked about favoring the black community – many openly discussed white fears after the campaigns. Richard Arrington, the black mayor of Birmingham, was clear on this point: "The transition creates uneasiness. I understand that" (quoted in Curry 1979). David Dinkins's slogan in New York in 1989, "Vote your hopes, not your fears," stressed the same point.[23]

---

[23] Media accounts echoed the sentiments of black candidates. In New York, for example, pollster Geoffrey Garin noted, "There is still a nervousness about any black candidate" (quoted in Borger 1989). Even in some of the less racialized contests, like the one that took place in St. Louis in 1993, reporters talked about white fears: "People are apprehensive and uncomfortable about what might happen in this city. There are people who think the city hall will collapse the next day" (Casmier et al. 1993).

TABLE 2.3 *The Transformation of the White Vote Between Black Challenger and Black Incumbent Elections*

	White Support for the Black Candidate
CONVENTIONAL POLITICS	
Candidate Quality	
Quality of White Opponent	−0.13 (0.07)*
Quality* Black Incumbent Election	−0.23 (0.11)**
Endorsements	
Democratic Party Endorsement	0.02 (0.05)
Party Endorsement* Black Incumbent Election	0.18 (0.08)**
Local Newspaper Endorsement	0.02 (0.04)
Newspaper Endorsement* Black Inc. Election	0.23 (0.12)*
RACIAL FEAR	
Percent Black of City Population	−0.07 (0.00)***
Percent Black* Black Incumbent Election	0.00 (0.00)
Racialization of Black Candidate's Campaign	−0.13 (0.06)**
Racialization* Black Incumbent Election	0.01 (0.09)
Black Incumbent Election	−0.30 (0.17)*
Constant	0.64 (0.11)***
Adj. R^2	0.72
N	48

Note: OLS regression. Figures in parentheses are standard errors.
***$p < 0.01$
**$p < 0.05$
*$p < 0.10$

In short, by three different measures – the aggregate white vote chief among them, but also the individual sentiments expressed by white residents, and the concerns voiced by black candidates themselves – there is evidence that racial fears played a critical role in these black challenger elections.

A Different Calculation in Black Incumbent Elections

But what happens the second time around? Is there, as the information model predicts, a real transformation in the nature of the white vote in black incumbent elections? A comparison of the aggregate vote in challenger and incumbent elections suggests that there is. Table 2.3 combines the results of the same set of black challenger and black incumbent elections and includes a series of interactions to directly determine if different factors matter more or less in the latter.[24] In the table, each variable that is not interacted with black incumbent elections measures the effect of that variable in black challenger elections. Each interaction directly assesses how much more or less that variable matters in black incumbent elections. Thus, reading down the table, the significant interactions and the largely insignificant individual variables indicate that it is only after black incumbents have been given a chance to prove themselves that conventional factors begin to play an important role. As experience with black leadership grows and fear about its consequences declines, "politics" begins to play a primary role in voters' choices.

More specifically, Table 2.3 reveals that conventional factors such as candidate quality and political endorsements matter much more in black incumbent elections than they do in challenger elections.[25] As evidenced by the significant interaction between candidate quality and incumbent elections, the weight that white voters put on the quality of the white opponent grew sharply from the challenger to the incumbent elections. White voters may not have cared who the white candidate was when he or she faced a black challenger; at that point, any white would do. But in black incumbent elections, white voters gave white candidates with experience in citywide office almost 20 percent more votes than candidates with no experience in political office. As one white politician put it, "Race is not as much of a litmus test as it once was. The issue now is who is the best qualified man" (*Sun Reporter* 1993). The reduction in white fears also appears to have increased white voters' attention to newspaper endorsements. These endorsements were essentially meaningless in black challenger elections, but endorsement by the main local newspaper increased white support in the average incumbent election by another 20 percent. As well, party endorsements helped in the black incumbent elections, even though they did not in the challenger elections. The local

[24] This type of ordinary least-squares regression clearly cannot tell us about the causal directions of these relationships. Given that Jacobson (1980) and others have demonstrated the endogeneity of campaign spending, challenger quality, and other resources in campaigns, it is possible that the causal arrows could be reversed. For the present purposes, however, all that matters is that conventional politics plays more of a primary role in black incumbent elections than in challenger elections.

[25] It is also worth noting that endorsements and candidate quality do not become more important in black incumbent elections simply because there is more variation on each measure in incumbent elections. As Appendix A shows, variance actually declines for most of these measures in black incumbent elections.

Democratic Party's endorsement delivered an additional 16 percent of the white vote on average when blacks ran as incumbents.

A second important conclusion to draw from Table 2.3 is that race still mattered in these elections. The fact that interactions with both of the racial fear variables are insignificant indicates that the size of the black population and the racial focus of the black candidate's campaign remained important to white voters. This is not surprising; even a brief review of these elections reveals that many of them were highly racialized. Chicago, New York, and New Haven, in particular, represent cases where the general trend toward increased white support and diminished racial tension did not apply.

At the same time, there is evidence that race and racial fears were generally less powerful in the incumbent elections. Further analysis indicates that racial fear lost half of its explanatory power: whereas the size of the black population and the racial focus of the black candidate's campaign alone account for 67 percent of the variation in the vote in black challenger elections, these two variables account for only 36 percent of the variation when white residents voted in black incumbent elections. As one reporter put it in Chicago, "Something has changed. The paranoia and ugly racism that ripped the city apart [four years ago] are largely absent this time" (Bosc 1987). Another observer of several black incumbent elections in 1993 simply stated, "Race has faded in many places" (*Sun Reporter* 1993). This conclusion was echoed in a recent study of mayoral voting in Houston (Stein, Ulbig, and Post 2005). Using three different surveys of voters in the city, the study found that racial considerations faded over the course of Lee Brown's tenure in that city. As the authors note: "Racial voting appears to be more influential in minority candidates' first electoral bids. In successive elections, voters come to rely more on their evaluations of the minority incumbent's job performance than their racial-group affiliation" (Stein, Ulbig, and Post 2005: 177). Though the magnitude of the change should not be overstated, it seems that white residents became less likely to base their votes on the race of the candidate and their fear of a black takeover in the incumbent elections. Instead when black incumbents ran for reelection, white residents seemed to more deliberately assess the pluses and minuses of their candidacies. As Sharon Watson put it in her account of mayoral bids in eight cities, "In [reelection] campaigns, while race remains a special factor, it did not seem to overshadow the campaign, as was true of the first elections. Race as an issue appeared neutralized somewhat" (1984: 172).

The Black Incumbent's Record and the White Vote

The analysis to this point has ignored an important aspect of black incumbent elections. If the information model is accurate and white voters change their minds about black leadership largely because experience with black incumbents disproves many of their fears, then a black incumbent's record in office should be an important variable shaping the white vote.[26] The model predicts that black incumbents whose policies take resources from the white community to serve the black community or who preside over cities with faltering economies should do less well than black incumbents who resist pro-black policies and govern under robust local economic conditions. To analyze the influence of black incumbents' records on the white vote, I assess a range of factors related both to overall conditions in each city and to the policies that each black incumbent enacted. Given that the main fears expressed by white residents before the election of a black mayor were a deteriorating economy, falling housing prices, and widespread crime, I included measures of each of these three factors in the model.[27] Since residents might logically also gauge black leadership by local government policy, I assess the impact of local government spending patterns on the white vote by including a measure of how much a city shifted resources from developmental spending toward redistributional functions such as social services, housing, and education during the black mayor's first term. Spending is obviously one of the arenas where black mayors can affect a large number of white residents, and any emphasis on redistributive spending is likely to be perceived by white residents as a strong signal of a black mayor's underlying preferences for serving the black community.[28]

---

[26] Obviously, this is not a relationship that is unique to black incumbents. Voters generally base their decisions at least in part on the record of the incumbent (Niemi and Weisberg 1993; Krosnick 1988; Downs 1957).

[27] Specifically, I include change in per capita income relative to the average change in per capita income for all metropolitan areas (Bureau of Economic Affairs 2005), change in median housing prices (Bureau of the Census 1973–2001), and change in the violent crime rate per 1,000 residents (Federal Bureau of Investigation 1969–2001). Despite the fact that incumbents are often not responsible for local economic conditions, incumbents who are lucky enough to serve during periods of relative economic gain tend to be rewarded, while those who lead during economic downturns are often punished (MacKuen, Erikson, and Stimson 1992; Lewis-Beck 1988).

[28] The exact measure is the change in the proportion of city government spending that goes toward redistributive policy (housing, education, and social welfare) minus change in the proportion of spending going to developmental policy (highways, streets, transportation, and airports) (Bureau of the Census 1964–2003). These categories represent a fairly standard division of spending in the urban literature (see e.g. Peterson 1981).

TABLE 2.4 *Determinants of the White Vote in Black Incumbent Elections*

	White Support for the Black Candidate
RACIAL FEAR	
Percent Black of City Population	−0.27 (0.16)
Racialization of Black Candidate's Campaign	−1.03 (0.36)**
CONVENTIONAL POLITICS	
Candidate Quality	
Quality of White Opponent	−0.20 (0.08)**
Endorsements	
Democratic Party Endorsement	0.21 (0.08)**
Local Newspaper Endorsement	0.21 (0.12)*
BLACK INCUMBENT'S RECORD	
Local Conditions	
Change in Per Capita Income	0.40 (0.45)
Change in Median Housing Prices	0.21 (0.09)**
Change in Crime Rate	−0.03 (0.08)
Policy	
Change in Redistributive Spending	−0.11 (0.44)
Constant	0.01 (0.20)
Adj. R^2	0.71
N	25

Note: OLS regression. Figures in parentheses are standard errors.
***$p < 0.01$
**$p < 0.05$
*$p < 0.10$

This analysis is displayed in Table 2.4, which presents the results of a regression explaining the aggregate white vote in black incumbent elections in the same set of twenty-six cities. With a small number of cases and eleven independent variables, the model in Table 2.4 stretches the limits of what regression analysis can do and should therefore be read with some caution.[29] Nevertheless, the results are suggestive.

The first conclusion is that there are signs of a link between the black incumbent's record and the white vote. The clearest evidence of this is that changes in the local housing market are significantly related to the white

Since residents may also be concerned about the fiscal health of a city, in alternate tests I include a measure of the city's debt as a percentage of the city's overall revenue.

[29] It is worth noting, however, that the basic results in Table 2.4 remain robust to a range of different specifications. In a series of alternate tests, I reran the analysis, dropping all nonsignificant variables or including only one measure for each factor (e.g. including only one variable for the incumbent's record). The basic conclusions did not change.

vote. If, contrary to white fears, housing prices do not collapse and home-owners do well under black leadership, white residents will tend to reward the black incumbent. This finding parallels emerging research on so-called performance models of mayoral approval (Stein, Ulbig and Post 2005; Howell and Perry 2004; Howell and McClean 2001). These recent studies have shown that in a small number of cities for which there are survey data white approval of incumbent black mayors is related to white evaluations of local economic conditions and white perceptions of city services.[30]

However, as Table 2.4 also reveals, for other aspects of the incumbent's record, the existence of any relationship to the white vote is less clear. None of the other factors assessing the incumbent's record significantly predicts the white vote. The most that can be said is that in all three cases the relationship between the incumbent's record and the white vote is in the expected direction.[31]

Thus, another interpretation is that the relationship between a black incumbent's record and the white vote is not nearly as strong as some might have expected. In only the one case – housing prices – is the incumbent's record significantly related to the white vote, and even here the magnitude of the effect is not large. For every one point increase in median housing prices, there is only a one-fifth of a point gain in white support for the black incumbent.

Why doesn't an incumbent's record matter more? Part of the answer may be related to the limitations of the empirical model. Too many variables and too few cases certainly cloud the analysis. The imprecise nature of the measures used in the analysis may also be a contributing factor. Whites, for example, may be more sensitive to housing prices and crime rates in their own neighborhoods than they are to overall changes at the city level. But a third and perhaps more critical answer here is the fact that almost all black incumbents exceed expectations. In the majority of the

[30] Given that in these surveys local conditions and services are evaluated subjectively by each individual respondent, there is a possibility of reverse causation – those who approve of the mayor tend to rate local conditions and services well. More work will have to be done to assess this connection.

[31] These regression results mirror bivariate analysis. Each of these three factors was individually correlated with the white vote in the expected direction, but in no case was the correlation statistically significant. The same can be said for the relationship between affirmative action in local government hiring practices and the white vote. In alternate tests, I included a measure of the increase in the proportion of the public employees who are African American during the mayor's term in office. These tests indicate that there is a negative but not significant relationship between affirmative action and the white vote in black incumbent elections.

cities in the data set, per capita incomes grew compared to the national average, and in only two cases were gains in per capita income outpaced by more than 2 percent by gains made at the national level. Median housing prices rarely fell. And although crime rates did rise in the average city, in most cases they did not rise at a rate appreciably faster than in the nation as a whole. Likewise, local government policy under black incumbents did little to substantiate white fears. The average city did not shift *any* resources from developmental projects to such redistributive programs as welfare, health, and housing, and in only two cases was more than 4 percent of the city budget transferred to redistributive functions. Finally, few of the cities stood out in terms of affirmative action policies. All but one increased black hiring under the black mayor, but only one city increased the proportion of blacks in the public sector by more than 5 percent. The lack of any dramatic change under black incumbents is not surprising, as these results mirror accounts from a range of existing studies. But it is important, because it represents a stark contrast with the expectations and fears of many whites. In essence then, the lesson is the same in almost every city. By maintaining tolerable or even relatively robust economic conditions and by choosing not to shift substantial resources away from the white community, black mayors, in almost all cases, demonstrate that black leadership does not appreciably hurt the white community. The bottom line is that black incumbents can help themselves by introducing policies that benefit the city but in the end all they have to do is not attack the white community. That is often enough to convince some white residents that they are worth supporting.

Individual White Residents and Learning under Black Incumbents

Although the changes in the vote outlined in Tables 2.2, 2.3, and 2.4 are important and certainly could be interpreted as showing that white residents learn from their experiences under black incumbents, we need to look at the sentiments expressed by individual white residents for direct evidence of white learning. These views reinforce the basic conclusions I have drawn from my analysis of the aggregate vote. At least among those who were willing to speak out, there was a strong sense of relief and a clear change in perceptions of black leadership. The comments of one Memphis resident are illustrative: "I get a feeling he is keeping the city from being split asunder by racial divisions. I thought there would be a lot of pressure on him from blacks to give in to all of their demands. I think he has been a mayor for all of the city" (A. Davis 1995). A voter in Los Angeles put it this way: "A lot of people were very suspicious and fearful before Bradley got in. But they never say anything now. I'm sure they have changed their opinions.... Most important, he is a good person. Whether he is black or white is immaterial" (*US News & World Report* 1975). In Atlanta, the head of a local civic organization also noted a change in white sentiments in that city: "A lot of people who thought they couldn't live with a black administration have found they can do so quite well" (Eisinger 1980: 77). Many whites did not change their minds about black leadership at all, and in some cities the change was more dramatic than in others. But for the most part, the sentiments of white voters in black incumbent elections are a far cry from the expressions of fear and uncertainty that surround black challenger elections.

Black candidates also made note of the learning process. Thirman Milner's comments are typical: "I ran up against racial issues in my first election with all the talk that crime would go up, the city would go down and I would only address black issues. But people began to see there are no racial distinctions when it comes to operating as a mayor" (Hagstrom and Guskind 1983). His views were echoed by Carl Stokes, Cleveland's first black mayor: "There are so many prejudices that impact upon voters. But once they've seen an individual in action and what they've been able to do, they discard some of those biases and fears and look at that candidate the same way they look at any other public official" (Vickers 1997: 23).

Another sign of learning that cannot be seen in the regressions in Tables 2.2, 2.3, and 2.4 is a dramatic shift in tone between the typical black challenger election and the typical black incumbent election. The black challenger elections tended to be intense, racially polarized affairs that were characterized by the media with phrases like "black versus white" (in the Flint election, 1983), "race-dominated" (in Chicago, 1983), and "highly polarized" (in Memphis, 1991). They often included highly provocative campaigns that played on white uncertainty and racial fears. But after a period of only a few years, these bitter, polarized elections often gave way to more ordinary affairs. In sharp contrast to black challenger elections, electoral contests with black incumbents were generally described with phrases that emphasized their lack of racial animosity: "low-key, almost dignified politicking" (in the Atlantic City election, 1986), "a colorless campaign" (in Atlanta, 1977), "ho-hum voters" (in Memphis, 1995), "a lusterless campaign" (in Cleveland, 1969), and "a humdrum affair" (in Denver, 1999). In Newark, for example, a black challenger election that had included numerous incidents of racial heckling, bomb threats, and even violence was followed four years later by a black incumbent election the *New York Times* characterized as "surprisingly uneventful" (May 12, 1974). Similarly, in Birmingham, four years after Richard Arrington's election bid "brought racial animosities in the city to their highest pitch since the civil rights demonstrations of 1963" (Raines 1979), his reelection run ended "with a biracial coalition and the largest victory margin in city history" (Russakof 1983). Incumbent elections in some cities, including Chicago, New York, and New Haven, did remain racialized and as such did not fit this pattern, but in the vast majority of cases there was a marked change in the nature of the election campaign.

Do White Residents Simply Give Up?

One possible confounding factor in the analysis to this point is "white flight." If a significant number of whites perceived black victory as certain and effectively gave up, choosing not to vote or to leave their city of residence altogether, the changes that we see in the white vote might be more apparent than real. To see if changes in the white vote are at least in part a function of white flight or selective nonvoting by whites, in alternate analysis I added two measures to the regression model in Table 2.4: voter turnout in each election and change in the city's white population between the challenger and the incumbent election. The regression results indicate that the white vote was not related to declining turnout or to white flight.[32] Other available evidence supports this conclusion. First, in cities where public opinion polls are available, the data show that white voters were not substantially more likely than non-voters to express support for black incumbents.[33] This strongly suggests that anti-black voters

[32] The model assesses the relationship between overall turnout and white support for the black candidate, but it seems likely that if turnout numbers for whites were available for all of these cities, white turnout would also prove to be unrelated to white support for the black candidate. White turnout is correlated with overall turnout at 0.97 for cities in which turnout by race is available. There is little evidence, moreover, of a relationship between the vulnerability of the black incumbent and turnout. White residents are no more apt to fail to vote in cities where blacks are the majority and could presumably determine the outcome of the election than they are elsewhere. White turnout actually drops less in majority black cities (5.5 point drop) than it does in minority black cities (8.7 point drop). Moreover, even if the first election was close and whites presumably had a real chance of reversing the outcome, white turnout dropped at about the same rate in these cities as it did elsewhere.

[33] Similarly, in cities where data are available by precinct or district, turnout falls at about the same rate across neighborhoods. White neighborhoods that were more opposed to the black challenger generally lost voters at about the same rate as white neighborhoods that had been more supportive of the black challenger (Sonenshein 1993).

were not selectively dropping out. Second, not that many white residents actually left their cities in the short period between the challenger and incumbent elections. The white proportion of the population declined by 2 percent on average across the cities – not enough to account for the changes in the white vote that are seen in Tables 2.2, 2.3, and 2.4 (Bureau of the Census 1994, 1990, 1978).[34] And those whites who did leave the cities were probably not especially anti-black in their thinking. Existing research indicates that whites who leave cities tend to be younger, wealthier, and better educated (Deane 1990). The poor, older, and less educated who are left behind because the costs of moving are too high are the people who are most likely to be racially intolerant (Bobo 1983; Rieder 1985). Thus, if anything, white out-migration should have led to a more rather than a less racialized white vote.[35]

Changes in the vote, changes in the tone of campaigns, and changes in the sentiments expressed by many white residents from challenger to incumbent elections all point to the conclusion that the information provided by black representation erodes the fears of many white residents and makes them more willing to consider supporting black leadership.

CHANGES OVER TIME

If black leadership is to represent a real turning point in American race relations, the effects that appear in the data set of twenty-six black mayors must extend to other candidates in other elections. Experience with one black incumbent, if it merely convinces white residents that a particular black incumbent is trustworthy, will only have a temporary and isolated effect. If, however, learning is more extensive and experience under black incumbents leads whites to fundamentally reevaluate the broader threat posed by black leadership and the degree to which black interests and white interests are in conflict, these elections could signal a new era in racial politics. Part of the answer to this question appears in Chapter 3 in a more detailed examination of white views under black representation, but a cursory look at the white vote for evidence of a gradual increase in

---

[34] This fits with other analysis, which indicates that the rapid out-migration of whites was largely stemmed by the time most of these cities had elected their first black mayors (Brown 1997).

[35] It is also worth noting that while race is often a factor in motivating moves from neighborhood to neighborhood, studies of inter-metropolitan migration suggest that racial motivations seldom explain moves into and out of larger cities (Koven and Shelley 1989; Long 1988; McHugh 1985; South and Deanne 1993; Stahura 1988).

TABLE 2.5 *Changes in Voting Behavior Over Time: Black Challenger Elections*

Decade (N)	Average White Support for Black Challenger (%)	Average Turnout (%)
1960s (2)	17	76
1970s (5)	21	67
1980s (13)	33	54
1990s (6)	34	41

support for black candidates over time can also tell us a little about how wide-ranging the effects of black leadership are.

In Table 2.5, I begin to test this proposition by examining white support for black challengers by decade in the twenty-six elections.[36] The analysis reported in the table suggests that white support for black candidates is in fact on the rise. Support for black candidates who run as challengers has increased markedly over time. The number of cases in each decade may be small, but the change is clear. Black challengers in the 1960s faced almost unanimous white opposition (83 percent of white votes). In the 1970s, white support for black challengers was, on average, 4 percent higher. In the 1980s, it grew by another 12 percent. By the 1990s, the average black challenger received the support of 34 percent of all white voters – certainly not an indication that race is now irrelevant, but nevertheless a big step from the fear and anti-black mobilization of the late 1960s.

Two other changes point to a similar transformation of the white vote over the same period. As the second column of Table 2.5 illustrates, turnout dramatically declined in black challenger elections over time. Overall, turnout dropped from an average of 76 percent in the 1960s to 41 percent in the 1990s. For the cities in which the data on turnout can be broken down by race, it appears that white turnout declined at roughly the same rate as overall turnout. It may well be that the election of a black candidate to office does not create nearly as much uncertainty and fear in the 1990s as it did in the 1960s.

An equally important change appears to have occurred in the tone and content of the white candidates' campaigns. Early black challengers faced

---

[36] A much stronger test of this proposition would assess white voter support for a random set of black challengers over time. Unfortunately, no such data set is available. Generally, only major contests in large cities have exit polls or pre-election polls, and smaller cities rarely have data on the racial and ethnic makeup of precincts, making it nearly impossible to obtain the vote by race in most local contests.

white opponents who tried to play on white uncertainty about black leadership. Since whites had little past experience with black leadership and no idea what to expect, white candidates could campaign effectively by playing on uncertainty. So, for example, in Los Angeles Sam Yorty could run against Tom Bradley in 1973 by stating: "You know what kind of city we've got. We don't know what we might get. So we'd be taking quite a chance with this particular kind of candidate." Similarly, in Chicago mayoral candidate Eddie Vrdolyak played on white concerns about the consequences of black leadership: "It's a racial thing. Don't kid yourself. I am calling on you to save your city, to save your precinct. We're fighting to keep the city the way it is" (quoted in Rivlin, 1992: 155). In Newark, the white police chief announced dramatically in 1970: "Whether we survive or cease to exist depends on what you do on [election day]" (quoted in Eisinger 1980: 15). In Atlanta, when Maynard Jackson ran in 1973, the slogan was, "Atlanta is too young to die."[37] But by the 1990s, whites had had the chance to evaluate the effects of black leadership in a range of major cities. Since Atlanta, Los Angeles, and other cities had done relatively well under black leadership, white candidates could no longer credibly claim that black leadership would mean the demise of the white community or that the city's police force would quit en masse if an African American were elected mayor. The old scare tactics faded out of existence.

There are other factors at work over this time period – increasingly strong norms against overt racism, and declining racial tension as the riots of the 1960s and 1970s faded into memory – so it is hard to know how much of these changes are actually due to white learning. But the end result is that more and more black challengers are winning office in majority white cities. In the 1960s, there were no black mayors of majority white cities with more than 50,000 residents. In the 1970s, 11 black candidates won election in these majority white cities. In the 1980s, the number increased to 15, while in the 1990s, 18 blacks won elections in majority white cities. Eighteen may not seem to be a large number, but it actually represents a sizeable portion of all big-city black mayors – 57 percent

---

[37] This phenomenon is not confined to black mayoral candidates, of course. When Harvey Gantt ran for the Senate in 1990, Jessie Helms countered with an advertisement depicting a white worker losing a job to a less qualified black man. Analysts felt that the advertisement was the turning point of the campaign. "The ad scared some whites, convincing them that Gantt was a threat to their future and ... propelled Helms to victory" (Frisby 1991: 14). Years earlier, George Wallace was much more direct: "If I don't win, them niggers are going to control this state" (quoted in Black and Black 1973: 736).

in 2001. When blacks were being elected in that year, white voters were critical to their success most of the time.

Changes in the white vote, in the kinds of campaigns white opponents run, and in the success rates of black candidates in minority black locales all hint at a sea change in the views and perceptions of a large segment of the white community. Though it is impossible on the basis of the data presented here to assign this change definitively to the effects of white learning from black leadership, they certainly leave open the possibility that experience with black leaders is fundamentally altering the nature of biracial politics in this country. To more directly assess changes in white attitudes and perceptions, in Chapter 3 I turn to a closer inspection of white racial views before, during, and after the election of blacks to the mayoralty.

But before we proceed, it is worth noting two qualifications. First, as Table A.1 in Appendix A makes clear, there is considerable variation across the cities in the data set. Although change in most cities led to greater acceptance of black candidates and less racialized political contests, black mayors in Atlantic City, Baltimore, Chicago, Durham, Flint, New Haven, New Orleans, New York, Philadelphia, and San Francisco faced more white opposition when they ran as incumbents than they did when they sought the mayoralty in the first place. Some of these cases can by explained by pointing to a poor local economy, a strong white challenger, or to more idiosyncratic events, such as scandals, but others cannot. Chapter 4 will delve more deeply into differences across cities and contexts and will try to link much of the variation in white reactions to differences in the local information environment. Nevertheless, the lack of positive change in many cities should give us some pause.

Second, even in the cities that did experience positive change, there is evidence that race continues to play a critical role even in black incumbent elections. And despite the changes noted here, blacks are still greatly underrepresented at the mayoral level. The ICMA reports that only 2.1 percent of all mayors in the nation are African American – well below the 12 percent of the national population that is African American (MacManus and Bullock 1993). Clearly, the nation has a long way to go before race no longer plays a role in mayoral politics. Expectations about the dawn of an era of interracial collaboration should be tempered.

3

The Transformation of White Attitudes

The last chapter revealed important changes in the white vote. Experience with black incumbency increased white support for black candidates and altered the nature of the white vote in biracial elections. These changes imply that whites are learning from their experience with black leadership, but the fact that some white voters begin to choose black candidates over white candidates does not tell us exactly *what* whites learn – how their views toward blacks change. The goal of this chapter is to focus directly on white views to try to understand what white voters learn during and after the transition from white to black leadership. The information that black incumbency provides appears to have a broad impact on white views. The tests analyzed here suggest that experience with black incumbents leads to positive changes in how many whites perceive black leadership and the larger black community. The changes are not always dramatic, but they are real. The results also show that everyone does not learn the same things from black leadership: among whites, Republicans and Democrats, in particular, appear to learn differently, and the result is a growing partisan divide on matters of race.

ASSESSING WHITE ATTITUDES

To assess changes in white racial attitudes and policy preferences under black mayors, I compared the attitudes of a representative sample of white respondents in cities with a white mayor to the attitudes of a similar sample of white respondents in cities with a black mayor. The least complicated and most direct test of white learning would examine the attitudes of a representative group of individuals in a city over time as they experienced the transition from white to black leadership. Unfortunately, this type of panel data is unavailable. In lieu of it, I utilized responses from the American National Election Study (ANES). The ANES contains an array of questions designed to gauge white racial attitudes and political orientation and is therefore a valuable tool for my purposes. Although the data are cross-sectional and thus do not follow the same individuals over time, I engage in a variety of tests to try to show that black leadership does, in fact, cause a change in white attitudes. Combined, these tests hopefully present a clear picture of change.

By pooling samples from the years 1984 to 1992, I obtained an ample number of white responses from a wide variety of cities with black and white mayors.[1] Details on the sampling, survey instruments, and other methodology concerning the survey can be found in Miller, and National Election Studies (1994). Data on the race of mayors and council members come from the National Roster of Black Elected Officials. Other data on city-level characteristics, such as racial demographics and median income, were drawn from the relevant census publications (Bureau of the Census 1964–2003; 1994; 1990).

I looked for change in white views on two basic sets of measures: perceptions of black leadership and feelings about the black community.[2] I chose these two areas because each addresses a critical aspect of the information model. If white residents learn anything from their experiences with black incumbents, it should be reflected first in their views of black leadership. When black incumbents do not target the white community but instead serve the interests of many members of the white community, whites should recognize this and the perception that black leaders pose a threat should be reduced. To see if perceptions of the threat posed by black leadership changed under black incumbents, I examined responses

---

[1] In this pooled sample, I included respondents from cities or primary areas with populations greater than 25,000. Within the sample, there are 1,605 white respondents living in eighteen cities with black mayors. These cities are 10 to 76% black. Across the whole pooled sample, there are 6,543 respondents from seventy cities represented in the data.

[2] Another important step in the learning process is for white residents to recognize the economic effects of black leadership. The ANES has one question that taps into this kind of learning: "How much real change do you think there has been in the position of black people in the past few years?" When I included it in supplementary tests, these tests appeared to show that the longer a city had experienced black leadership, the more likely white residents were to believe that the pace of racial change had slowed. Since answers to this question could be interpreted less as an objective measure of racial change and more as a liberal indictment of American society, the conclusions to be drawn about white learning from this result are not clear.

to the following question: "Some say that the civil rights people have been trying to push too fast. Others feel they haven't pushed fast enough. How about you: Do you think that civil rights leaders are trying to push too fast, are going too slowly, or are moving about the right speed?"[3] This particular question in some ways represents a difficult first test. Since the question does not refer to local leaders and local politics, whites would have to generalize from their experiences with local black leadership to all black leadership in order for there to be a change on this measure.[4] The advantage of this particular question, however, is that it also taps into broader aspects of race relations. Bobo (1983) has argued that this question is a key indicator of the state of racial conflict, and tests indicate that responses to the question are significantly correlated with recent or imminent changes in local racial policy making (Bobo 1983). Thus, the measure provides a reasonable assessment of race relations, and any improvement in white views on it should be considered significant.

A second important question about white learning is whether white views about the black community as a whole change under black leadership. Whites may learn that black leadership is less threatening but, nevertheless, they may not change their views about the larger black community. If white residents do not believe that local black leaders represent the interests of the black community, then they may feel that the black community still represents a significant threat. To assess this larger change in white attitudes, I examined white responses to all other ANES questions in the pooled sample that tapped views about the black community without getting into specific policy debates. Of these questions, the most general measure of white views toward blacks was a black feeling thermometer. For the feeling thermometer, white respondents were asked how "warmly" or "favorably" they felt toward blacks as a group on a scale from 0 to 100. I reversed the scale to get a measure of anti-black affect. Since different respondents can assign very different meaning to the same

---

[3] Answers to the question were coded as follows: (1) too fast, (0.5) about the right speed, (0) too slowly.

[4] The task is made even tougher by the fact that this question, and the others, are embedded in the ANES, a survey that focuses on national politics. However, given the extensive media coverage of black mayors and the intense fears that many white respondents seem to have about black leadership at the local level, there is reason to believe that white views even on more national or general questions will be affected by their experiences with a black mayor. If this assumption is incorrect, and white responses to these questions do not reflect the knowledge that white residents have obtained from living under black mayors, then we should expect to find no relationship between experience under a black mayor and white attitudes.

value on the scale (that is, what does a value of 60 mean?), I controlled for each respondent's feelings toward whites on a similar reversed feeling thermometer.[5] The result is a measure of how negatively respondents felt toward blacks as a group relative to their feelings toward whites – a measure that is akin to in-group favoritism (Tajfel 1981).[6]

A second measure of whites' overall views of the black community comes from the four remaining race questions in the pooled sample: (1) "It's really a matter of some people not trying hard enough; if blacks would only try harder they could be just as well off as whites." (2) "Irish, Italian, Jewish and many other minorities overcame prejudice and worked their way up. Blacks should do the same without special favors." (3) "Over the past few years, blacks have gotten less than they deserve." (4) "Generations of slavery and discrimination have created conditions that make it difficult for blacks to work their way out of the lower class." In each case, respondents were asked whether they agreed or disagreed with the statement and how strongly.[7]

On the surface, each of these four questions addresses a different issue. Yet each focuses on one central element of race relations: the extent to which blacks face barriers in American society. The four questions are not only linked conceptually, they are also linked empirically. Answers to the four questions are highly correlated, with inter-item correlations ranging from a low of 0.39 to a high of 0.59. Thus, I was able to create what I call a *racial resentment scale* using these four questions.[8] If black representation does change white views about blacks as a group, then it should be reflected in both the measure of anti-black affect and the racial resentment scale.[9]

---

[5] Since some respondents tend to be high raters and others low raters, in alternate tests I standardized responses by controlling for each respondent's mean score across an array of six feeling thermometer measures. The following results are almost identical with or without feelings toward whites controlled, and with or without standardizing by the mean. The scale has a mean response of 0.55 (std. dev. = 0.10).

[6] This scale can also be viewed as a measure of prejudice (Hurwitz and Peffley 1998; Allport 1954). The more whites prefer whites as a group over blacks as a group, the more they can be seen as prejudiced.

[7] For each question, responses were (1) disagree strongly, (2) disagree somewhat, (3) neither agree nor disagree, (4) agree somewhat, and (5) agree strongly.

[8] This scale is almost identical to a racial resentment scale developed by Kinder and Sanders (1996).

[9] To create the scale, responses to each question were ordered from least to most sympathetic to blacks. Individual responses were then added together, and the scale was normalized to a 0–1 range. The reliability of the scale is high, with a Cronbach's alpha of 0.77. The scale

To try to ensure that any differences in white attitudes between black-run and white-run cities are really a function of black leadership, I controlled for demographic and socioeconomic factors known or suspected to affect white racial attitudes. The model includes the following control variables: (1) personal socioeconomic characteristics – age, education, income, gender, employment status, home ownership, and the number of years the respondent had lived in the city; and (2) contextual variables – portion of the city that is black, level of urbanism, year of the interview, and residence in the South.[10] All independent variables were coded o to 1 for ease of interpretation.[11] Coding and descriptive statistics for these variables are included in Appendix B.

is centered on a value of 0.60, indicating that most white respondents are slightly more resentful than they are sympathetic on these questions. Scores are distributed normally. Standard deviation is 0.24. I tried two alternate tests to ensure the robustness of my results. First, I repeated the following analysis with each individual question, rather than the whole scale. Although statistical significance usually declines, there are few substantive changes to the results. Second, I used maximum likelihood estimation confirmatory factor analysis to develop a latent factor representing the main theme of these four questions. When I substituted the latent factor into the following analysis, the results were almost identical.

[10] I also include in each model a dummy variable for cities that are within twelve months of the transition to the first black mayor of a city. I do so for two reasons. First, there is likely to be heightened racial tension during the transition year. As a result, white respondents may be less rather than more racially tolerant in the period surrounding the election of a city's first black mayor. Second, white residents in cities that have just been taken over by black mayors have had little experience with black leadership and hence little time to learn what the consequences of black leadership are.

[11] One possible confounding factor is white flight. The rapid outmigration of a large number of anti-black white residents under black mayors could clearly affect the remaining mix of white racial attitudes under black incumbents. As noted in Chapter 2, there are several factors that suggest this is not a primary factor here. First, the rapid outmigration of whites was largely stemmed by the time these surveys were taken (Frey 1980). Between 1980 and 1990 in the cities included in this survey, the proportion of each city's population that was black increased by 2%. Moreover, the proportion of the population that was black increased only marginally faster in cities that had black mayors during this period (2.3% increase). Second, in the analysis, I control for the number of years a respondent has been living in a community. If changes in white attitudes were due to racially conservative whites moving out, one would expect that longer stays would be associated with more liberal racial attitudes. This is decidedly not the case. If anything, whites who live longer in their communities are less racially tolerant and more resentful. This seems to confirm research on migration patterns, which indicates that because moving is expensive, whites who leave cities tend to be younger, wealthier, and better educated (Deane 1990). The poor, older, and less educated who are left behind are the people who are most likely to be racially intolerant (Bobo 1983; Rieder 1985).

Finally, to help assuage fears that the changes we will see in white attitudes under black mayors are not the result of especially racially tolerant white communities electing black mayors, I compared the racial attitudes of white residents in cities prior to the election of a black mayor with the attitudes of whites in cities that did not elect black mayors. Across the attitudinal measures looked at in this study, there were no consistent or substantial differences between the two groups of white residents. In other words, whites in cities that elected black mayors were not especially racially tolerant before the arrival of a black mayor.[12] It is only after years of experience under a black incumbent that differences emerge. Given that the main factors driving the election of black mayors are the size and resources of the black community (Karnig and Welch 1980), it probably should not be surprising to find that white racial views in cities electing black mayors are not unlike white racial views elsewhere.

IMPROVED ATTITUDES UNDER BLACK MAYORS

Whites do appear to learn from their experiences under black representation. As illustrated by Table 3.1, whites who live in cities governed by black mayors have significantly more positive racial attitudes than whites who live under white mayors. First, under black mayors, as one might expect, there were clear changes in how whites perceived black leadership. White residents who experienced black mayoral leadership were less apt to believe that black leaders were pushing too hard. Given that this particular question can also be viewed as a measure of perceived racial group conflict, there is at least some evidence here that the election of blacks to office diminishes racial tension, though the change is not dramatic.[13]

Importantly, it is not just whites' views of black leadership that changed under black mayors. Feelings toward the black community as

---

[12] It should, however, be noted that whites in cities that were just about to elect black mayors were slightly more liberal or Democratic leaning than whites in other cities (analysis not shown).

[13] Part of the reason why differences between the two types of cities are not very pronounced may be that whites who live in cities with white mayors are observing black mayoral leadership from afar and are themselves learning from those observations. Although it is unlikely that this distance learning will have the same effect as actually living under a black mayor – witnessing first hand that one's own community did well under black leadership is probably very different from reading about economic trends in another city in the newspaper – it is quite possible that learning is occurring in a range of circumstances.

TABLE 3.1 *The Impact of Black Representation on White Racial Attitudes*

	Views of Black Leadership	Views of the Black Community	
	Blacks Pushing Too Hard[b]	Anti-black Affect[1]	Racial Resentment[a]
Black Mayor (1 = yes 0 = no)	−0.21 (0.12)*	−0.02 (0.01)***	−0.04 (0.01)***
Education	−1.5 (0.16)***	−0.05 (0.01)***	−0.21 (0.02)***
Income	0.04 (0.17)	−0.00 (0.01)	−0.01 (0.02)
Age	1.2 (0.21)	0.04 (0.01)***	−0.01 (0.02)
Gender (1 = male)	0.23 (0.08)***	0.00 (0.01)	0.02 (0.01)***
Ideology (1 = liberal)	−2.1 (0.21)***	−0.06 (0.01)***	−0.27 (0.02)***
Party ID (1 = Democrat)	−0.55 (0.14)***	0.01 (0.01)	−0.02 (0.01)
Employment Status (1 = unemployed)	−0.62 (0.23)***	−0.00 (0.01)	0.01 (0.02)
Years Living in City	0.11 (0.13)	0.01 (0.01)	0.03 (0.01)**
Percent Black in City	0.66 (0.28)**	0.04 (0.01)***	0.13 (0.03)***
Level of Urbanism	0.05 (0.16)	0.01 (0.01)	−0.07 (0.02)***
South (1 = yes)	0.30 (0.10)***	0.01 (0.00)***	0.03 (0.01)**
1986	−0.24 (0.15)		
1988	−0.30 (0.14)**	0.02 (0.01)***	0.04 (0.01)***
1990	−0.24 (0.16)		−0.04 (0.01)***
1992	−0.38 (0.13)***	−0.02 (0.01)***	0.01 (0.01)
First Year of Black Mayoralty (1 = yes)	−0.13 (0.19)	0.01 (0.01)	0.01 (0.02)
Constant		0.59 (0.01)***	0.88 (0.02)***
Intercept 1	−4.1 (0.25)***		
Intercept 2	−0.64 (0.23)***		
Adj. R²/pseudo R²	0.15	0.09	0.21
χ²	424		
N	2597	2914	2461

Note: Figures are unstandardized coefficients with their standard errors.

***p < 0.01
**p < 0.05
*p < 0.10
[a] Ordinary least squares.
[b] Ordered logit.

a whole also appear to have shifted. Whites who lived under black mayors were significantly more likely to feel warmly toward the black community. For many whites, experience with black leadership also seems to have led to a diminution of racial resentment. White residents in cities with black mayors were substantially more sympathetic to black

interests and more understanding of the barriers facing the black community.[14]

A Causal Connection?

Thus far, my analysis of Table 3.1 has overlooked an important issue.
Given the cross-sectional nature of the data, it is possible that the causal
arrow is reversed: cities with more tolerant white residents could be more
likely to elect a black mayor rather than the opposite. Although the available evidence seems to suggest that the presence of a black mayor in a
city depends much more on the size and resources of the black community than on the characteristics of the white community (Karnig and
Welch 1980), I nevertheless conducted several different tests on this point.
In each case, the results were the same: each model suggests that black
mayoral leadership does lead to less negative views of blacks and black
leadership.

The first test is a two-stage least-squares model that uses instrumental
variables to try to address the question of causality. It is described in detail
in Appendix B, and the results of the model are displayed in Tables B.1
and B.2 in the appendix. This alternate test strongly suggests that white
views on race are significantly more positive under a black mayor than
they are under a white mayor even after the possibility of reverse causality
is taken into consideration. As an additional check on the link between a
black mayoralty and white racial attitudes, I reanalyzed the data with a
different sample of respondents. In this second alternate model, I included
only white respondents from cities that have had a black mayor at some
point in their history. Since all of the cities in this new sample elected black
mayors at some point, any positive change in white attitudes under black
leadership is less likely to be the especially racial tolerant cities electing
black mayors and is more likely to be directly related to experience with
an incumbent black mayor. The results, which are displayed in Table B.3

---

[14] One might object that the model in Table 3.1 does not take into account all of the
potentially relevant factors in the local environment. Perhaps white attitudes depend on
the class makeup of the black population or the city-level mix of partisanship. However,
alternate test revealed no such links. Although both the class makeup of the black community and the percentage of Republicans in the city were related to the presence of a
black mayor (see Table B.3), their inclusion in these models did little to affect the overall
results. I could find no city-level contextual factor that eliminated the link between a
black mayoralty and white attitudes.

in Appendix B, corroborate the findings in Table 3.1. In this more select group of cities, the analysis reveals once again that under black mayors anti-black affect declines, racial resentment wanes, and whites perceive less racial group conflict.

When Do Whites' Attitudes Change?

One last way to try to ensure that the changes we see under black mayors are real is to look at changes over the course of black mayoral leadership in a city. If changes in white racial attitudes really are a function of information garnered from the actions of black incumbents, then we should see whites beginning to feel less and less threatened and expressing increasingly positive racial attitudes as the years go by under a black mayor. In Table 3.2, I test this proposition. Here we are only including white respondents from cities that currently have a black mayor. The dependent variables are the same: I consider attitudes toward black leadership and views of the black community (anti-black affect and the racial resentment scale). The independent variable in this case is the length of time a city has had a black mayor. In order to ensure that the results are not skewed by racially tolerant respondents from one or two cities that have had decades of black mayoral leadership, I normalized the years of black leadership in each city.[15] This allowed me to compare the views of respondents reporting at the beginning of a black mayor's tenure with respondents reporting later in the tenure of a black leader.[16] It is worth noting that across the entire white American population there has been no overall improvement on these particular racial attitudes, and on some questions whites in America actually feel more negatively toward blacks than they did decades ago (Schuman et al. 1997). Thus, positive changes under black mayors are not the result of a general improvement in racial attitudes over time.

[15] Thus, length of time under black leadership is measured on a scale from 0 to 1, with 0 being the first year a black mayor was elected and 1 being the last year the city had a black mayor. To create the scale, I simply add up the number of years the city has had a black mayor in office (excluding any interim years in which a white mayor held office). I then calculate the number of years the city has had a black mayor at the time of the survey for each respondent and divide the latter number by the former.

[16] As a secondary test, I repeated the analysis with a nonnormalized scale (the number of years under black leadership). The results were almost identical, but the level of significance of the effects of black leadership on white racial attitudes declined in some cases.

TABLE 3.2 *How Time Under Black Leadership Affects White Racial Views*

	Views of Black Leadership	Views of the Black Community	
	Blacks Pushing Too Hard[2]	Anti-black Affect[b]	Racial Resentment[a]
Years Under a Black Mayoralty (1 = last year, 0 = first year)	0.75 (0.52)	−0.05 (0.02)***	−0.15 (0.04)***
Education	−1.8 (0.33)***	−0.05 (0.01)***	−0.22 (0.03)***
Income	−0.05 (0.39)	0.00 (0.01)	−0.00 (0.03)
Age	1.4 (0.48)***	0.04 (0.02)**	−0.00 (0.04)
Gender (1 = male)	0.16 (0.17)	0.00 (0.01)	0.02 (0.02)
Ideology (1 = liberal)	−2.5 (0.47)***	−0.06 (0.02)***	−0.28 (0.04)***
Party ID (1 = Democrat)	−0.61 (0.30)**	0.01 (0.01)	−0.02 (0.03)
Employment Status (1 = unemployed)	0.05 (0.59)	−0.00 (0.02)	0.02 (0.04)
Years Living in City	−0.03 (0.31)	0.01 (0.01)	0.03 (0.02)
Percent Black in City	0.77 (0.52)	0.02 (0.02)	0.08 (0.04)**
Level of Urbanism	0.38 (0.40)	−0.01 (0.01)	−0.07 (0.03)**
South (1 = yes)	0.39 (0.22)*	0.01 (0.01)	0.03 (0.02)
1986	−0.34 (0.39)		
1988	−0.73 (0.38)*	−0.02 (0.01)**	0.05 (0.02)**
1990	−0.94 (0.44)**		−0.02 (0.02)
1992	−1.6 (0.47)***	−0.01 (0.01)	0.08 (0.03)***
Constant		0.62 (0.02)***	0.96 (0.04)***
Intercept 1	−4.3 (0.65)***		
Intercept 2	−0.61 (0.61)		
Adj. R^2/pseudo R^2	0.20	0.08	0.21
χ^2	138		
N	622	800	800

Note: Figures are unstandardized coefficients with their standard errors.
***p < 0.01
**p < 0.05
*p < 0.10
[a] Ordinary least squares.
[b] Ordered logit.

The results here are not totally uniform, but there does appear to be a clear link between the length of time a white respondent has lived under black leadership and at least some of his or her views. In particular, Table 3.2 reveals a significant positive relationship between time under a black mayor and white views of the black community. As time passes and white residents' experiences with black leadership grow, whites feel less resentful and more warmly toward the black community. Alternate tests also show that the longer a city has experienced black leadership, the more likely whites are to believe that the pace of racial change is slowing. In other words, as time goes by, white residents are more apt to recognize that black leadership does not mean racial upheaval. At the same time, there is no clear link in Table 3.2 between time under black mayoral leadership and white perceptions of black leadership. As the years went by, whites did not become more likely to say that black leaders were not pushing hard. Whether this is because this particular question did not tap into local politics effectively or because there is some other intervening variable is unclear. Without panel data definitive answers are hard to come by.

One thing we can do is look at events in these cities over time to see if they mirror the pattern of positive change that we see in this public opinion analysis. Accounts from the bulk of the cities do suggest that time and experience with black mayoral leadership are important variables. Atlanta is a typical case: Maynard Jackson's mayoral victory was followed by a period of bitter racial confrontation. Only with the passage of time did the true impact of a black mayoralty become clear. Specifically, it was only after Jackson played a pivotal role in breaking a strike of low-paid, mostly black garbage workers that he began to receive more support from the white community. According to one advisor, Jackson's actions helped make whites "less paranoid" (Scott 1977). Similarly, the beginning of Mayor Coleman Young's tenure in Detroit was marked by considerable racial strife (Rich 1987). Only after Young proved to white residents that he could govern the city fairly did racial tensions decline. After Young prepared an austerity budget that cut city services and laid off nearly 4,000 workers, his electoral support grew, and by the time of his reelection, his two white primary opponents could muster only a combined 19 percent of the white vote (Scott 1977). This anecdotal evidence confirms that it takes time for white residents to assess the impact of black leadership, just as it takes time for a black incumbent's actions to reduce white uncertainty enough to alter white attitudes toward the black community.

A review of Tables 3.1 and 3.2 reveals two other interesting findings. First, the results suggest that the size of the black population is negatively related to white views of blacks and black leadership. The higher the percentage of blacks in a city, the more racial conflict whites perceive and the more racially resentful they are. This finding fits into a long line of research that has shown that white attitudes are closely shaped by the size of the local black population.[17] In most of these studies, as the black population grows, race relations deteriorate.

This relationship does, however, raise an important question. Why is there a negative relationship between a larger black presence and white attitudes on one hand and a positive relationship between the presence of black leadership and white attitudes on the other? Why do the actions of blacks in positions of authority seem to quell white fears, while the presence of a large black population seems to increase racial tensions? I argue that the critical difference between the positive effects of black leadership and the negative effects of a larger black population is the control that black leaders have over their actions and the white community. What may make black political leaders different from black neighbors or co-workers and consequently why black representation should provide more credible information that alters white views is the fact that when blacks assume political office, it marks one of the first times that blacks have authority to enact policies or make changes that could harm the white community. This perceived authority or control not only makes black political leadership especially threatening, it also makes the actions of black leaders especially informative. If whites believe that a mayor has considerable power to influence events (as surveys show they do), then the fact that black leadership does not hurt white interests can be seen as credible evidence that blacks are not out to get the white community. In contrast, the behavior of blacks in most other situations can be dismissed because whites can surmise that black behavior was constrained.

If my interpretation is accurate, then these results help us to understand the dynamics of interracial contact, suggesting that whites change their

---

[17] In particular, a higher percentage of blacks in the local community has been linked to increased white on black violence (Corzine, Creech, and Corzine 1983), an increased sense of threat among whites (M. Taylor 1998; Fossett and Kiecolt 1989; Giles and Evans 1986), higher levels of white bloc voting (Murray and Vedlitz 1978), greater white support of racist candidates (Giles and Buckner 1993; Black and Black 1973), more conservative racial policy preferences (Glaser 1994), greater support for segregation (Pettigrew and Campbell 1960), suppression of black voting (Matthews and Prothro 1963), and decreased interracial friendship (Shaw 1973). Judging by these studies, white Americans seem to be keenly aware of and very threatened by the presence of minorities in their neighborhoods and cities. However, it is important to note that others have found either no relationship between the size of the black community and whites attitudes (Bledsoe et al. 1995) or a positive relationship (Welch et al. 2001; Kinder and Mendelberg 1995; Carsey 1995).

views of black leaders only when they receive information that they perceive as credible. In particular, these findings corroborate recent research in social psychology, which is increasingly finding that *how* group members receive information about out-groups is more critical than *what* information they receive (Scarberry, Ratcliff, and Lord 1997; Bar-Tal 1997).[18]

The second interesting finding to emerge from Tables 3.1 and 3.2 concerns the link between white racial views, political ideology, and partisanship. Both tables report a fairly strong relationship between identifying as a Republican and holding conservative ideological views and holding more negative views of black leaders and the black community. This suggests that there may be important differences in attitudes toward blacks across different segments of the white community. Given that all whites do not feel the same way about the black community, we should probably not expect that all whites will respond the same way to black leadership. In particular, some whites may be less affected by the information black incumbents provide.

Who Changes Their Mind?

Given the clearly divergent racial agendas of the Republican and Democratic parties and the link between Republicanism and more negative views of the black community illustrated in Tables 3.1 and 3.2, one might predict that white Republicans will be more resistant to the information that black representation provides (Carmines and Stimson 1989; Huckfeldt and Kohfeld 1989; Kinder and Sanders 1996; Kinder and Sears 1981). White Democrats, on the other hand, may be much more receptive to having a positive view of blacks and black leadership, particularly since such an attitude fits into their political views more broadly. If this were true, one should find that most if not all of the positive change in racial attitudes and voting behavior that occurs under black mayoral leadership is confined to white Democrats.

In Table 3.3, I test this proposition by separating out the responses of white Democrats, white Republicans, and white Independents to black

---

[18] As I mentioned in the Introduction, the exceptional effects of black mayoral leadership on white attitudes echo a series of studies in experimental psychology that suggests that one of the few times whites really change their attitudes about blacks is when they know that blacks are free to choose their actions (Wilder, Simon, and Faith 1996). The link between mayoral authority and attitude change also fits with formal models in political science that have shown that actions by individuals are uninformative unless the individual is in control and has the power to choose a different course of action (Lupia and McCubbins 1998).

TABLE 3.3 *How Time Under Black Leadership Affects the Views of Democrats, Republicans, and Independents*

	Views of Black Leadership	Views of the Black Community	
	Blacks Pushing Too Hard[b]	Anti-black Affect[a]	Racial Resentment[a]
Years Black Mayor	0.57 (0.52)	−0.08 (0.02)***	−0.18 (0.04)***
Years Black Mayor* Democrat View	0.01 (0.37)	−0.08 (0.02)***	−0.07 (0.04)**
Years Black Mayor* Republican View	−0.42 (0.36)	0.12 (0.02)***	0.14 (0.03)***
Education	−1.7 (0.31)***	−0.06 (0.01)***	−0.22 (0.03)***
Income	−0.04 (0.38)	0.01 (0.02)	0.01 (0.03)
Age	1.5 (0.46)***	0.04 (0.02)**	0.01 (0.04)
Gender (1 = male)	0.10 (0.17)	0.01 (0.01)	0.02 (0.02)
Ideology (1 = liberal)	−2.6 (0.46)	−0.06 (0.02)***	−0.28 (0.04)***
Party (1 = Democrat)	−0.95 (0.58)*	0.15 (0.02)***	0.14 (0.05)***
Employment Status (1 = unemployed)	0.20 (0.59)	−0.00 (0.02)	0.01 (0.04)
Years Living in City	0.13 (0.29)	0.01 (0.01)	0.02 (0.02)
Percent Black in City	0.01 (0.01)	0.03 (0.02)	0.09 (0.04)**
Level of Urbanism	0.41 (0.39)	0.01 (0.01)	−0.05 (0.03)*
South (1 = yes)	0.38 (0.21)	0.01 (0.01)	0.03 (0.02)
1986	−0.46 (0.38)		
1988	−0.80 (0.37)**	0.02 (0.01)*	0.05 (0.02)**
1990	−0.94 (0.42)**		−0.02 (0.02)
1992	−1.6 (0.4)***	0.02 (0.01)	0.09 (0.02)***
Constant		0.54 (0.02)***	0.88 (0.05)***
Intercept 1	−4.7 (0.65)***		
Intercept 2	−0.95 (0.61)		
Adj. R²	0.21	0.14	0.22
χ²	154		
N	658	800	800

Note: Figures are unstandardized coefficients with their standard errors.

***p < 0.01

**p < 0.05

*p < 0.10

[a] Ordinary least squares.

[b] Ordered logit.

mayoral leadership.[19] The dependent variables are the same racial attitude questions examined earlier. The only change to the model is that in Table 3.3 I interact the years under a black mayor variable with dummy variables for Democratic and Republican Party identification. Independents become the baseline group. To gauge how white Independents respond to time under black leadership, one need only look at the coefficient for "Years Black Mayor." To determine how Democrats (or Republicans) respond to time under black leadership, one has to add the coefficient for the "Years Black Mayor – Democrat" (or Republican) interaction term and the coefficient for "Years Black Mayor" together.

Table 3.3 shows that, as expected, white Democrats, white Republicans, and white Independents respond differently to black representation. First, the more time the white Independents in the sample spent under black mayoral leadership, the more positive their racial views became: as the years under a black mayor went by, white Independents felt less anti-black affect and expressed less racial resentment. Changes were even more pronounced and positive for white Democrats: in two of the three cases, white Democrats' views improved even more rapidly than those of white Independents. Republicans, however, responded less positively to time under a black mayor. On two of the three attitudinal measures, Republican views improved significantly less than those of Independents. Adding the Republican interaction term with the "Years Black Mayor" term it appears, in fact, that there was little to no change in the level of racial resentment and anti-black affect among white Republicans. The same pattern emerges if one does not look at change over time under black leadership but instead simply compares whites in cities with a black mayor to whites in cities with a white mayor, as was done in Table 3.1. White Democrats who lived in cities with a black mayor had significantly more positive views of blacks than white Democrats who lived in cities with a white mayor. By contrast, white Republicans' racial views changed only marginally. This suggests that some white Republicans either ignore or discount the words and actions of black incumbents. Given this resistance to the information that black leadership provides, it seems reasonable to argue that a racial prejudice or racial stereotype model of political behavior may more accurately describe the views of some Republicans than an information model. In short, the information model may not apply to all whites equally.

---

[19] Independents are self-identified Independents or respondents who listed no party affiliation.

The same pattern is also evident when one looks at the actual vote in mayoral elections involving black incumbents. As noted in Chapter 2, in the few cases where voting data are broken down by both race and party identification, the evidence suggests that the bulk of the increase in white support for black incumbents came from white Democrats (Sonenshein 1993; Pettigrew 1976). White Republicans, in contrast, tended to vote against black candidates whether they were challengers or incumbents. This suggests that racial considerations are most consequential for white Democrats (see Hurwitz and Peffley 1998 on this point). Whether white Democrats support black leadership seems to be greatly affected by their views of blacks, while white Republicans may have a range of reasons for opposing black candidates that may or may not include racial considerations.[20]

The end result of these divergent patterns is that black representation has a polarizing effect on the white community. Democrats become more and more racially liberal, while Republicans' views stay largely the same. In fact, the racial attitudes gap between white Democrats and white Republicans more than doubles in size under black mayoral leadership. Table 3.4 illustrates this growing gap by presenting the difference between mean Democratic views and mean Republican views across the same series of racial questions. As column one of Table 3.4 reveals, the gap between white Democrats and white Republicans in cities with a white mayor was rather small. On one of the three questions, the difference is not even statistically significant ($p < .05$). But in cities with a black mayor, the gap between white Democrats and white Republicans on each indicator doubled or more than doubled. On matters of race,

---

[20] Although one could argue that this pattern is the result of the defection of racist white Democrats from the party, there are two factors that make this highly unlikely. First, since most Democratic defectors become Independents rather than Republicans, one would expect any negative change to be among Independents, not Republicans. Second, if this pattern is due to racial realignment, one would expect that the pattern would be more pronounced in the South, where racial realignment was itself most pronounced. Additional tests, however, reveal no clear difference in the pattern between Southern and non-Southern cities. Third, by all accounts, racial realignment was a slow, gradual process. Thus, it is a stretch to argue that realignment can account for changes in the Democratic and Republican votes that occur in the same city over a four-year period. Not enough Democrats defect in a four-year period to change the Democratic vote as much as it changes in many cities. Finally, it seems unlikely that the gradual defection of whites from the Democratic Party over time could account simultaneously for the differences in the views of different white partisans who live under black mayors and for differential changes in the views of different white partisans as the years under black leadership go by.

TABLE 3.4 *Black Representation and the Polarization of the White Community*

	Difference Between Mean Democratic and Mean Republican View	
	Cities Without a Black Mayor	Cities With a Black Mayor
Sense of Black Threat[a]	−0.06**	−0.11**
Anti-black Affect[a]	−0.01	−0.03**
Racial Resentment[a]	−0.04**	−0.11**

Note: Indicates that difference between Democratic and Republican mean is significant.

*p < 0.10
**p < 0.05
***p < 0.01
[a] All dependent variables coded 0–1.

black representation means even greater division between Democrats and Republicans.

IMPLICATIONS

The tests in this chapter indicate that experience with black mayors can lead to improved white views of black leadership and significant positive changes in white attitudes toward the black community at large. These changes are all consistent with an information model of white behavior. When blacks are perceived to have the power to hurt white interests and when by all accounts they do not do so, many whites may interpret that experience as a sign that blacks and black leadership are not as bad as they may have feared and their attitudes appear to change accordingly. All of this fits well the information model. None of it is predicted by a racial prejudice or a social dominance view. We thus have a fairly clear test and fairly compelling evidence in favor of the information model. We also have fairly strong evidence that many whites in American cities are far from prejudiced. They are open to change and willing to look at the black community in a more positive light.

At the same time, the data also indicate that black representation has significant limitations. Not everyone seems to "learn" from black leadership. The change that occurs within the white community, when considered in the aggregate, is apparently largely to be confined to Democrats and Independents. It seems as if part of America remains prejudiced and is unwilling or unable to change. Moreover, the limited nature of change to date is evident in accounts of policy divides from many of the cities included in the data set. Despite years and often decades of black mayoral leadership, whites and blacks continue to differ over minority contract set-asides, police behavior, public schools, and downtown versus neighborhood development, among other things (Rivlin 1992; Stone 1997). At least over the short term, black representation has only a limited impact on the "extraordinary racial divide" that separates white and black America (Kinder and Sanders 1996: 28).

4

Learning Across Different Cities

To say that black representation generally leads to significant positive change in white racial attitudes and white voting behavior is not to say that white Americans in all contexts are equally likely to be affected by black leadership. Indeed, if the information model is accurate, then white reactions should vary sharply depending on the local information environment. In this chapter, I begin to consider how context affects both the information that whites receive from black leadership and the nature of their response to that leadership. White reactions to black leadership depend greatly on the amount of control black leadership is perceived to exercise over local policies and conditions. The higher the level of perceived control, the more information whites obtain from black leadership and the more positively they respond to black incumbents.

A brief account of events in two different cities, Memphis and New York, highlights the enormous variation in white reactions to black leadership and raises important questions about why white residents respond so differently in different contexts. Memphis and New York are particularly interesting because the two cities followed similar patterns before the election of a black mayor and only diverged after that mayor entered office. In both cities, black mayoral leadership came only recently and only after overcoming significant white opposition.

In Memphis, the first black mayor was elected in 1991. The late arrival of a black mayoralty in Memphis was not the result of a lack of effort on the part of the black community. In every election between 1971 and 1991, black candidates vied for the mayoralty, with widespread support from black leaders and black voters. But every time a black candidate ran for election, the white community in Memphis responded with almost unanimous support for the white candidate. The most successful of the black challengers, Otis Higgs, managed to win a paltry 10 percent of the white vote in 1975. In each election, whites won by trumping African American turnout (Wright 2000). Given this history, it is no surprise that the white vote was once again squarely behind the white candidate on October 4, 1991, when another black challenger, Willie Herenton, sought the mayoralty. Despite the fact that Herenton's campaign tried to avoid racial issues, and despite the fact that there were few major policy differences between Herenton and his white opponent, white voters in Memphis once again refused to support the black challenger. In what has been described as "one of the most racially polarized mayoral elections in urban American history," Herenton was opposed by 98 percent of white voters, who turned out in record numbers to try to defeat the black candidate (Pohlman and Kirby 1996: xv; Wright 1996). Fortunately for Herenton and his black supporters, the outcome of this election was different. An African American finally took over the mayoralty.

What makes the Memphis story so remarkable is what happened *after* Willie Herenton assumed power: decades of heated white opposition faded away, and support for black leadership grew dramatically. By Herenton's fourth year in office, a citywide poll revealed that three-quarters of all whites in the city approved of the job that he had done and a slim majority thought he should be reelected (A. Davis 1995; Polhman and Kirby 1996). Later that year, Herenton, running as an incumbent, received the support of nearly 40 percent of all white voters (Hobbs 1995). Four years later, in 1999, he won again with half of the white vote, prompting the *Commercial Appeal*, the city's main newspaper, to highlight the "unprecedented unity" surrounding the election (Goad 1999). In his third reelection bid, in 2003, Herenton faced no serious opposition – white or black.

This turnaround in white political behavior in Memphis seems all the more noteworthy when Memphis is contrasted with New York City. African Americans in New York City have also long had a difficult time getting elected. Historically, black representation on the city council and other elected offices in the city has been well below parity (Logan and Mollenkopf 2003; Mollenkopf 1986). As John Mollenkopf has noted, "New York City has not incorporated minorities and...has not produced policies that are especially aimed toward minorities" (1986: 591). Thus, when David Dinkins ran to become the city's first black mayor in 1989, most observers were not surprised to find the city racially polarized in response. Despite Dinkins's repeated attempts to appeal to the city's white voters by stressing nonthreatening themes, such as fiscal prudence and law and order, he managed to garner only 28 percent of the white vote (Kaufman 1998; Arian et al. 1991). Nevertheless, Dinkins became the city's first black mayor.

In sharp contrast to events in Memphis, after Dinkins was elected, black leadership in New York was met with anything but growing acceptance. In fact, race relations in the city appeared to get worse rather than better with Dinkins in office (Sleeper 1993). The next four years were marred by a series of high profile racial incidents. And when Dinkins ran for reelection, racial polarization actually increased. In the 1993 election, 78 percent of white voters opposed Dinkins – an increase that was just enough to give his white opponent, Rudy Giuliani, the victory (Kaufman 1998). Black leadership in New York City was over almost before it began.[1]

These examples suggest that in some cases black leadership leads to racial conciliation, while in other cases it leads to continued, if not heightened, racial antagonism. According to the information model, the patterns we see across cities should be a function of the quality of the information that black leadership provides the white community. When experience with a black mayor gives white residents clear, concrete information about the effects of black leadership on the white community, changes in white behavior should be pronounced. In contrast, when whites' information about black leadership is limited or uncertain, change in white behavior should be minimal. But why do white residents get more information in some cities than in other cities?

For whites, it is critical to know whether a black leader or someone else is responsible for the ongoing well-being of the white community. The more that blacks are free to enact their own agendas and to

---

[1] A factor that makes Dinkins's failed reelection bid in New York particularly surprising is the liberal nature of the white vote in that city. Why did an incumbent black Democrat lose his reelection bid in a city that is generally so liberal? Part of the answer, I will argue, is racial threat and fears of blacks eventually taking control. Dinkins was the recognized leader of a large black community and that scared many whites – even liberal whites. When Dinkins sided with the African American community and failed to act decisively against violent black incursions into the white community, it scared whites even more. Who knew where the city was going? The result was a small shift in the white vote that helped thwart Dinkins's reelection bid. This is, however, not the entire story. An economic recession, a terrorist bombing of the World Trade Center, and increased voter turnout in more conservative Staten Island due to a referendum on that island's secession all cut into Dinkins's liberal base.

overcome any constraints imposed by the white community, the more whites will attribute their ongoing well-being to black leadership, and the more insight they will gain into the interests of blacks and black leaders. One implication of this logic, as I have explained, is that racial demographics play a critical role in whites' perceptions of black leaders. Specifically, changes in white behavior should vary predictably across three types of cities: majority black cities, majority white cities, and racially balanced cities.

In cities where blacks are the majority of the population and the dominant political group, it is easy for whites to link local conditions to the interests and policies of black leadership. In these cities, when the world under black leadership remains very similar to the world under white leadership, many whites interpret this as a sign that they have little to fear from black leaders. Blacks could have changed things and they chose not to. But in other types of cities, the information provided by black incumbency is more limited. Where whites are the clear majority and dominate the political arena, the election of a black mayor does not represent a real transition of power from the white community to the black community. Whites still do not know what would happen if the black community truly had control. As a result, the actions of a black mayor in a majority white city provide only limited information, and changes in white behavior are moderate. In racially balanced cities, the information provided by black leadership is even less clear. The election of a black mayor will not necessarily lead to black control of the local political process, but a black mayoral victory will likely put blacks on the cusp of power.[2] This has two important effects. First, it is likely to spur white elites into action. Rather than cede control of local political resources, whites will mobilize to prevent blacks from taking control. The result in many cases is policy paralysis. Because no one is clearly in control and a black agenda is never realized, most white voters receive little new information from the black mayoralty. Second, the rough balance of power between the black and white communities raises considerable uncertainty about subsequent elections. In any future election, with the right outcome, a black-led coalition really could gain control and take over the local political arena. With little new information and the possibility of black control becoming much closer, white opposition to black leadership is likely to increase in these cities.

[2] In the racially balanced cities that are examined in this book, blacks held on average one-third of the city council seats at the time the first black mayor was elected.

TESTING THE EFFECT OF RACIAL DEMOGRAPHICS
ON THE WHITE VOTE

To test these predictions, I divided the twenty-six cities with black challenger and black incumbent elections into three groups. Cities with populations that were more than 55 percent white were coded as majority
white, those with populations that were 45 to 55 percent white were
coded as racially balanced, and those whose populations were less than
45 percent white were coded as minority white.[3] I chose these cutoffs
because they adhere to previous empirical research.[4] However, the exact
cutoff points chosen to distinguish each type of city are not critical.[5]

Table 4.1 illustrates that white reactions to black leadership are clearly
dependent on racial demographics in the ways predicted by the information model. In minority white cities, white support for the same black
candidate increased by an average of 16.3 percent. This gain roughly
doubled the level of white support in these cities – from 16.1 percent in
black challenger elections to 32.4 percent in black incumbent elections.
In majority white cities, white support increased by an average of only

---

[3] The majority white cities are Charlotte, Cleveland, Kansas City, Los Angeles, Minneapolis,
Rockford, and Seattle. The racially balanced cities are Chicago, Dallas, Durham, Flint,
Houston, New Haven, New York, Philadelphia, and San Francisco. The minority white
cities are Atlantic City, Baltimore, Birmingham, Gary, Memphis, Newark, Oakland, and
Trenton.

[4] Grofman and Handley (1989) have found that congressional districts that are 40 to 60%
black elect black representatives about half the time. Cameron and his coauthors (1996)
have suggested that the point of equal opportunity to elect a black candidate is generally
less than 50% black. The literature on schools has similarly found that at around 50%
white, the balance of power between white and black students is most precarious and the
intensity of competition between races is highest (Longshore 1988; Crain, Mahard, and
Narot 1982; Bullock 1976).

[5] Alternate cutoffs (e.g. 40 to 60% white) lead to similar patterns of behavior across cities.
Also, whether one institutes cutoffs based on the size of the white population, the size of
the black population, or the relative size of the two populations, the results are essentially
the same. The main reason why these different specifications lead to similar results is
that most of these cities had very small Asian American and Latino populations at the
time that they elected black mayors. On average, 92% of the residents of these cities
were black or white. Thus, focusing on the size of the white population is essentially the
mirror opposite of focusing on the black population. In large part because of the small
size of their populations, Asian American and Latino voters tend to play a limited role
in the elections under consideration. Of course, there are exceptions, like Chicago, where
Latinos can provide the margin of victory for either a white- or black-led coalition. Given
the relatively small size of the Latino and Asian American populations in these cities, it is
extremely difficult to try to measure and assess their reactions to black leadership in any
systematic way.

TABLE 4.1 *Change in Political Behavior from Black Candidacy to Black Incumbency: The Impact of the Racial Balance of Power*

	Change in:			
	Percent White Vote for Black Candidate	Margin of Victory	Percent Turnout	Black Incumbent Reelection Rate
Minority White	19.6	19.6	−6.4	100% (8 of 8)
Racially Balanced	−7.5	−7.7	−4.4	63% (5 of 8)
Majority White	7.1	14.3	−9.9	100% (7 of 7)

6.2 percent (from 42.2 percent to 48.4 percent).[6] And in racially balanced cities, white support actually *decreased* by an average of 2.9 percent.

Not surprisingly, these changes in the white vote affected the outcome of each contest. Whether or not black incumbents won reelection was greatly dependent on whether they faced a racially balanced, minority white, or majority white electorate. In the minority and majority white cities, black incumbents won reelection every time, while in racially balanced cities, the black incumbent won reelection only about half of the time (5 out of 8 cases). The margin of victory in black mayoral elections was similarly dependent on the racial balance of power. On average, the margin of victory for the black candidate decreased by 7.7 percentage points in racially balanced cities. In contrast, the margin of victory increased by an average of 19.6 percentage points in minority white cities and 14.3 points in majority white cities. Measures of overall turnout conform to this same pattern. The turnout decline in majority or minority white cities seems to suggest that the often intense white mobilization against the black challenger had faded by the time the candidate came up for reelection. The somewhat smaller turnout decline in racially balanced cities, by contrast, suggests that white fears and concerns remained relatively high in these cities even when blacks ran as incumbents.

It would seem, then, that white reactions to black leadership closely mirror the predictions of the information model. In minority white cities, whites became much more accepting of black leadership. In majority white

---

[6] The more limited increase in white support in majority white cities might at least in part be due to the fact that white support is slowly approaching a maximum threshold. Candidates, after all, rarely get unanimous support. It is, however, worth noting that mayoral elections are usually not close. The average margin of victory in mayoral elections is 24 percentage points (Hajnal, Lewis, and Louch 2002). Given that successful mayoral candidates typically win a large majority of the vote, it is unlikely that the 48% white support we see here is pushing a maximum threshold.

cities, change was positive, but not as strong. And, in racially balanced cities, whites were just as opposed to black incumbents as they were to black challengers. All of this suggests that there is a link between the level of black control of the local political arena, information, and white behavior.

TESTING COMPETING EXPLANATIONS

Could other more conventional political factors – candidate quality, endorsements, and the incumbent's record – account for the differences in whites' reactions in different kinds of cities? To try to ascertain if changes in white behavior were in fact related to the information environment rather than to other features of the local political arena, I undertook more formal multivariate analysis of the change in the white vote. In this analysis, I incorporated the same range of features of the local political arena that I used in the investigation of black challenger and black incumbent elections in Chapter 2. To assess the impact of basic features of the campaign, I took into account changes in newspaper endorsements, the Democratic Party endorsement, and the quality of the white opponent. To see if the black incumbent's record affected the change in the white vote, I included three features of the local environment that were likely to have been most prominent in white voters' minds, given the fears they expressed when black challengers first entered office: change in per capita income, change in median housing prices, and change in the local crime rate. To determine if the policy actions of the black mayor also mattered, I added a measure of the degree to which the black mayor's administration shifted spending from development to redistribution – presumably a change that would most dramatically benefit the black community at the expense of at least some of the white community.[7] Finally, to investigate if the racial content of the black candidate's campaign influenced the white vote, I included a measure of the degree to which it shifted from being race neutral to racially focused. Although I have tried to make this list as comprehensive as possible, other factors in the local environment, such as the local political culture, might also have played a role in these contests. Details about the coding and sources of each of the variables are included in the Appendix to Chapter 2.

---

[7] In alternate tests, I also looked to see if greater pursuit of affirmative action in public hiring affected changes in the white vote, but I found no link. The lack of an effect was likely due to the fact that most black mayors pursued affirmative action at a very moderate pace.

The number of independent variables and the limited number of cases once again stretch the limits of what an ordinary least-squares regression can do, but the results do seem to fit a clear pattern: where blacks have more ability to control local events, whites seem to learn more from their experiences with black leadership and appear to be more willing to support black incumbents.[8] After controlling for an array of variables related to the campaign and the incumbent's record, the results in Table 4.2 indicate that racial demographics have a substantial effect on changes in the white vote. All else being equal, the model suggests that white support grows 12 percentage points more in minority white cities than it does in racially balanced cities. The difference between white majority cities and racially balanced cities is not nearly as stark, but there is at least some indication that whites learn more in majority white cities than they do in racially balanced cities.[9] Table 4.2 also indicates that racial control is not the only variable that influences the white vote. Race enters into the calculus of white voters in other ways. Black candidates who move away from racialized campaigns toward more race-neutral campaigns tend to garner a larger share of the white vote. Similarly, when fears of increasing crime are not borne out by experience with black mayoral leadership, white residents appear to grow more accepting of that leadership. None of the other features of the incumbent's record or the campaign is significantly related to the white vote, but it is worth noting that for every variable in Table 4.2 the coefficient is in the right direction, and in some cases, such as party and newspaper endorsements, is reasonably close to being significant. It may be that better measures of the campaign and the incumbent's record would reveal clearer relationships.

RACIAL DEMOGRAPHICS AND THE TONE OF MAYORAL ELECTIONS

The extent to which racial demographics shape both the information environment and white reactions can also be seen in the racial tone of elections. Changes in the tone or racial mood of campaigns in each type of city follow a pattern very similar to the vote. In racially balanced cities, the reelection bids of black incumbents tend to retain a high level of

---

[8] Alternate tests dropping some of the independent variables and bivariate correlations led to roughly the same set of findings as those demonstrated in Table 4.2.

[9] In the model in Table 4.2, the coefficient for the white majority is positive but not quite significant. Bivariate tests reveal a positive and significant correlation between change in the white vote and a dummy variable for majority white cities.

TABLE 4.2 *Determinants of Change in White Support for the Black Candidate*[a]

	Change in White Support for the Black Candidate
RACIAL CONTROL	
White Minority City[b]	0.18 (0.07)**
White Majority City[b]	0.07 (0.06)
Percent Black	0.00 (0.26)
CAMPAIGN BASICS	
Candidate Quality	
Change in Quality of White Opponent	−0.10 (0.11)
Endorsements	
Change in Democratic Party Endorsement	0.12 (0.14)
Change in Local Newspaper Endorsement	0.14 (0.11)
Racial Focus of the Campaign	
Change in Black Candidate's Racial Focus	−0.31 (0.13)**
INCUMBENT'S RECORD	
Local Conditions	
Change in Per Capita Income	0.49 (0.72)
Change in Median Housing Prices	0.18 (0.11)
Change in Crime Rate	−0.01 (0.00)*
Policy	
Change in Redistributive Spending	−0.58 (0.45)
Constant	−0.24 (0.23)
Adj. R^2	0.45
N	25

Note: OLS regression. Figures in parentheses are standard errors.
**$p < 0.01$
*$p < 0.05$
$p < 0.10$
[a] All variables and their sources are described in detail in Appendix B.
[b] The excluded or comparison group is racially balanced cities (45% to 55% white). White minority coded as <45% white. Majority white coded as >55% white.

racial tension. In Chicago, for example, when Harold Washington ran for reelection in 1987, he faced opponents who did not hesitate to play the race card. The racial theme of the slogan chosen by Washington's primary opponent, Jane Byrne – "Jane Byrne: A Mayor for All Chicago" – was clear to all involved. Similarly, Ed Vrdolyak, Washington's main opponent in the general election, made "bold use of racial themes throughout his campaign" (Grimshaw 1992: 192). In Philadelphia, another racially balanced city, there was also considerable racial hostility in the black incumbent election. When Wilson Goode ran for reelection in 1987, the local media saw the election as "a campaign in black and white" (quoted in Adams 1994). Goode's opponent, Frank Rizzo, was "pilloried by the press as a race baiter" and at one point simply stated, "Vote white" (P. Taylor 1987). Accounts in Cleveland, another racially balanced city, also highlighted the role of race in the black incumbent's first reelection bid. In 1969, when Carl Stokes ran for reelection, the campaign focused in large part on a police shootout in an African American neighborhood, and, according to Levine, "despite disclaimers from both sides, the race issue again dominated Cleveland politics" (1974: 59).

In contrast, in minority and majority black cities, black incumbent reelection bids tended to be more subdued affairs that almost always focused on the incumbent's record and the traditional array of policy issues that any candidate, black or white, would face. Norm Rice's reelection in Seattle was dubbed by many as a foregone conclusion. Emmanuel Cleaver's reelection bid in Kansas City was greeted with widespread apathy. And Richard Arrington's reelection bid in Birmingham was so calm and racially civil that the national press ignored it. Arrington himself lamented: "Since we didn't have any [racial] animosity, we didn't get any attention" (Russakof 1983). The tone of incumbent elections in these cities suggests that uncertainty surrounding black leadership and fears about what might happen after the next election had, at least in part, been erased by the tenure of the first black mayor.

This pattern of change across cities has an important implication for the literature on racial context and interracial dynamics. As discussed, much of the scholarship on racial context has found that the larger the local black population, the greater the level of racial animosity (see, e.g., Key 1949; Giles and Hertz 1994). And indeed, Chapter 3 demonstrated a linear relationship between the size of the black population and the negativity of white views. This chapter's analysis suggests, however, that once a black candidate assumes an important leadership position, the simple linear relationship no longer holds.[10] Because the reality of black control turns out to be less menacing than the threat posed by the possibility of black control, racial tension appears to peak in cities where black control is imminent but not yet in place. Thus, the racial divide often remains exceptionally high in racially balanced cities and ironically declines markedly in cities where blacks are more numerous and presumably more able to take over.

---

[10] For a similar argument about racial balance, see Blalock (1967) and Longshore (1988).

TABLE 4.3 *The Impact of the Racial Balance of Power on Black Incumbent Reelection Rates*

City Demographics	Incumbent Reelection Rate
Minority White	81% (61 of 75 cases)
Racially Balanced	65% (13 of 20 cases)
Majority White	77% (24 of 31 cases)

A BROADER RANGE OF CASES

Information and racial control appear to play a key role in these twenty-six cities, but can they account for electoral outcomes across a wide range of cases? To answer this question, I once again looked at the outcome of every black incumbent reelection bid in the twentieth century in every city in the United States with over 50,000 people.[11] When we shift to this more complete set of cases, the same pattern emerges. Outcomes in black incumbent elections across the United States have been strongly related to a city's racial balance of power. As Table 4.3 reveals, in minority white cities, black incumbents win almost all of their reelection bids (81 percent). In majority white cities, they are slightly less successful: they win 77 percent of their reelection bids. But in racially balanced cities, black incumbents win only 65 percent of the time.

The data presented in this chapter suggest that when whites can hold black leaders accountable for the lack of negative change that occurs under their watch, then these leaders' tenure in office will provide valuable information to white voters about the effects of black leadership. This, in turn, will lead to greatly increased white support and almost certain reelection. But in racially balanced cities, black mayoral control is often too precarious and racial competition too intense for white residents to know who is to blame or credit for their continued well-being. In such cities, white fears remain, elections continue to be highly racialized, and black politicians have a more difficult time getting reelected. In short, information and uncertainty appear to play a critical role in the decisions of white voters.

---

[11] Each city is also coded as majority white, racially balanced, or minority white at the time of the election. The cutoffs are the same as those employed for the smaller data set: majority white (over 55% white), racially balanced (45 to 55% white), and minority white (under 45% white). Alternate tests that break down cities based on the size of the black population or the relative sizes of the black and white populations reveal similar patterns.

The pattern of white voting across cities that this chapter has identified may have practical implications for redistricting decisions. Many have advocated the creation of more racially mixed districts, both because blacks have a good chance of winning office in this type of district and because they may maximize black substantive representation (Grofman and Handley 1989; Lublin 1997; Cameron, Epstein, and Halloran 1996). My results indicate, however, that black politicians may have a more difficult time getting reelected in racially balanced arenas and that the creation of racially competitive districts could actually lead to an increase in racial tension.[12] It is by no means clear that the pattern we see across cities will be found in legislative districts or other types of geographic contexts, and thus much more investigation of this phenomenon is required. Nevertheless, those drawing the lines should at least begin to consider two new concerns that have generally been previously overlooked: reelection rates and the level of black-white conflict associated with different racial demographics.[13] Both of these concerns may lead legislators who favor greater black representation away from supporting the creation of racially balanced districts.

This chapter has shown that patterns of change in white support can be linked to the amount of control that black incumbents are able to exercise over the local political arena. The patterns evident here certainly fit the expectations of the information model. Thus, there is little doubt that the information model provides at least a plausible explanation of changes in white behavior. But these simple correlations do not actually show us how information is or is not translated by white residents in a given community. In order to connect changes in white behavior more directly to changes in the information environment, in the next two chapters I examine two cases of black mayoral leadership in much more detail. The goal of these two chapters is to follow the process of racial learning and to directly link the actions of black incumbents to specific changes in the views and actions of white residents.

---

[12] Interestingly, as noted earlier, studies at the school level also suggest that racial tensions may peak in racially balanced communities (Longshore 1988).

[13] These are obviously only two of the possible criteria by which a district can be judged. One might also want to consider how district lines affect substantive representation, descriptive representation, and a host of other issues (see Mansbridge 1999; Cameron, Epstein, and Halloran 1996; Lublin 1997; Swain 1995).

5

Black Mayoral Leadership in Los Angeles

None of the data presented to this point allows us to follow the course of black leadership in a single city to see daily, monthly, or even yearly changes. This is an important omission, because learning under black incumbents is a *process*. What we have seen so far is a glimpse into the outcome of that process, but statistical data provide little insight into exactly what information is provided by black leadership, how that information is transmitted, and ultimately how it is interpreted by city residents. In this chapter, I begin to address this omission by presenting more direct evidence of the process of racial learning. Specifically, I follow the actions of black mayoral leadership and the attitudes and actions of white residents before, during, and after the transition from white to black leadership in Los Angeles. The goal is to demonstrate as clearly as possible how information from black incumbency is translated into changes in white attitudes and behavior.

I focus on Los Angeles for both practical and theoretical reasons. On a practical level, data constraints confined my choices to cities that had substantial empirical records of white views during a black mayoralty. Unlike almost all other cities that have experienced black mayoral representation, Los Angeles has mayoral exit polls that allow for analysis of the white vote in several contests, and several of these polls included questions assessing white racial concerns. This allows me to gauge the effects of racial views on the white vote at different points in time. Coupled with rich primary and secondary accounts of Mayor Tom Bradley's record in Los Angeles, these polls allow for perhaps the most comprehensive assessment of white reactions to black leadership available in any city.

On a theoretical level, moreover, Los Angeles under Tom Bradley offers an interesting test case. When he was elected in 1973, Bradley became one of the first black mayors in the country, so his tenure marked one of the first times that white Americans could gauge the consequences of black leadership in an important elected office. Thus, we might expect learning to be particularly pronounced here. In addition, Bradley's long tenure as mayor (twenty years) allows for a more refined assessment of how white attitudes and actions change over time. Even if the process of learning is a slow one, it should still be evident in Los Angeles. A more extensive account of the motivations behind my case selection is included in Appendix C.

In this chapter, I assess three different aspects of the learning process. First, to what extent did a lack of information about the consequences of black leadership play a role in black challenger elections? If the information model is accurate, a lack of concrete information about the consequences of black leadership for the white community should be one of the central features of black challenger campaigns. To test this hypothesis, I detail the views and concerns of white residents during Bradley's two campaigns to become the city's first black mayor, and evaluate the role racial concerns played in the white vote in these two contests. Second, what information did black incumbency provide? Here, I review Bradley's policy initiatives and their impact on the economic vitality of the white community to show that Bradley's tenure did little to harm white Angelenos. And third, was information provided by black leadership translated into changes in white attitudes and behavior? In particular, did white residents update their beliefs about blacks and black leadership? Again, if the information model is accurate, at least some whites should have taken the limited impact of black leadership on the white community as a sign that black leaders were not out to get them, racial concerns should have played a declining role in the white vote over time, and whites should have been more willing to vote for a black candidate in subsequent elections. I test this last set of hypotheses by looking at changes over time in overall white support for Bradley, in the determinants of the white vote, and in the sentiments expressed about Bradley. Once again, I contrast the information model with a racial prejudice model and a white backlash model. If the racial prejudice model fits Los Angeles, there should have been *no change* in white views or actions under a black mayor. If the backlash model is accurate, whites should have *increased* their efforts to try to reverse black gains and oust black leadership.

For this narrative of Los Angeles politics, I rely primarily on newspaper reporting and primary accounts of events in the city. However, I also draw on previous analyses when they provide further insight. All of this is supplemented with in-depth analysis of two public opinion polls: one conducted in 1969, the year of Bradley's first mayoral bid and one from 1980, the midway point of Bradley's mayoral tenure. Both are described in more detail in Appendix C.

BLACK CHALLENGER ELECTIONS: LIMITED INFORMATION AND WHITE FEAR

To begin to assess the information model, I examined Tom Bradley's two bids to become the first black mayor of Los Angeles (his unsuccessful bid for the mayoralty in 1969 and his successful campaign in 1973) to see if uncertainty about black leadership led to racial fears and opposition to Bradley's candidacy. The results closely fit the information model. Almost every aspect of both elections points to acute racial concerns about Tom Bradley and widespread fear about how black leadership could affect the white community.

While the evidence is anecdotal in nature, the white Angelenos who were interviewed in the days and weeks before the 1969 election were often very clear about their fears of black leadership. These individuals regularly expressed deep-seated concerns about the potential consequences of black leadership for the white community. The comments of Jo Ann Des Ruisseaux were typical: "I just don't like all these Black Panther people that are hanging around [Bradley's] campaign. I know he denies it, but where there's smoke, there's fire" (Reich 1973b). Many focused on black in-migration as a real threat. One white resident lamented: "If we have a colored mayor we'll have colored people pushing us out of the city. The whole city will be black if Bradley wins" (Reich 1973a). A citizen from Encino echoed this concern about a black victory: "You know what this means? There'll be blacks all over this place next month. They'll be all over Encino. You're not gonna recognize this town" (Seidenbaum 1973). Others did not mention specific threats, but suggested that the consequences of Bradley's election could be dire for the white community.

Perhaps the most persuasive evidence of the important role that uncertainty and white racial concerns played in these two contests comes from analysis of the white vote itself. Whether whites voted for or against

TABLE 5.1 *Key Factors Driving the Vote for the Challenger Tom Bradley*[1]

	Change in the Probability of Voting for Bradley (%)
RACIAL CONCERNS	
Bradley Favors Blacks	67
Concerned About Black Gains – Not Concerned	−54
THE WHITE INCUMBENT'S RECORD	
Satisfied With Public Services – Dissatisfied	Not Significant
Satisfied With Economic Gains – Dissatisfied	Not Significant
POLITICAL IDEOLOGY	
Conservative – Liberal	27
Republican – Democrat	37
RACIAL PREJUDICE	
Racially Prejudiced – Not Racially Prejudiced	Not Significant

[1] Predicted probabilities derived from logistic regression in Table C.1 in Appendix C.

Bradley depended more than anything else on their concerns about Bradley and black leadership. One poll from the 1969 runoff between Bradley and Sam Yorty – who was running for reelection – is particularly illuminating. In Table 5.1, I present an account of the main factors driving the white vote in that election.[1] The predicted probabilities in the table are derived from a logistic regression that assesses the effects of racial concerns, Yorty's record as an incumbent, racial prejudice, political ideology, and socioeconomic status. The survey, variables, and full model are detailed in Appendix C.[2]

Several important conclusions emerge from this analysis. First, concerns about how black leadership would affect the white community dominated white voters' decision making. Whether or not whites supported Bradley depended principally on the simple question of whether or not they thought Bradley would serve black interests at the expense of white interests. If a white respondent thought that Bradley "would show more favoritism to his supporters than most other mayors," that person was 67 percent less likely to support Bradley than if the voter thought Bradley would be evenhanded. Similarly, if whites were concerned about black political and economic gains and felt that blacks would "push themselves

[1] There is, unfortunately, no comparable survey of white voters in 1973.
[2] The survey is a pre-election poll of white suburbanites in Los Angeles conducted by the National Opinion Research Center shortly before the run-off election between Bradley and Yorty.

where they're not wanted," they were 54 percent less likely to vote for Bradley. Fears about losing out to blacks clearly were central to the white vote.[3]

The other important and unique aspect of the Bradley-Yorty contest was the fact that the white vote was unrelated to Yorty's record as an incumbent in the mayor's office. As Table 5.1 indicates, whether or not white residents were satisfied with city services under Yorty and whether or not they were satisfied with their personal economic gains over the previous five years had little effect on whether white voters chose Bradley or Yorty. The white vote was not about the white candidate or the past. It was instead about the black candidate, the future, and concerns that black leadership might harm the white community.

At the same time, Table 5.1 reveals that racial concerns were not the only factor that mattered in the white vote. Nonracial concerns, including political ideology and party identification, played a modest role in the contest. Liberals and Democrats were somewhat more likely than conservatives or Republicans to support Bradley – although the difference was not as large as one would traditionally expect. Self-identified liberals were only 27 percent more likely to support Bradley than those who viewed themselves as conservative. In the end, Bradley received considerably more white support than other black challengers who were gaining office in other big cities at around the same time. Overall, he garnered 32 percent of the white vote in 1969 and 46 percent in 1973 (Halley, Acock, and Greene 1976). By contrast, successful black challengers in Cleveland, Gary, Newark, and Atlanta, the four other big cities electing black mayors around the same time, won only between 15 and 17 percent of the white vote.

The fact that nonracial concerns did sway some white voters in Los Angeles and the relatively widespread white support for Bradley when he ran as a challenger is exactly what one would expect given that the black community in Los Angeles was much smaller and posed less of a threat than the black population in these other majority black cities. In 1969, Los Angeles was a majority white city, and African Americans made up only 17 percent of the population. Los Angeles' demographics meant that whites would likely retain firm control of the local political arena,

---

[3] Equally importantly, as Table 5.1 shows, being prejudiced against blacks had no significant effect on the vote. Specifically, holding negative stereotypes of blacks (thinking blacks are less intelligent than whites) played no direct role. It was not simple prejudice that structured the vote, but expectations about the future and fears about black leadership.

even if Bradley were elected. Uncertainty played a role in Los Angeles but concerns about black leadership in this majority white city were less pronounced than were white fears in cities where blacks really could "take over."

The media in Los Angeles echoed this analysis of the white vote. Most of the stories run by the *Los Angeles Times* highlighted in one way or another the important role that white fears about black leadership played in Bradley's bids to become mayor.[4] Kenneth Reich, in particular, saw "a distinct note of concern about a black man in the mayor's office" (1973a). His interviews of white Angelenos "indicated that the racial issue remains highly important this year."[5]

White concerns about what might happen if blacks were allowed to take over also came through in the campaigns that Bradley and his opponent ran. Yorty, in particular, designed his two campaigns against Bradley to highlight all of the unknowns surrounding a black victory. In both 1969 and 1973, the theme of Yorty's campaign was typified by the following statement: "We know what kind of a city we've got. We don't know what we might get [if Bradley is elected]. So we'd be taking quite a chance with this particular kind of candidate" (Bergholz 1973b). Time and time again, Yorty accused Bradley of being a radical who was anti-police and pro-communist. He repeatedly raised questions about the future of Los Angeles under black leadership. "Will your family be safe?" asked one advertisement. "Will your city be safe with this man?" queried another (Bollens and Geyer 1973). There was, Yorty argued, a real chance of "losing the city" (Boyarsky 1973c). In short, Yorty clearly felt that the best way to defeat his black opponent was to play on white fears about the unknowns surrounding black leadership.

Yorty was not the only candidate who realized that white Angelenos were afraid of black leadership. Bradley also knew that concerns about black leadership were widespread, and he did everything he could to try to assuage those fears in his campaigns as a challenger. By avoiding any

---

[4] See e.g. Boyarsky 1973a; 1973b; 1973c; 1973d; 1973e; Bergholz 1973a; Paegel 1973; and Reich (1973a; 1973b).

[5] More extended scholarly accounts that were written in the years after the elections reaffirmed the central role of racial fears. In fact, it is quite remarkable that of the dozen or so studies that examined the two elections in depth, every single one concluded that fear and uncertainty plagued Bradley's bid for the mayoralty. The following accounts all point to the critical role uncertainty played in Bradley's two challenger elections: Bollens and Geyer 1973; Hahn, Klingman, and Pachon 1976; Halley, Acock, and Greene 1976; Jeffries and Ransford 1972; Kaufman 1998; Kinder and Sears 1981; Litwin 1981; Maullin 1971; Payne and Ratzan 1986; Pettigrew 1972; Robinson 1976; Sears and Kinder 1971; Shiesl 1990; Sonenshein 1989; 1993; Watson 1984.

mention of racial issues, downplaying his connections to black activists, and focusing his campaign on law and order, Bradley made it clear that his was not a "black" campaign. He did not bring in any well-known black leaders from outside the city, he campaigned largely in white neighborhoods, and he did not talk about the issue of race except to occasionally deny that it was an issue. As Sonenshein put it, "Bradley forces went to great lengths to reassure white and Hispanic voters that Bradley would be fair to all" (1989: 343).

After he lost in 1969, Bradley and his advisors were certain that racial fears had cost him the election. They were determined not to let white fears dominate his second challenger bid (Payne and Ratzan 1986b). Thus, in 1973, Bradley's efforts to reassure white voters greatly increased. He repeatedly stressed his ties to the Los Angeles Police Department and focused much of his campaign on conservative law and order issues (Boyarsky 1973c). When Yorty focused media attention on a Black Panther who had endorsed Bradley, Bradley's response was swift and decisive: "I do not seek, I do not want, and I reject the endorsement. I have always been opposed to such a philosophy" (Paegel 1973).

What all of this evidence, both quantitative and qualitative, suggests is that uncertainty about black leadership was widespread among white residents in Los Angeles when Bradley ran as a challenger. Bradley may have had a record as a moderate on the city council, but whites in Los Angeles had never experienced an African American in control. The experiences that white Angelenos did have – the Watts Riot, periodic violent racial flare-ups, and growing demands from the black community – undoubtedly led many to expect the worst.

THE INFORMATION EFFECTS OF BRADLEY'S TENURE

In this section, I review Bradley's tenure in an effort to see what his agenda looked like, how well he was able to enact that agenda, and how the economic and social well-being of white Los Angeles changed under his mayoralty. The bottom line is that if whites were watching Bradley to see what black leadership meant to the white community, what they saw and experienced under Bradley suggested that black leadership was not a serious threat to their well-being.

Bradley's Pro-Development Agenda

Although there were some areas in which Bradley pushed for modest gains for blacks, the main theme of his administration, according to almost all observers of Los Angeles politics, was economic development, and in particular downtown development (Saltzstein 1986; Sonenshein 1993; Regalado 1991; 1992; M. Davis 1992). As part of this pro-development agenda, Bradley maintained a fiscally sound administration. In his first years, he cut city expenditures by 10 percent and was able to balance the city budget without raising taxes (Payne and Ratzan 1986b). There was also no real redistribution of income or any real change in spending priorities under Bradley (Regalado 1992; Jackson and Preston 1994; Anderson 1996).[6] Over the twenty-year period of his tenure, local government redistributive expenditures grew only 0.9 percent as a percentage of total government expenditures (Bureau of the Census Bureau 1964–2003).

The core of Bradley's policy agenda had little, if anything, to do with race. Bradley, in fact, tried hard to avoid racial controversies and regularly vowed to serve all racial groups. In his first speech as mayor, he pledged that he would "be mayor of all of Los Angeles" (Payne and Ratzan 1986a: 135). And on most racial issues, Bradley's regime was silent (Jackson 1990; Sonenshein 1993). As Sonenshein has noted, "On such tinderbox issues as school busing, Bradley has been utterly invisible" (1990: 40). In 1979, when an LAPD officer shot Eulia Love, a black woman, aggravating racial tensions, Bradley's response was "feeble," according to many observers (Anderson 1996). Bradley's administration did provide some real, concrete benefits for blacks in the city. In a regime that many felt was at least "initially transformative," Bradley fought to ensure greater oversight over the Los Angeles Police Department, and he attempted to open the doors of city government to previously excluded groups (Sonenshein 1993). Minority contracting expanded, and more blacks were hired as commissioners and in other positions of authority (Jackson and Preston 1994).[7] Bradley also helped to increase the number and size of federal grants for poverty and public housing spending when these funds were widely available in the 1970s (Keiser 1997; Sonenshein 1993). But these efforts were modest. Under Bradley, black employment in city government only increased from 20 percent in the Yorty years to 24 percent in the 1990s (Sonenshein 1993; Joyce 1994). Indeed, it is unclear whether affirmative action in Los Angeles proceeded at a faster pace than it did

---

[6] The biggest change in government under Bradley, according to Sonenshein (1993) was the incorporation of business. As one Chamber of Commerce executive put it, "Business was made a managing partner in running the city" (Litwin 1981: 87).

[7] Black commission appointments increased from 6% under Yorty to 20% in 1991 (Sonenshein 1993).

in other cities without black mayors (Jackson and Preston 1994; Litwin 1981; Eisinger 1983).

In short, Bradley did not show any sign that he was interested in a "black takeover." All of these actions – and inactions – on the part of the Bradley administration likely served to reassure white Los Angeles that black leadership was relatively safe for the white community.

Ongoing White Prosperity

More importantly, the end result of Bradley's tenure was ongoing white prosperity and no change in the relative economic status of white and black Los Angeles. If anything, whites gained under Bradley, while much of the black community fell behind. Los Angeles experienced an extended period of economic expansion during Bradley's tenure (Litwin 1981; Oliver, Johnson, and Farel 1993; Ong and Blumenberg 1996; Regalado 1992; Schwada 1989; Sojo and Scott 1996). At a time when many other cities went downhill, Bradley helped to transform Los Angeles into the largest industrial center in the United States (Sonenshein 1993). Overall, the median family income of the city's residents grew by 5.3 percent between 1969 and 1989, marginally better than the average for urban America (Ong and Blumenberg 1996). Importantly for the white population, these gains had a disproportionate impact on the upper end of the wage distribution. Of the hundreds of thousands of new jobs created during Bradley's administration, most were for highly skilled, well-educated white workers (Ong and Blumenberg 1996). Most of the development occurred downtown, where white business interests benefited (Sonenshein 1993). On the other end of the spectrum, in Los Angeles' poor black communities, there were limited positive developments; if anything, economic fortunes deteriorated under Bradley.[8]

---

[8] Bradley's mayoralty did little to alleviate poverty and the variety of social ills that plagued much of black Los Angeles (Anderson 1996; Bunch 1990; M. Davis 1992; Keiser 1997; Jackson and Preston 1994; Oliver, Johnson, and Farrel 1993; Ong and Blumenberg 1996). Areas such as Southcentral Los Angeles suffered a slow decline. In Southcentral between 1973 and 1990, the poverty rate, the unemployment rate, and the proportion of residents on welfare all grew (Ong and Blumenberg 1996). By 1990 in Southcentral, unemployment exceeded 50%, welfare dependency stood at 25%, the poverty rate was 30%, and 56% of the adult population were high school dropouts (*Los Angeles Times* 1992). In other words, the efforts of Bradley's administration "stopped short of the population most in need" (Anderson 1996: 351). The fact that Bradley had not met black expectations was confirmed by considerable disenchantment within the black community, which became more and more evident as Bradley's tenure went on (M. Davis 1992; Sonenshein 1990).

The racial status quo that had seemed to many to be threatened by the onset of black leadership survived the twenty years under Bradley. A variety of economic and social indicators revealed no change in the relative well-being of blacks and whites during Bradley's tenure. In 1969 in Los Angeles, black male median earnings (controlling for education and labor force experience) were 70 percent of white earnings. In 1989, the figure was a virtually identical 69 percent (Ong and Blumenberg 1996). Income inequality data reveal an increasing gap between wealthy, mostly white Los Angeles and poor, disproportionately black Los Angeles over the same period. Between 1969 and 1989, the GINI coefficient grew from 0.37 to 0.44, and the poverty rate increased from 10.9 to 15.1 percent (Ong and Blumenberg 1996). As the *Los Angeles Times* noted in 1989, "An already yawning racial gulf between rich and poor is growing" (2: 6). For anyone who watched, the lesson was clear: whites could support blacks without hurting their own well-being.[9]

DID WHITES LEARN IN LOS ANGELES?

Did whites, in the end, learn this lesson, updating their beliefs about Bradley and black leadership? If the information model is correct and Bradley's tenure did demonstrate to white residents that black leadership was not in conflict with white interests, then uncertainty about Bradley and black leadership should have declined. And as uncertainty declined, perceptions about the meaning of black leadership should have changed, racial concerns should have faded in importance in subsequent elections, and more and more whites should have supported Bradley. All of this is borne out by the evidence.

Growing White Support and Falling Turnout

The most obvious change in white behavior was increased white support for Bradley's leadership. When Bradley was first elected, he faced record white turnout, and most white voters voted against him. But as Table 5.2

---

[9] It is also important to note that Bradley's governing coalition faced little serious opposition during most of his tenure (Jackson 1990; Sonenshein 1993). Even though Bradley's mayoral powers were somewhat limited, what he proposed was often pretty close to what Los Angeles got. Thus, white residents would have had a hard time pointing to anyone else in the city as being responsible for the direction of policy under Bradley's administration.

TABLE 5.2 *White Support for Bradley Over Time*

	White Vote for Bradley (%)	Voter Turnout (%)
1969	32	76
1973	44	75
1977	53	42
1981	58	45
1985	62	35
1989	47	23

illustrates, as white residents gained more and more experience with black leadership, most of this opposition faded. In Bradley's first reelection bid, white support increased to 53 percent, and he won all but one city council district. By 1979, polls showed Bradley with a 76 percent approval rating. One year later, the *Los Angeles Times* exclaimed, "Bradley is, within the liberal community, unassailable" (Sonenshein 1993: 179). In 1981, Bradley's approval reached 85 percent, and he won 58 percent of the white vote that year. Four years later, he garnered a record 68 percent of the city vote, capturing 62 percent of the white vote and winning every district – including the conservative white Valley districts that had mobilized in 1969 and 1973 in such great numbers to prevent what they thought was a black takeover. It was only after scandals and a poor showing in the California gubernatorial race tarnished his reputation that Bradley's winning percentage dropped for the first time, in 1989. He chose not to run for a sixth term in 1993.

Remarkably, over a sixteen-year period, Bradley's support in the white community nearly doubled. A losing black challenger had been transformed into a five-term mayoral juggernaut.[10] By the end of his tenure, Bradley's support among white residents was not too different from his support among black Angelenos. In 1990, blacks on average rated Bradley as a 68 on a 100-point feeling thermometer. Whites weren't that far behind

[10] Analysis of the mayoral vote in key city council districts confirms Bradley's growing support among all sectors of white Los Angeles. Over the five elections from 1969 to 1985, Bradley's support among white liberals grew from 51 to 58 to 62 to 69 to 74%. Among conservatives, the increase in support was not nearly as dramatic, but it was nevertheless impressive. Over the same five elections, conservative white support for Bradley grew from 31% to 50%. Among moderate white and Latino wards, Bradley's support went from 44% in 1973 to 60% in 1985 (Sonenshein 1993).

at 57.[11] In short, by the end of Bradley's tenure, something resembling racial consensus had crept into the mayoral politics of the city.

The direction of the vote was not the only sign in Los Angeles that racial concerns surrounding black leadership had declined. Another possible indication of diminished fear was the steep drop in voter turnout. Turnout in Bradley's mayoral contests plummeted from a record high of 75 percent in 1969 to 42 percent in 1977, 37 percent in 1981, 35 percent in 1985, and 23 percent in 1989. The 23 percent turnout in 1989 represents a record low for the city, and it occurred despite the fact that many observers felt that Bradley had a real chance of losing that year. The fear that had motivated so many white residents to try to prevent a black takeover appears largely to have disappeared over the course of Bradley's tenure.

The Declining Role of Race Among White Voters?

A less obvious but equally important change under Bradley was the diminishing role racial concerns played in campaigns and in the white vote. Just as the information model predicts, the racial concerns that dominated the calculus of white voters in Bradley's two challenger candidacies slowly faded with time. As each year went by and whites gained more experience with black leadership, Bradley's record as an incumbent became more and more critical to white voters.

Bradley's first reelection bid in 1977 began the trend and is particularly illustrative. In many ways, Bradley faced a difficult electoral context that year. In the interim four years, Los Angeles voters had moved markedly to the right. As the election results would later show, in most of the city's municipal and school board elections, voters opted for more conservative candidates than they had in the past (Sonenshein 1993). Moreover, during the campaign, Los Angeles was facing a racially divisive school busing controversy, a highly unfavorable setting for any black candidate.[12] Alan Robbins, Bradley's chief opponent, tried to use this context to his advantage. Just as Yorty had done before him, Robbins attempted to make race relevant in the campaign, repeatedly trying to incite white racial concerns about Bradley and black leadership by raising the issues of crime and

---

[11] The increase in white support for Bradley is even more impressive when one considers the conservative drift of the Los Angeles electorate. Bradley was increasingly successful during a period in which Los Angeles' white voters favored fiscally conservative propositions (e.g. Prop. 13 in 1978, Prop. A in 1981, and Prop. 1 in 1985).

[12] All through the campaign, the busing controversy received more coverage than the campaign did.

busing, among others. He accused Bradley of allowing the school system "to be set on an almost irreversible path toward extensive forced busing" (Reich 1977a). He criticized Bradley's cuts in police spending, and he accused Bradley of being soft on crime. He even went so far as to hand out thousands of rape whistles. As one city hall observer noted, "Bradley is black and the whole Robbins campaign is subtly directed toward playing upon it" (Reich, 1977a). In the end, though, Robbins's efforts failed.[13] Although the attention that busing received indicated that race was still an important issue in Los Angeles, the results of the election suggested that most whites did not fear Bradley. With Bradley running as an incumbent, there was no run-off. There was no widespread white mobilization. In short, there was no contest. White voters supported Bradley in large numbers, white business provided Bradley with strong financial backing, and turnout declined precipitously. In contrast to the 1969 and 1973 elections, racialized voting did not follow a racialized campaign.

On this point, most observers agreed:

There were two overriding reasons for Mayor Tom Bradley's overwhelming victory – his own substantial record of achievement over the past four years and the diminution of race as a factor in Los Angeles politics. The fact that Bradley is black was significant in his two previous campaigns for mayor. There were similar, more indirect efforts this year to place a negative emphasis on race.... But the voters, to their credit, saw more merit in Bradley's pledge to work for peaceful compliance.... We also commend the voters of this city for appraising Bradley on the basis of performance, not of race. (*Los Angeles Times* 1977)

Even Bradley agreed that racial concerns had largely dropped out of the equation. In a *Los Angeles Times* article entitled "Race Banished as Vote Issue," Bradley was quoted as saying, "You know that this city could rise above race, could rise above economic circumstances, could rise above politics, to elect a mayor on his qualifications, character, and confidence in the progress of ideas" (Reich 1977b). Bradley went on to claim that white voters had lost their fear of black leadership. They had learned that a black mayor was not the end of the world: "This time, there was not such an important issue to be proved.... [White voters] were sure enough, ready, and willing to vote for a man who was black" (Reich 1977b). In short, the 1977 election provided ample evidence that experience under

---

[13] This time, against Robbins, Bradley did not even have to counter with a conservative law and order campaign, as he had done before, against Yorty, to assuage white fears. Instead, he simply campaigned on his record in office.

Bradley as mayor had allayed white fears concerning Bradley the black candidate.

Subsequent elections told a similar story. The 1981 election was an almost exact repeat of 1977. In 1981, Bradley faced his old nemesis, Yorty. And Yorty went with the same white fear campaign he had used in 1969 and 1973. Race, crime, and fear were the order of the day for the campaign. "People are afraid in this town. They're afraid to go out at night and afraid to go out in the daytime," Yorty declared (Dowie 1981). Though the campaign was the same, the reaction was not. This time around, Yorty was sharply criticized for his racist attacks and his efforts to incite white fear. As the campaign went on, in fact, Yorty was forced to tone down his attacks (Payne and Ratzan 1986b). Also in contrast to 1973, Bradley did not respond to Yorty's vitriol. Bradley's commercials did not mention Yorty or his tactics. There was none of the law and order campaign that Bradley had used in 1973 to assuage white fears. There was also little mention of his 21-year career on the LAPD. Bradley ran on his record as mayor, and the results were impressive. He won 64 percent of the vote to Yorty's 32 percent, and he carried every council district in the city. Bradley became the first mayor of Los Angeles to win a third term without a run-off. A *Los Angeles Times* editorial applauded the city's white voters for ignoring Bradley's race: "Just as encouraging was the absence of race as a dominant issue in Sam Yorty's battle to unseat the black mayor" (*Los Angeles Times* 1981).

The story of the 1985 and 1989 mayoral elections is somewhat different, but the conclusion is the same. In both elections, race and racial issues took a back seat to other city and voter concerns. In 1985, for the first time, Bradley's main opponent did not use race in his campaign. John Ferraro did run a negative attack campaign, but the issue was never race. Unlike previous elections, there was a plethora of issues to choose from. Ferraro tried to win votes by coming out against a city metro line and by voicing opposition to a proposed property tax hike. The two big issues in the election turned out to be Bradley's support for offshore oil drilling and whether or not Bradley would run for governor the next year. In Payne and Ratzan's view, "The issues were the focus of the campaign, and race seemed, for the first time, to be of little concern to either the candidates or the voters" (1986b: 329). In 1989, the names of the challengers changed, but the script was largely repeated. Race had ceased to be the central element in Los Angeles mayoral elections.

Empirical analysis of local newspaper coverage helps to confirm the declining role of race in mayoral campaigns. In Bradley's challenger

TABLE 5.3 *Main Factors Driving Approval of Bradley*

	Impact on Support for:	
	Bradley the Challenger	Bradley the Incumbent
RACIAL CONCERNS		
Concerned about Black Gains – Not Concerned	58%	Not Significant
INCUMBENT'S RECORD		
Satisfied with the City Conditions – Dissatisfied	Not Significant	−46%

Note: Predicted probabilities derived from logistic regressions in Table C.2 in Appendix C.

campaigns, race was *the* issue. Both in 1969 and 1973, race dominated campaign coverage (Graber 1984). Far outweighing all other issues, race was mentioned in half of all coverage of the 1973 election (Sylvie 1995). For anyone who cared to listen, read, or watch, Bradley's mayoral challenge was more than anything else a racial battle between a black and a white candidate. But all of this changed after Bradley was elected mayor. In Bradley's mayoral reelection bids, the media slowly ceased to focus on race. Graber's (1984) analysis of campaign coverage in Los Angeles reveals a substantial decrease in the frequency with which the issue of race was raised in local newspapers. Bradley's race had been replaced by Bradley's record.

VIEWS OF BRADLEY AS CHALLENGER AND INCUMBENT

Another way to see if experience with black leadership fundamentally altered white views in Los Angeles is to compare the factors driving white support of Bradley as a challenger with the factors driving white support of Bradley as an incumbent. If the information model is accurate, this kind of comparison should reveal a sharp decline in the importance of racial concerns and a sharp increase in the importance of the incumbent's record. This is exactly what we see in Table 5.3. The table contrasts the factors driving white approval of Bradley in 1969, when he first ran as a challenger, with the factors driving white approval of Bradley in 1980, after he had already led the city for seven years.[14] The predicted probabilities in the table are derived from two regressions that assess the effects of racial concerns, the incumbent's record, racial prejudice, political

[14] I focus on the 1980 poll because it is the only citywide poll during Bradley's administration that includes measures of white racial attitudes.

ideology, and individual socioeconomic status. The surveys, variables, and full models are detailed in Appendix C.

The contrast between white views and concerns before Bradley was elected and white views and concerns seven years into Bradley's tenure is dramatic. As the first column of Table 5.3 illustrates, when Bradley ran as a challenger, the election was largely about racial concerns. Fears about the possible consequences of black leadership dominated the white vote, and the incumbent's record played no role. Whites' support for Bradley, the black challenger, over Yorty, the white incumbent, was unaffected by their feelings about how well the city was doing. Rather, support for Bradley was almost wholly shaped by concerns about the future and the fear that Bradley would serve black interests.

In sharp contrast, views of Bradley the incumbent were not significantly tied to racial concerns. The racial fear that had shaped the white vote in Bradley's challenger election appears to have faded as whites gained experience under Tom Bradley and as the reality of black mayoral leadership proved better than expected. Even more important, as the information model would predict, support for Bradley as an incumbent was largely a function of the information that his tenure had provided. If whites thought the city had fared well under Bradley, they generally supported him. Those who felt "things in Los Angeles" were going well were 46 percent more likely to have a favorable view of Bradley than those who felt that Los Angeles was faring poorly. In other words, the key factor driving white views of black leadership was Bradley's policy record. And since the majority of whites thought the city had fared well under Bradley, Bradley's record was critical to his ongoing success.[15]

Whites who were interviewed in greater depth in the years after Bradley entered office echoed this transformation and in so doing highlighted the important role that information played. One white resident of Los Angeles put it this way: "A lot of people were very suspicious and fearful before Bradley got in. But they never say anything now. I'm sure they have changed their opinions.... Most important, he is a good person. Whether he is black or white is immaterial" (boatshop worker interviewed by the *US News & World Report* 1975). Mark Murphy, the editor of the

---

[15] Additional analysis suggests that Bradley's record on race was also critical. When a question asking about whether or not black-white relations had improved over the course of Bradley's tenure was added to the incumbent regression in Table 5.3, it was significant. All else being equal, whites who felt that black-white relations had improved over the course of Bradley's tenure were 21% more likely to approve of Bradley's mayoralty than those who thought that race relations had deteriorated.

Los Angeles Times, expressed a similar opinion: "Tom Bradley is beyond black in the eyes of most of the people of L.A. Most of us think of him simply as our mayor" (*US News & World Report* 1975).

Bradley was also well aware of this change in white perceptions. Indeed, he felt that it was one of the greatest accomplishments of his career, both for the city and for the country (Ingwerson 1981): "Race, in my judgment, was not a relevant issue. Never should have been. But it took the experience of the people to be convinced that it should not and would not become a factor in how you serve the interests of this city. And having seen that demonstration, I don't think anybody can make a case now or in the future that the color of a candidate's skin is a factor and should be of any significant concern" (Ingwerson 1981).

Pollsters, too, knew that experience with Bradley and black leadership had transformed white views. In Bradley's two challenger elections, the common view among political pundits was that racial concerns about black leadership were an important liability that prevented many, if not most, white voters from supporting him. As one prominent pollster put it, "In essence, Tom Bradley contributed to the [white] backlash sentiment by being black in a de facto segregated society" (Maullin 1971: 51). But according to the same pollsters, just a few years later, something had changed for Bradley the incumbent. Bradley was widely recognized as an important asset to his liberal coalition. In this revised analysis, Bradley, the man, was the key to his electoral success. At the end of Bradley's tenure, Sonenshein wrote: "In the broadest sense, a major resource of the coalition has been Bradley's popularity. This public appeal is the product of his style and of the meaning attached to having a successful Black mayor" (1993: 185). Similarly, in an article in 1989 that marveled at Bradley's ability to avoid criticism and gain reelection, Schwada concluded, "Because he's politically bland and non-threatening, he can move in all circles" (1989: 102). Bradley's tenure and the information it provided had transformed black leadership from being a major threat to the white community into something that sparked little to no negative reaction.

The lessons from this study of Los Angeles' mayoral politics, then, are fairly clear. Racial learning did occur in Los Angeles. White support for Bradley was never absolute. Many white residents never voted for Tom Bradley, and a large number never trusted him or black leadership. But many white residents did change their minds about Tom Bradley and black leadership. Just as the information model predicts, experience with black mayoral leadership appears to have led to a fundamental transformation of white views and a greater willingness to support the black incumbent.

After living for years under Tom Bradley, white Angelenos' uncertainty about black leadership faded and was replaced by a much more reasoned and positive assessment of black leadership and the gradual diminution of a black-white divide in the mayoral politics in the city. By enacting a fairly racially neutral agenda that helped ensure ongoing white prosperity, Bradley had proven to many whites that black leadership was worth supporting.

At the same time, it is important to note that by focusing exclusively on mayoral politics under Bradley this chapter has obscured three potentially important trends. First, by focusing on Tom Bradley's words and actions, this chapter has ignored a range of factors outside of black leadership that could have contributed to changes in the white vote in Los Angeles. Over this time period, there were, for example, fairly dramatic changes in the racial demographics of the city and the state. If rapid Latino and Asian American immigration represented more of a threat to whites than did the presence of a relatively small and stable black population, then growing support for Bradley might signal less about acceptance of blacks and more about growing fears of Latino and Asian American power.[16] Other trends, such as the migration of white voters into the city and the state, continued economic growth across the state, and variations in the ideological leaning of the state's voters, could also have influenced the white vote. Although racial learning seems to have played an important role, it is not at all clear that it was the only factor affecting the white vote in Los Angeles over this period.

A second missing feature of this chapter is a discussion of race relations outside the arena of mayoral politics. This is an important omission because an exclusive focus on mayoral politics obscures considerable racial discord in the city. Black mayoral leadership may have had an important effect on white political behavior, but it is not clear how far that racial learning process extended. Even a cursory examination of race relations in the city reveals that black representation is no panacea for the array of racial conflicts facing the city, and the nation. Bradley's initial victory appears to have lessened racial tensions across the city, and for a decade few instances of severe racial conflict erupted. But subsequent developments reveal ongoing racial divides in the city. The 1992 riots are the most obvious example of the continued importance of race in

---

[16] The fact that whites in California used direct democracy to target Latinos more than blacks or any other group over this period lends some credence to this theory (Hajnal, Gerber, and Louch 2002).

Los Angeles, and there have been many other episodes of racial conflict – some of which have repeated old patterns, and others that have demonstrated new tensions (Fears 1998; Gold 2001; Newton 1998).[17] It is clear that whites, blacks, Latinos, and Asian Americans continue regularly to disagree over how the city's resources should be allocated. In the end, experience with black leadership is unlikely to be able to alter the underlying interests of any of these groups. If blacks, whites, Latinos, and Asian Americans truly want different policies, minority representation will do little to end racial conflict. If, however, members of these groups want the same things from their government, then minority representation may help them to recognize their similar interests. Thus, the lesson from Los Angeles' recent history is an optimistic one only in a very limited sense.

Finally, a focus on black leadership overlooks important developments in Asian American and Latino leadership in the city. The unsuccessful mayoral candidacies of Michael Woo in 1993 and Antonio Villaraigosa in 2001 and the successful mayoral bid of Villaraigosa in 2005 highlight a range of new and extremely variable racial divisions. Woo's candidacy resulted in a fairly strong inter-minority coalition and seemingly widespread white opposition to Asian American leadership.[18] Villaraigosa's 2001 bid pointed to a sharp black-Latino divide and only somewhat less widespread white opposition to minority leadership.[19] And Villaraigosa's 2005 electoral victory resulted in a much more moderate black-Latino divide and sharply increased white support for the Latino candidate. In Chapter 7, I will look more closely at these new forms of minority leadership. However, it may be too early to offer much in the way of definitive generalizations about how Asian American and Latino leadership will ultimately affect racial dynamics in Los Angeles and other cities. The mixed results we see in these three elections and the, as of yet, small number of cases of Latino and Asian American leadership make it difficult to reach any conclusions.

---

[17] The increasingly central battle between blacks and Hispanics over each group's political representation in the city is perhaps the most important new facet of the city's racial dynamic.

[18] Woo captured 69% of the Asian American vote, 86% of the black vote, and 57% of the Latino vote but only 33% of the white vote (Kaufman 1998). At least some of this white opposition could, however, have been generated by Woo's strongly liberal stances on a range of issues.

[19] In the 2001 primary, according to a *Los Angeles Times* poll, only 26% of white voters supported either of the two Latino candidates and in the general election, 59% of white voters in the city opposed Villaraigosa.

Another question this study of Los Angeles cannot answer is why some cities do not conform to the same pattern of growing white acceptance of black leadership. As we saw in Chapter 4, in a small minority of cities, whites respond to black leadership with ongoing white opposition and persistent racial tension. In Chapter 6, I follow the course of black mayoral leadership in Chicago to try to understand why whites in racially balanced cities do not change their minds about black leadership.

6

Black Mayoral Leadership in Chicago

Although black representation in most cases leads to decreased racial tension and greater acceptance of black incumbents, there are a select number of cities where racial tension remains high, voting continues to be highly racially polarized, and few new white voters begin to support black leaders despite years under black leadership. The goal of this chapter is to look much more closely at the course of black leadership and white learning in one such city to try to understand and explain the lack of change.

Chicago represents perhaps the most famous case of ongoing white resistance.[1] Voting figures in the city tell a story of unrelenting white opposition to black leadership. Harold Washington actually lost white support when he ran for reelection and none of the eight black candidates who have sought the mayoralty after Harold Washington's tenure has managed to garner more than 10 percent of the white vote in a primary or general election. Whites in the city seem no more willing to support black mayoral leadership today than they were in the days before Washington assumed office. The obvious question is why has experience with black leadership produced little, if any, change? Why didn't white voters in Chicago begin to accept and support black mayoral leadership as they did in other cities?

---

[1] Another important reason to focus on Chicago is the extensive empirical record on mayoral and racial politics in Chicago. A range of primary accounts and a number of in-depth polls detail white attitudes and views before, during, and after Harold Washington's tenure as mayor allowing for a detailed assessment of the information model and its alternatives.

In Chapter 1, I suggested that information and control were the critical variables explaining variation across cities – in particular, in accounting for the lack of change in a small number of racially balanced cities, such as Chicago. Racially balanced cities are different, I argued, for two reasons. First, in racially balanced cities, black incumbency provides little information to white residents because it is unclear whether the black or the white community is in control of the local political arena, and as a result it is unclear who should be blamed or credited for conditions in the city. Rather than experiencing the effects of a black mayoralty, white residents are apt to witness a battle for control between black and white elites that ends in stalemate. Second, the precarious balance of power between the black and white communities in racially balanced cities means that any additional black victory takes on added significance, as any black victory could lead to a black takeover. The limited information provided by experience with black leadership and the impending possibility of real black control should, according to the information model, prevent white support for black leadership from growing and in some cases even inspire whites to increase their efforts to prevent a black takeover.

To see if this information story can account for the lack of change in white political behavior in Chicago, I will address a series of questions about three different stages in the racial learning process. First, did white fears about the possibility of black leadership in Chicago mirror white concerns in other cities? Second, how does the information provided by black leadership in the city of Chicago differ from the information provided by black leadership in most other cities? In particular, did Harold Washington's tenure as mayor provide whites with less credible evidence about the consequences of black leadership? Third, is a lack of information reflected in ongoing white fears and continued white resistance to black leadership?

This review of these different stages in Chicago suggests that a lack of credible information can plausibly account for ongoing white resistance in the city. Harold Washington's tenure provided much less information to white residents than other cases of black leadership because Washington was prevented by a white-led coalition in the city council from enacting his agenda. Since a black agenda was never realized, white residents did not know what would happen if a black mayor actually got control of the city. The situation was exacerbated by the fact that blacks were moving closer to achieving control of the city's political apparatus. Toward the end of Washington's tenure, his coalition won two seats on the city council to create an even 25:25 split. Another loss at that point could easily have pushed the precarious balance of power between the black and white communities in favor of the black community. In this context, it made sense to many whites in Chicago to continue to oppose black mayoral leadership.

As plausible as the information account may be, lack of information is certainly not the only factor that could have contributed to enduring white opposition in Chicago. Later in this chapter, I will examine a number of other factors related to the electoral context that could have influenced the white vote. Most of these factors cannot easily account for ongoing white resistance but it is impossible with just one case to rule out all factors. Thus, the conclusions of this chapter at best will be tentative.

CONCERNS ABOUT BLACK LEADERSHIP

To see if information – or more specifically a lack of information – could have contributed to ongoing white aversion to black leadership in Chicago, it is important to establish that whites in Chicago felt many of the same fears that other whites in other cities felt when faced with the prospect of black mayoral leadership. A review of the sentiments expressed by white residents, the tactics of the candidates, and patterns in the white vote all strongly suggest that whites in Chicago were, in fact, just like whites in other cities. They were uncertain and afraid. Just as in other cities with serious black challengers, the uncertainty that surrounded black leadership was acknowledged, explicitly or implicitly, by almost everyone who participated in the election.

White residents were relatively open about their fears and concerns. For many white residents, the prospect of black leadership implied nothing short of disaster. "[It's] more than an election," one voter opined. "We're fighting for everything we have this time" (Kleppner 1985). Another said: "The story is going around here 'Go in your room and lock your door for two days if Washington is elected'"(Peterson 1983b). "If Harold Washington is elected mayor," a third city resident predicted, "it will be the worst disaster in Chicago since the Chicago fire" (quoted in Rivlin 1992: 191).

Often, the fear was generalized. If a black man is elected, bad things will happen. But frequently, it focused on one terrifying possibility: neighborhood integration. As one white resident put it, "I don't know how to say this, but most people are afraid he is going to exert all of his powers for the black community and the white community is going to get nothing. My fear is that he's going to try to push racial integration, which is fine as long as I don't lose money on my house . . . because I can't take the loss (Coleman 1983a). A Democratic Committee member concurred, explaining, "[My constituents] are giving me a message of racial pride . . . They're afraid of scattered-site housing. They're concerned about the stability of our neighborhoods" (in Rivlin 1992: 185–6). "People have lived here all their lives," a resident of one white neighborhood explained. "It's a nice area and they want to hold onto what they have" (Morganthau 1983). Jesse Jackson put it more succinctly and perhaps more accurately than anyone else: "Black people were energized. White people were traumatized" (quoted in Kleppner 1985: 187).[2]

As in other cities facing the possibility of black leadership, the white candidate attempted to play on these racial concerns. "Epton, before it's too late!" became the rallying cry of Washington's white opponent in the general election. Mirroring Sam Yorty's racialized campaigns in Los Angeles, Bernard Epton asked white voters to consider what would happen if a black man were elected to run the city: "Will he obey the law? Will he do what he promises?" (Kleppner 1985: 205). And, as in other cities, the black candidate had to respond. Washington, while primarily focused on mobilizing the black community, tried to allay white fears whenever possible.[3] His campaign theme, "A Mayor for All Chicago," was part of an inclusive campaign that often explicitly told whites that they would be included: "Our concern is to heal. Our concern is to bring together. . . . I want to reach my hand in friendship to every living soul in this city." Washington also took more concrete steps to try to reduce white fears. Jesse Jackson was "all but banished" during the general election

---

[2] The importance of white fear was highlighted by the media and other political observers, who generally concluded that the 1983 election was about white racial concerns rather than about political reform, candidate qualifications, or any number of other potentially relevant issues. The *Washington Post* called Chicago a city "engulfed in fear" (1983). A review of public opinion polls taken during the 1983 contest simply concluded that "Washington scared white people" (Rivlin 1992: 173). Another account in the *Chicago Tribune* compared white fears in Chicago to the fears of white Southerners facing the civil rights movement: "It is understandable why some segments of this city fear the kind of change the election of Harold Washington as mayor signifies. It was the same fear felt by the South during the civil rights struggle 20 years ago and in cities all over this country in the years since" (quoted in Levinson 1983: 213). Another journalist tried to describe what it was that whites feared: "Simply put, the fear in this and other white ethnic wards of the city is that Washington's election would cause a redistribution of power and resources. White neighborhoods would suffer" (Peterson 1983b).

[3] Washington's campaign is best characterized as two campaigns, one focused on black Chicago and the other focused on white Chicago. Each campaign had separate offices and different leadership. In front of white audiences, Washington pressed for racial unity, fiscal conservatism, and reform. In front of black audiences, he preached an "It's our turn" philosophy.

campaign, and Washington made sure he spent more time in white Chicago than any of his opponents spent in black Chicago (Rivlin 1992). He even announced the formation of a mostly white transition team in the last weeks of the campaign to try to prove to white Chicagoans that their interests would be considered.

Despite Washington's efforts, racial fears appeared to dominate the white vote.[4] The aggregate vote total is the most obvious evidence of this fear. In the Democratic primary, Washington received only 8 percent of the white vote. In the general election only about 20 percent of white voters supported him. In short, few whites in Chicago seemed willing to vote for a black mayoralty. What makes this white opposition to Washington more telling is that it broke voting patterns that had held for decades. To vote against Washington in the general election, white Chicagoans had to support the Republican nominee – something they had been loathe to do since the 1930s. In the decades before Washington entered the scene, the Republican nominee for mayor had never garnered more than 5 percent of the vote. But when Harold Washington ran on the Democratic Party ticket, 79.3 percent of all white Democrats did the unthinkable and voted Republican (Kleppner 1985). An "unchallenged bastion of Democratic voting strength" had suddenly become a competitive bipartisan city.[5] And whites clearly did not flock to Epton because he was a great candidate: he was a total unknown prior to the campaign, had never won an election, was regularly criticized for being a poor speaker, and was viewed as being moody and temperamental, having twice spent time in a mental hospital. By all accounts, if he had not been facing a black candidate seeking to become the city's first black mayor, Epton would have garnered next to no support.[6] What seemed to motivate white voters was race. A range of analyses of exit polls, precinct returns, and pre-election surveys all found that race was more critical than any other issue in the election (Baker and Kleppner 1986; Day, Andreason, and Becker 1984; Kleppner 1985).[7] White fears and racial concern were also reflected in remarkable white voter turnout. A record 83 percent of eligible white adults registered for

---

[4] In the end, the only thing that saved Washington was record black turnout (80.1% of registered voters) and all but unanimous black support (Lewis, Taylor, and Kleppner 1997).

[5] Moreover, the 1983 election did not mark a trend to more Republican voting. Since Washington died, no Republican mayoral candidate has won more than 5% of the citywide vote.

[6] Overall, Bernard Epton won 49% of the vote.

[7] My own analysis of an NBC/Associated Press primary election poll suggested that the single most important determinant of the white vote was how important whites felt it was that Harold Washington was black.

the general election, and of these registered voters a record 80 percent turned out (Lewis, Taylor, and Kleppner 1997). The actions of white Chicagoans when faced with the prospect of black leadership were not all that different from those of whites in other cities. What set Chicago apart is what happened after Washington entered office.

WHAT INFORMATION DID WASHINGTON'S TENURE PROVIDE?

If whites in Chicago were as concerned about the consequences of black leadership as were whites elsewhere, why didn't experience with black leadership reduce these concerns? The simple answer is a lack of information. By all accounts, Washington was never given a chance to govern, and, as a result, could not prove that black leadership would not hurt white interests. The efforts of white Chicagoans at various levels inside and outside of city government successfully blocked almost all of Washington's agenda.

The most visible and most effective resistance came from white members of the city council. Even before Washington's inauguration, his white foes on the city council had hatched a plan to usurp power. During the first session of council, the anti-Washington coalition changed the electoral rules of the council and took charge of all of the city council committees. The infamous council wars were on. Chicagoans quickly grew accustomed to the rhythm of city politics under this new administration: "Washington or one of his council allies, – the Washington 21 – introduced an ordinance. It failed twenty-nine to twenty-one. The Vrdolyak 29 introduced an alternative, which passed twenty-nine to twenty-one. Washington vetoed it, and there the matter remained deadlocked" (Rivlin 1992: 233). This pattern continued for almost three and a half years. Over that period, almost every single ordinance that Washington's administration introduced was voted down.

In the first year, a vital downtown development faltered, a proposed new public library failed to move forward, a historic Chicago theater rejuvenation project could not get off the ground, and a key piece of city real estate, the Navy Pier, remained undeveloped. Even O'Hare airport was threatened with a shut-down in 1984. Washington's first two budgets were rejected by the Vrdolyak 29. What's more, Washington could not get much done with city government, because he was not able to gain influence over the bureaucracy. His appointments to various positions in city government were consistently held up by white opposition on the city council. Over eighty key Washington appointments were held hostage.

The appointments languished – two hundred days later, four hundred days later, six hundred days later (Rivlin 1992: 263). Thus, from day one of Washington's term, his administration was essentially cut off at the knees. For every action by the Washington's administration, there was an equal and opposite reaction. A headline in the weekly magazine *Newsday* said it all: "Harold Washington: In Charge, But Not In Control" (Miller 1989).

The inability of Washington's black-led coalition to pass its preferred policies ultimately meant that black representation provided very little information to white Chicago. Because Washington's agenda was never enacted, white residents in Chicago could neither reward him nor punish him for conditions in Chicago, and they could not know what would happen if Washington and his black-led coalition were ever able to gain control of the local political arena. Whites could have inferred something from what Washington's coalition *wanted* to pass. But even here, the message was mixed, and thus the likely consequences of black control somewhat unclear. On the one hand, Washington pursued policies that were not threatening. He took steps to try to balance the budget and cut the city payroll. He also talked repeatedly about reform and being fair and open to all parts of Chicago. But on the other hand, Washington took actions that whites could easily have perceived as hostile. He tried to push affirmative action and the redistribution of funds from downtown to the neighborhoods. He also proposed record-breaking tax increases.[8] He occasionally made statements that whites could interpret as a threat to their ongoing well-being. At one point, for example, he asserted, "Every group, when it reaches a certain population percentage automatically takes over. They don't apologize.... they just move in and take over" (quoted in Graber 1984: 72). In short, Washington's record was too limited, too inconsistent, and had too many potentially threatening elements to convince most white voters that they had little to fear from black leadership.

What whites could have easily learned over the course of Washington's tenure was that blacks were getting closer and closer to controlling the local political arena. The last six months of Washington's first term had already tilted the precarious balance of control in favor of the African American community. Special city council elections gave pro-Washington

---

[8] Only on taxes was Washington successful. In 1987, he was able to pass major tax hikes. By contrast, over the four-year period from 1983 to 1987, redistributive expenditures (social services, education, housing, and community development) actually decreased by 0.3% as a percentage of total government expenditures (Bureau of the Census 1964–2003).

forces control of exactly half of the city council seats. With the council vote divided 25:25 on most issues, Washington could regularly determine the outcome by casting the deciding vote.[9] Moreover, although many of Washington's efforts at affirmative action had been stymied, there was, nevertheless, slow growth in the African American presence at all levels of city government. Under Washington, the proportion of city government workers who were black rose from 26 to 30 percent, and the proportion of black policy makers increased from 23 to 33 percent. Blacks still did not hold enough positions to unilaterally control the operations of city government, but with some help from liberal whites and other minorities, they were very close to attaining a dominant governing coalition. Finally, whites were losing ground in the electorate as well. In 1980, whites made up over half of Chicago's voting-age population (54 percent), but that number was rapidly declining (down to 47 percent in 1987). The pendulum was swinging, and it was clear that another Washington victory, coupled with electoral success on the council and other arenas of local politics, could push blacks over the top.

ONGOING WHITE CONCERNS

Given that Washington's tenure offered little information about black leadership to white residents, and given that blacks were that much closer to gaining control of the local political arena, one would expect whites who had feared black leadership in the first place to continue to be anxious about black representation. This is exactly what a review of events in Chicago reveals. An array of evidence indicates that many whites in Chicago continued to be concerned about the possibility that blacks would take over.

White concerns were reflected most directly in public opinion polls throughout Washington's tenure. Early in his term, polls showed that three-quarters of whites thought Washington was "out to get them" (Rivlin 1992: 243). When asked their opinions in later polls, white Chicagoans continued to state their fear of Washington and black leadership. Washington's own pollster continued to find that whites perceived Washington as "hostile and threatening" (Rivlin 1992: 240). Donn Bailey, a black sociology professor at Northwestern University, described the white response to Washington's campaign for reelection: "There's a deep

---

[9] With that power, Washington's coalition managed to pass significant legislation, raising taxes and expanding tenants' rights.

fear among the white people. I can understand it. They think we're going to treat them the way they've treated us" (quoted in Rivlin 1992). These fears often spurred whites into action. Groups such as the Save Our Neighborhoods, Save Our City coalition, an organization that fought black encroachment into white neighborhoods, rapidly expanded their memberships under Washington.

Not everyone openly expressed these fears, and, by some accounts, white fears had moderated somewhat by the time Washington ran for reelection.[10] One local pundit argued that "the city is calmer now, because white Chicagoans have learned that a black mayor is not the end of the world. Harold Washington has served four years and the Sears tower is still standing" (Bosc 1987). Several white residents recounted to reporters the positive lessons they had learned under four years of black leadership in Chicago. One retired white security guard, for example, pointed to the lack of racial tension and the provision of city services in white neighborhoods: "Actually Washington has performed pretty good. As far as him splitting the city in half, I don't think so. I don't see marches, things like that. It's peaceful in the city. Police and fire protection, garbage pickup – they're as good as they were before he got elected. Who knows? I may end up voting for [Washington]" (Camper 1987). But in the end, it seemed as if Washington's tenure was not enough to convince the security guard and others like him to actually support black leadership. Judging by the aggregate vote, most white Chicagoans remained wary of blacks and black leadership. In his reelection bid, Washington won few new white converts. In fact, after four years of black leadership, white support marginally declined. Washington garnered only 14 percent of the white vote in the primary and a similarly small 15 percent of the white vote in the general election.

More telling than the aggregate white vote is an account of why individual white Chicagoans continued to oppose Washington. Unlike in most other cities with black incumbents, whites in Chicago were often willing to admit that race and racial fears still mattered. Almost three-quarters felt that race would be a central factor for white voters (Neal 1986). More than 40 percent of whites admitted to pollsters that they would personally consider race when voting in the upcoming election (Davidson 1987). Even more important, unlike the white vote in reelection bids in other cities, the

---

[10] White turnout did decline, suggesting that at least some white concerns had diminished. Turnout of registered white voters dropped from a record high of 67% in 1983 to 59% in 1987 (Lewis, Taylor, and Kleppner 1997).

white vote in Washington's reelection bid did not seem to be closely tied to Washington's record. Despite the fact that more than half of white voters (55 percent) thought that race relations in the city had actually improved or were not getting worse under Washington, and the fact that half of white voters believed that their own quality of life had either improved or stayed about the same under black leadership, Washington garnered only 15 percent of the white vote. It was also impossible to point to party or political ideology as the reason for the high level of ongoing white opposition to black leadership. Once again in 1987, almost 80 percent of white Democrats voted against their own party to oppose Washington in the general election. Finally, the white vote against Washington in 1987 was clearly not a vote in favor of a particularly attractive white candidate. Over a third of whites who voted for Washington's opponent in the general election admitted that they were voting to "stop another candidate from being elected."

What appeared to matter most was not what had happened over the previous four years – a period that offered little information to whites – but what might happen in the future. The possibility that the city would fall apart if blacks gained control continued to motivate white Chicagoans. One exit poll showed that concerns about the future were so extreme that almost a third of white Chicagoans were "seriously thinking about moving out of Chicago." A northwest side resident put it in the following way: "Our neighborhood is really changing. We wonder what the neighborhood will be like" (Belsie 1987). These concerns about the future clearly affected the vote. Of those white Chicagoans who saw "bad times" coming, only 4 percent supported Washington in the general election. By contrast, 30 percent who saw good times ahead were willing to support Washington. Overall, the vote in Washington's reelection bid was more like a black challenger election than a black incumbent election. Party allegiances meant little, candidates meant little, and nonracial issues played a secondary role. Black incumbency had not provided enough information to convince whites that they need not fear another black victory.[11]

The nature of the 1987 campaign also suggested that racial concerns were still prevalent in the white community. Although the candidates'

---

[11] The range of figures for the 1987 election are based on analysis of three citywide polls: an *ABC News* primary pre-election tracking poll, an *NBC News* primary exit poll, and an *ABC News* general election exit poll. Unfortunately, given the limited and incomplete set of questions in each individual survey, no multivariate analysis could be performed.

campaigns that year were, by most accounts, more muted than the heated and racially explicit campaigns of 1983, there were still signs that both Washington and his white opponents were acting as if white fears still mattered. Both of Washington's main opponents, Jane Byrne in the primary and Ed Vrdolyak in the general election, tried to highlight the dire straits whites would be in if blacks were able to gain control of the city (Grimshaw 1992). Vrdolyak was the most direct: "If [Washington] is reelected, the sad fact is there won't be another chance for us.... his dream, our nightmare" (Rivlin 1992: 361). Byrne was more subtle, but the racial tone of her primary campaign was also evident. White campaign workers were also quick to use the ongoing threat of black leadership to their advantage. Elmer Filipini, the 30th ward precinct captain, proclaimed, "If Washington wins, in four years they'll be 100,000 or more whites moving out of the city of Chicago" (Secter 1987). In response, Washington's campaign tried to address these fears by muting Washington's rhetoric. There was no "It's our turn" statement this time. Washington smiled more, hired more white bodyguards, and avoided most racial policy questions. But in the end, his actions did not matter. White Chicago had not changed its mind about black leadership. The same racially divided world that Washington had taken charge of in 1983 was still there in the final year of his first term. The campaigns, the nature of the vote, and the fact that Washington got only 15 percent of the white vote all strongly suggest that white fears remained prevalent. Four years had gone by but the theme seemed not to have changed: 'Who knows what will happen if blacks gain control?'

CHICAGO AFTER WASHINGTON

Although Washington won in 1987, he had little opportunity in his second term to demonstrate to white residents what black control of the local political arena would do to the white community. Half a year into his second term, he died of a heart attack. The city council then appointed Eugene Sawyer, an African American who was part of the old machine, as acting mayor. But Sawyer served as a caretaker for only a little over a year before losing in the primary in 1989 to Richard M. Daley, the son of longtime Chicago Machine boss Richard J. Daley. Black mayoral leadership was over almost before it had really begun – certainly before black leadership had been given a real chance to prove itself.

The result was that the fears and concerns that white Chicagoans expressed in various ways during the Washington years seemed to persist

TABLE 6.1 *White Support for Black Mayoral Candidates in Chicago*

Election/Year	Black Candidate	Whites Voting Black (%)
Primary 1983	Harold Washington	8
General 1983	Harold Washington	20
Primary 1987	Harold Washington	14
General 1987	Harold Washington	15
Primary 1989	Eugene Sawyer	8
General 1989	Timothy Evans	6
Primary 1991	Danny Davis	7
General 1991	Eugene Pincham	2
Primary 1995	Joseph Gardner	5
General 1995	Roland Burris	6
Primary 1999	Bobby Rush	4

Sources: Lewis, Taylor, and Kleppner (1997); Alkalimat (1986); Rivlin (1992); and author's analysis of 1999 *Chicago Tribune* election poll.

in subsequent years. As illustrated by Table 6.1, over two decades after the end of Washington's tenure, the pattern of extremely racialized voting continues.[12] Although more recent contests have been void of the explicitly racialized campaigns that marked the election in 1983, the white vote in each subsequent contest suggests that whites in Chicago continue to have real concerns about black leadership. In every election since 1987, black candidates have lost against a nearly unanimous white bloc vote. In the first post-Washington election, Eugene Sawyer, despite his ties to the Democratic Machine, garnered only 8 percent of the white vote in his primary bid in 1989.[13] Subsequent black challengers have fared even worse with white voters. Despite winning the majority of the black vote, Tim

[12] There are certainly exceptions to this pattern at different levels of office. The successful Senate campaigns of Carol Moseley-Braun and Barak Obama are two of the most prominent. However, even in these two cases, it is not clear how supportive white Chicagoans were of black leadership. Despite almost unanimous black support, Obama actually lost Cook County in the primary before winning a majority of the white vote in Cook County against another black candidate in the general election. Braun did win 53% of the statewide white vote but she lost much of that white support in her reelection bid (Oden 1996).

[13] The 1989 election provided further evidence that white racial concerns about black leadership, and not the candidates or the campaign, continue to determine the white vote. The election turned out to be the most racially polarized contest in Chicago history despite the fact that the campaign was "the least vociferous" in decades and the fact that Sawyer was a longtime machine supporter.

Evans, Danny Davis, Eugene Pincham, Joseph Gardner, Roland Burris, and Bobby Rush all were opposed by more than 90 percent of white voters in their bids for the mayoralty between 1989 and 1999.[14] This pattern of ongoing white opposition suggests that little has changed in Chicago and that much of white Chicago stills fears the onset of black control.

ALTERNATE EXPLANATIONS FOR CONTINUED WHITE OPPOSITION

The information model offers a plausible explanation for why white Chicagoans continue to oppose black leadership, but it is by no means the only factor that could have contributed to ongoing white resistance to black leadership. There are lots of reasons why white voters might oppose black candidates and lots of other things that might make Chicago different from other cities. In this section, I consider a range of basic factors related to the local political arena during Washington's tenure that might have played an important or even primary role in sustaining white opposition to his candidacy. Logically, if Washington's tenure coincided with a downturn in the local economy, if Washington or his opponents played the race card more than they had in his first contest, if Washington was able to raise less money in his reelection bid, if political endorsements favored his opponent more in his reelection bid, or if he faced a more qualified opponent, then Chicago might be different from other cities, not because of the lack of information black leadership provided but instead because local political conditions turned against the black candidate.

However, none of these accounts offers a ready explanation for continued white aversion to black leadership. There was no marked decline in local economic conditions, there was no increase in the racial nature of the campaigns, and Washington enjoyed the usual advantages of incumbency – money, endorsements, and relatively inexperienced opponents. However, even after going through this process, I cannot definitively point to information as the cause of white actions in Chicago. Although the four factors that I discuss are the main factors usually cited as being critical in urban elections, they, by no means, represent an exhaustive set of potentially relevant conditions. Other less quantifiable aspects of Harold Washington the candidate or Chicago the city could have contributed to the outcomes. Harold Washington was, in many ways, different from the

---

[14] Black voters were nearly united in their support for most of these black candidates. In all of the elections between 1989 and 1999, black candidates for mayor garnered at least three-quarters of the black vote.

typical black candidate. His occasionally overtly racial campaigns and his vow to reform the machine suggested that more was at stake in Chicago than in other cities.[15] The city of Chicago, itself, was, in some respects, also not typical. Intense racial segregation and a long history of a powerful and sometimes corrupt Democratic machine are just two of the features that set Chicago apart. With only one case and only one pattern to be explained – no decrease in white opposition to black leadership – it is impossible to rule out all of these potentially important influences. The available evidence may point to information as the main cause of sustained white opposition in Chicago but any and all conclusions regarding the racial learning process in Chicago are necessarily tentative.

Of the many factors that could have limited Washington's support, a downturn in the local economy is perhaps the most likely suspect. Over and over again, economic conditions have been a central factor governing the vote in American elections (Fiorina 1981; Erikson 1989). However, economic conditions in the city of Chicago did not deteriorate under black leadership (Keiser 1997; Fasenfest 1989; Wievel 1989; Fremon 1988). Contrary to the fears of many white voters, under Washington per capita income actually increased, and unemployment figures saw marginal

---

[15] Did Washington lose some white support because he continued to press for reform of city government? Probably. In both 1983 and 1987, Washington called repeatedly for an end to patronage, the opening of the local governmental process, and an equitable distribution of city funds. Unlike most previous politicians in Chicago, Washington also refused to compromise with his machine predecessors once in office. This stance certainly frightened white politicians, who opposed Washington at every turn. And the actions of white machine politicians likely helped spur white opposition to Washington. Among other things, the actions of white elites certainly helped to highlight the precarious balance of power in the local political arena and prevented black leadership from proving itself. But it is also clear that a lot of white opposition to Washington preceded rather than followed white elite actions. As soon as Washington won the primary in 1983 and it became clear that he had a chance to take over the city, much of white Chicago mobilized into action. As Kleppner and others have noted, "It was a spontaneous and enthusiastic outpouring from the grass roots, a groundswell. At that point, most of the white committeemen were probably still stunned by Washington's nomination and...took the election of any Democratic nominee for granted" (Kleppner 1985: 191). Moreover, in 1987, white Chicagoans continued to oppose Washington even though white machine politicians were fighting each other to see who would challenge Washington. Despite the fact that the machine could not produce one "great white hope," white voters still chose to vote against Harold Washington in 1987. By almost all accounts, white fears had little to do with reform issues either. As the *New York Times* put it, "Say what they will, Democrats defecting in such numbers in Chicago are not just concerned for the probity of the Democratic machine or candidates. Many white Chicagoans simply fear...the idea of a black mayor" (1983a). In short, much of the sustained white opposition would likely have been there with or without the issue of reform.

improvement.[16] Equally important, there was no marked change in the relative economic status of the black and white communities. Blacks did get a few more jobs, more appointments, and more contracts from city government, but the change was far from dramatic and did not greatly affect the welfare of most of the black or white communities (Joyce 1994; Fremon 1988). The major problems facing poor, black Chicago were as bad in 1987 as they had been in 1983.[17] In short, there was little in Chicago's economy under black leadership that should have generated the extraordinary white opposition Washington faced in his bid for reelection.

The lack of change in the white vote also cannot be attributed to the increased racialization of either Washington's or his opponents' campaigns. In 1987, both Washington and his opponents toned down the racial rhetoric in their campaigns. Washington was by no means a color-blind politician in 1987, but most agreed that his second campaign was muted compared to his first (Rivlin 1992; Holli and Green 1989; Miller 1989). Washington's campaign manager, Jackie Grimshaw, described it this way: "Our approach this time is more intellectual than emotional" (quoted in Rivlin 1992: 366). There was no Task Force for Black Political Empowerment, no talk about taking over, and Washington "generally steered clear of any mention of race" (Rivlin 1992: 366). After a passive performance in a debate with Vrdolyak, Washington complained, "My own campaign did something to me that Vrdolyak could never do. They cut my balls off" (quoted in Miller 1989: 303). Instead of focusing on race, Washington campaigned largely on his record, highlighting his fiscal responsibility while continuing to talk about neighborhoods and reform. Nor did Washington's opponents play the race card in 1987 to the same extent they had in 1983. Racial slurs largely dropped out of the campaign (Holli and Green 1989). Several ostensibly nonracial issues actually got some air time (Grimshaw 1992; Fremon 1988; Davidson 1987). Byrne, the primary challenger, talked a lot about crime. Washington's general election foes also spent time and resources addressing the issues of taxes and Chicago's poor schools. Race and white fears may have still been on everyone's mind, but, with a couple of notable exceptions, these racial concerns were not the topic of conversation. Whites who voted against

---

[16] Between 1983 and 1987, per capita income grew 5.7% (Bureau of the Census, 1964–2003). Immediately prior to Washington's arrival, 11.7% of Chicago was unemployed. Just before his first reelection bid, unemployment stood at 9.3% (Bureau of the Census).

[17] In 1987, poverty stood at over 20%, and one in five Chicagoans had no health insurance (Fremon 1988; Rivlin 1992). The Chicago Housing Authority was still in crisis, and Chicago's public school system was viewed as one of the worst in the nation.

Washington in 1987 did not do so, then, because they had been exposed to an exceptionally racialized campaign.

Washington's inability to attract more white voters when he ran as an incumbent cannot be explained away by pointing to a lack of incumbent resources. In 1987, he was able to greatly outspend his opponents. In the general election, Washington raised $6.3 million, over twice as much as his closest competitor, Ed Vrdolyak, who raised $2.3 million. In 1987, Washington also managed to get all but a few of the city's major endorsements, including firm support from the city's two major newspapers. He was officially endorsed by the Cook County Democratic Party. And, for the first time, in 1987 many prominent local white Democrats actually campaigned at his side, while other influential Democrats chose to sit on the sidelines rather than actively campaign for Washington's opponent, as they had done in 1983. There was no clear trend in candidate quality and overall little link between the white vote and candidate quality across Washington's four primary and general elections. Whether Washington faced the incumbent mayor, the assumed heir to the Daley machine, a relatively unknown and inexperienced candidate, an ex-mayor trying to make a comeback, or three white opponents (the most successful of whom began with negative poll ratings unmatched in city history), his white support remained more or less constant (Holli and Green 1989).[18] It appeared that "anybody but Harold" was the choice of almost 90 percent of white Chicago.

All told, Washington was a powerful incumbent who under normal circumstances would have substantially increased his share of the white vote. But in 1987, blacks were on the verge of real power, and nothing about Washington's track record, his opponents, or his campaigns had demonstrated to white voters that their fears were unwarranted. After four years of stalemate, fears of what would happen if blacks gained control of Chicago politics appeared to be a critical force behind white aversion to Washington and black leadership.

---

[18] The fact that Washington could garner no more than 15% of the white vote in the general election in 1987 despite facing three white opponents whose campaigns were largely aimed at ousting each other and who, with the exception of Vrdolyak, whose "disapproval" rating stood at 64%, had little name recognition and limited political experience was perhaps the strongest sign that candidate quality was largely irrelevant in these contests (Holli and Green 1989). As confusing and as unappealing as the white candidates were, their shortcomings did not prevent white voters from uniting to serve one electoral goal: the defeat of Harold Washington.

Ultimately we cannot know for certain that a lack of information about black leadership played the central role in sustaining white opposition to black candidates in the city. There are just too many potentially relevant factors and not enough data points to rule them all out. However, if there is a lesson from Chicago, it seems to point to the importance of information. Without credible information about how black leadership affects the white community, little change seems to occur in the arena of local racial politics. If black leadership is prevented from enacting its agenda, whites get less information. As a result, fears about black leadership and highly racialized voting patterns are likely to persist. Ironically, white racial fears prevent white residents from learning that their fears are largely unwarranted since the closer blacks get to gaining control and being able to prove themselves to the white community, the more motivated whites are to prevent that takeover. This conclusion does not bode well for the future of race relations in Chicago. Today, whites represent only 42 percent of the city's population, and the balance of power between whites and blacks remains precarious.[19] Whites are very unlikely to want to cede control at any point in the near future, and thus one could predict that the black-white divide in Chicago will endure.

The future in other racially balanced cities seems less clear. The data that I have presented in this book are not particularly encouraging. Across all of the racially balanced cities that I examined in Chapter 4, white support for black candidates actually declined when those candidates ran for the first time as incumbents. And even today, mayoral politics in cities such as Philadelphia and New York can hardly be viewed as racially harmonious. However, some racially balanced cities have shown signs of improved race relations. In Houston, for example, the last two mayoral elections have ended with multiracial coalitions supporting the winner. In other racially balanced cities, black mayors have been given more of a chance to enact their agendas. Black mayors in Dallas and Hartford, for example, were able to put forward programs without incurring massive white counter-mobilization. Whites may thus be getting important information from black leadership in these cities. In addition, immigration is altering the basic racial dynamics of mayoral politics in many racially balanced cities. The growth of the Latino and Asian American populations in cities like San Francisco and Houston has certainly complicated

---

[19] In large part, whites have been able to retain control by garnering support from the growing Latino population.

the electoral equation, as both black- and white-led coalitions vie for the support of these other minority groups. Thus, the future of race relations in these cities depends upon a range of factors as diverse as racial learning and immigration and there is at least some chance that white aversion to minority leadership will diminish.

7

Other Cases Where Information Could Matter

This book is ostensibly about race – about how black mayors affect the views and votes of their white constituents. But the story presented in the preceding chapters is also very much about information and how credible information can fundamentally alter individual views and intergroup dynamics. In this chapter, I consider the implications of information for other types of political transitions. I begin this task by reviewing how and why information matters in the interactions between black mayors and their white constituents. I then assess a variety of other cases to see if they could plausibly fit an information-based account of behavior. In each case, I ask two questions. Is the case structured in a way that suggests that information should matter? Does the evidence point to learning? The goal in each case is not to demonstrate or prove learning. In fact, the evidence that I put forward in each case will be extremely limited. I merely wish to point to cases where the presence of learning is plausible enough to warrant further investigation.

According to the information model, the key to learning is that experience with new representation provides credible information. In order to provide this, new leaders must be perceived to have real control over outcomes and policies. The more that new leaders have the power to influence the well-being of one community, the more credible is the information the members of that community get from their experience with the new leaders, and the more likely they are to learn. Power and credible information are not, however, the only conditions necessary for learning to occur. In addition, for credible information to lead to a change in views and votes, residents must have exaggerated expectations. They must have unrealistic concerns that stem from a lack of information and the use of inaccurate stereotypes. For new leaders to reduce these fears and stereotypes, moreover, they must not use their new power to harm another group.[1] It is the decision *not* to enact harmful policies that is both surprising and informative.

To explore whether the information model can be applied more broadly, I examine three additional cases below: whites' reactions to black members of Congress, African Americans' reactions to black mayors, and whites' reactions to Latino and Asian American elected officials. I also very briefly consider whether the information model might be applied to a range of nonracial political transitions both inside and outside the U.S. context. Each case fits the information model to a greater or lesser extent.

BLACK INCUMBENTS IN CONGRESS

If information really does structure white reactions to black leadership, it should not only explain variation in white responses across cities but also account for different white reactions across different types of political offices. The more that a particular political office can control local policies and affect local conditions, the more white residents should learn from that position, and the more positively they should respond to the presence of a black incumbent in that office.

Incumbents in Congress have a lot of power – often more than mayors, whose powers are limited by city charters – but there are two key differences that make it easier to connect black mayors than black members of Congress to local conditions. First, incumbents in Congress do not have the power to act unilaterally. Unlike a mayor, legislators must obtain the support of a majority of their colleagues to enact policies. Second, since members of Congress are in Washington and often deal with national issues, they are less frequently blamed or credited for outcomes at the local level. Mayors, by contrast, are viewed as being primarily responsible for

[1] Another important assumption behind the information model is that residents can and do acquire information about the impact of the new leadership. Given the relatively low levels of political knowledge evident in the mass public (Campbell et al. 1960; Delli Carpini and Keeter 1996), there is some doubt as to whether most individuals are likely to acquire information about new leadership. However, as I noted in Chapter 1, residents do not need a lot of information to learn from new leadership. They need only know that new leadership exists and that their own well-being – or the well-being of their community – has not changed under these new leaders. If the conditions of the information model are met and residents do have real concerns about new leadership, then there is reason to believe that most residents will have the motivation to acquire this limited information.

local policy and local economic conditions. Moreover, although Congress can appropriate considerable funds for local projects, their actions are less likely to have a direct, visible effect on local conditions. From education to police protection to garbage collection, the implementation of most local policies occurs under the control of local government. All of this means that it is harder to tie a local outcome to the actions and interests of an individual legislator.[2] If any politician is to be blamed or credited, it will probably be the mayor. Since it is easier to track the effects of black mayors than it is to track the effects of black members of Congress, black mayoralties should provide more credible information to white residents than do black Congress members. As a result, we should expect fewer positive changes in white behavior under incumbent black members of Congress than under incumbent black mayors.

In undertaking this comparison, I cannot provide the same analysis of Congress members as I did for mayors. The main problem is that most black members of Congress win in majority black districts and many, if not most, face only black challengers. With few biracial elections and few cases with large white voting populations, it is difficult to undertake rigorous empirical analysis of the white vote in all but a few elections. I will simply review the relevant results from a number of existing studies that have examined white voting patterns in black incumbent congressional elections and present my own data on incumbent reelection rates.

To begin to see if black incumbency at the congressional level affects white votes, I collected data on the outcome of every black incumbent reelection bid in Congress in the twentieth century. As with black mayors, the first point to note about black incumbents in Congress is that they win almost all of the time. In the last century, African American members of Congress won reelection an impressive 97 percent of the time (302 out of 312 cases). This rate of success puts black incumbents in Congress roughly on a par with white House members, who generally win reelection over 90 percent of the time (Stanley and Niemi 1992).

What is more important for our purposes is how black incumbents do when facing white voters. Here, the results are also fairly clear. In the thirty-three cases where a black incumbent went up for reelection in a majority white district, the reelection rate was an equally impressive

---

[2] Another important factor limiting the information provided by black legislators is that they are invariably in the minority in the legislature. In the House, black members hold less than 10% of the seats. No state has close to a majority of black legislators. Thus, whether a policy passes or not is usually not dependent on the preferences of black legislators.

94 percent. These reelection rates cannot tell us if black candidates garner more white support as incumbents, but they do at least tell us that there is no widespread white backlash.

Importantly, the success of black incumbents stands in stark contrast to the failure of black challengers. Although there is no complete record of how many African American candidates have run for Congress, it is clear that few have been successful in districts where white voters controlled the outcome. Of the 6,667 House elections in white majority districts between 1966 and 1996, only 35, or 0.52 percent, were won by blacks (Canon 1999). And even when blacks won, it appears that most white voters opposed them. In the bulk of studies that have assessed white support for successful black challengers, the results suggest that only about a third of white voters ultimately voted for the black challenger (Bullock and Dunn 1997; Voss and Lublin 2001).[3] In other words, white voters appear to be resistant to the prospect of black leadership at the congressional level, and many try hard to prevent blacks from winning office. Once a black representative or senator is in office, however, this resistance seems to fade. Even in cases where white voters could oust black incumbents in Congress, they almost never choose to do so.

A set of five reelection bids deserves special attention here. In the early 1990s, the Supreme Court struck down the districts of five black House members and effectively forced then to run for reelection in newly redrawn districts that no longer had black voting majorities. Most civil rights activists and many academics felt the Supreme Court decisions would spell doom for black representation in Congress (Reeves 1997). Laughlin McDonald, the director of the southern regional office of the American Civil Liberties Union, predicted "a bleaching of Congress" (Sack 1996). The Reverend Jesse Jackson called the Supreme Court's move "a kind of ethnic cleansing" (Sack 1996).[4] But to almost everyone's surprise, the 1996 congressional elections told a very different story. In that year, all five black members of Congress who ran for reelection in newly

---

[3] In addition, there are often signs that racial prejudice is a determining factor in the white vote in these contests. For example, the white vote in Edward Brooke's attempt to become the first popularly elected African American senator was closely correlated with indices of prejudice (Becker and Heaton 1967).

[4] Within the black community, anger at the court's actions was pronounced. An editorial written by one of the black incumbents stated: "Five Supreme Court Justices have done to [blacks] in Louisiana what no hooded Ku Klux Klan mobs were able to do in this decade – remove a [black] from Congress. The federal district court created a district where David Duke, a former Klan leader, will have a far better chance of election than Cleo Fields [the black incumbent]" (Fields and Higginbotham 1996).

redrawn minority black districts won their races – and with substantial white support. In perhaps the two most surprising cases, Cynthia McKinney won the 11th District in Georgia with the support of an estimated 31 percent of white voters, and Sandford Bishop carried approximately 36 percent of the white vote to victory in Georgia's 2nd District (Bullock and Dunn 1997). Equally important, but perhaps less surprising, none of these five black incumbents lost an election in the ensuing years. Given that before 1996 less than 1 percent of previous elections in the nation's majority white congressional districts had produced a black victor, this string of African American victories is quite striking (Canon 1999). It suggests that incumbency is a powerful tool for black candidates at the congressional level. As Cynthia McKinney put it, "My victory says more about the power of incumbency than anything else" (quoted in Bullock and Dunn 1999: 15). As challengers, black candidates almost never win when they face white voters. As incumbents, they almost always win.

The key test of the information model is not simply whether black incumbents win or whether they win with white support but rather if they win with *more* white support than they had as challengers. Although data that allow an assessment of this change in the white vote are limited, one study has attempted to measure change in white support during and after the transition from white to black leadership. Bullock and Dunn (1999) examine changes in white support between challenger and incumbent elections for a handful of black candidates who ran in the South in the 1990s. The results varied from candidate to candidate, and some of the black incumbents in their sample did lose white support over time. However, when all of their cases were looked at together, white support did increase. On average, black candidates garnered about 3 percentage points more white support when they ran as incumbents in 1996 then when they ran as challengers in 1992. This is certainly not an overwhelming shift in the white vote, but it may be enough to suggest that some learning was occurring.

Another way to assess the importance of information and racial learning is to see if racial considerations prevent at least some white voters from supporting black incumbents. In other words, is the level of white support for black incumbents less than it would be for similarly situated white incumbents? Here, the results are quite mixed. In perhaps the most expansive study of black incumbent congressional reelection bids, Highton (2004) used exit poll data to find that, after campaign spending, partisanship, the presidential vote, and demographics had been controlled for, white voters were not less willing to support black incumbents than white incumbents.[5] By contrast, Gay (1999) and Voss and Lublin (2001) employed ecological inference across a smaller number of Southern House elections to find that whites were, on average, 8 to 10 percent less likely to support black incumbents than white incumbents. If Highton's exit poll reports can be believed, it appears that whites' racial concerns largely disappear by the time black members of Congress run for reelection. If estimated election returns more accurately reflect the white vote, however, there is evidence that when blacks run as incumbents, these fears, although not overwhelming, are still present.

If the information model works at the congressional level, white voters should be more and more willing to support black congressional candidates as more blacks gain office around the country. Here, the data are much more limited but nevertheless suggestive. In the last four decades, there has been a slow but steady increase in the number of black members of Congress who represent majority white districts. The number grew from zero in 1960 to one in 1970, two in 1980, four in 1990, and six in 2000. Although the number of blacks representing white districts is still very small, the six blacks who come from majority white districts represent a significant percentage of all black members of Congress: in 2000, 16 percent of all black members of Congress represented districts where whites were the majority of voters. Many factors likely contributed to this expansion, but the increased willingness of white voters to support black challengers for Congress certainly seems to have helped to push blacks closer to parity in the House.

Much more research needs to be done, but overall, the evidence seems to suggest that incumbency at the congressional level has a real but limited effect on white voters. Incumbency would appear to lead to modest gains in white support for black candidates and may be leading to a diminished role for race in the voting booth. The modest changes that we see under black incumbents in Congress fit well with an information model of white behavior. Given that blacks in Congress exercise little direct control over local policy or local conditions and given that it is difficult to gauge the impact of black leadership at the congressional level, one would expect experience under a black incumbent to influence only a small number of whites.

[5] Highton (2004) examines about 18,000 white votes in 357 contested House elections (37 with black incumbents) in 1996 and 1998.

AFRICAN AMERICANS AND BLACK ELECTED OFFICIALS

Another interesting potential application of the information model is the case of African American voters. In the accounts of mayoral politics that I have presented in this book, I have not given a great deal of attention to black voters. But clearly, in these cities and elections, black voters played a critical role. Without their support, few black challengers would ever have won office. Obviously, the fate of black incumbents is intricately tied to the decisions made by black voters. Do they learn from their experience with black mayoral leadership as well? Just as it was for white residents, prior to the election of black mayors, black residents had not seen black leaders in positions of real authority over the white community. Indeed, much of the available evidence suggests that many members of the black community had very high expectations of black political leadership. One account notes that "everyone was optimistic life was going to get better" (Donze 1998). Another refers to "an almost revolutionary rise in expectations" (Span 1983: 55). Despite the fact that black residents likely had more informed and more nuanced views of the black community than did whites, there appears to have been considerable room for learning among African Americans.[6] Equally importantly, African American residents lived through the same events and witnessed roughly the same information. Thus, there is at least some reason to suspect that information should matter for African Americans as well.

A brief review of elections in the cities highlighted in this book suggests that experience with black leadership did in fact change African Americans' views and political behavior. In the same way that experience under black mayors taught white voters that they have little to fear, experience under black leaders seems to have taught African Americans that they could not expect black leaders to be able to redress deep-seated racial inequalities. The early euphoria surrounding black electoral victories seems in many cases to have been replaced by more reasoned assessments of black leadership. As one black resident of New York put it, "It's become clear that [Dinkins] has not produced dramatic changes and probably won't" (Hicks 1993). Others were even more direct. In Los Angeles, a black voter complained: "To put it bluntly, [Bradley] just hasn't done a

---

[6] Surprisingly, it is not clear whether African Americans always hold different views of the black community from whites. Surveys of white and black Americans reveal that African Americans tend to hold similar stereotypes about the black community and black candidates (Schuman et al. 1997; Williams 1990).

hell of a lot for black folk" (Litwin 1981: 88).[7] A retiree in Gary expressed a similar view: "It's been 28 years of black mayors and I don't see what they have done" (Kendall 1995). Though this evidence is anecdotal, it suggests that time under black incumbents has taught some African Americans that black political representation cannot easily or quickly solve the black community's basic economic problems.[8]

A drop in turnout is perhaps another sign of black learning and diminished expectations regarding black leadership. Intense mobilization and record black turnout in black challenger elections slowly gave way to average or even record low turnout in black incumbent elections. As one reporter in Newark put it: "They danced in the streets in 1970. They walked to the polls in 1974, and they crawled to the polls in 1978" (Oreskes 1981: 29). Across the twenty-six cities examined earlier, black turnout fell from an average of 66 percent in black challenger campaigns to 59 percent when the same candidates first ran for reelection a few years later. In many subsequent elections, black turnout dropped even further. In Detroit, for example, black turnout slowly declined during Coleman Young's tenure to the point where just under a third of registered black voters were going to the polls in his later bids for reelection (Rich 1987). And in a range of cities from Los Angeles to New Orleans to Memphis, successive elections with black incumbents similarly saw lower and lower figures for black participation (Jackson and Preston 1994; Wright 2000). Although a number of factors likely contributed to declining black participation, frustration with the pace of change under black incumbents may very well have played an important role. As one account put it, "the reality of governance generated less enthusiasm than its prospect" (Peterson 1994: 2).

Even more telling, perhaps, is the increasing willingness of some black voters to favor white candidates over black candidates.[9] While the trend

---

[7] At times, this frustration has been extreme. One black councilwoman in Cleveland was particularly negative: "The mayor doesn't represent the black community. The mayor is bought and sold by the power structure in this city" (Milbank 1993: A1).

[8] Despite what appears to be widespread frustration about the pace of change, African Americans still seem to garner psychic benefits from black representation. Tate (2003) and Bobo and Gilliam (1990) have both shown that black leadership leads to increased trust and efficacy among African Americans.

[9] This trend was not apparent in the first few years of black leadership. Across the 26 cities examined earlier, black voters were just as supportive of black mayoral incumbents (95% of blacks supported them on average) when they ran for reelection for the first time as they were of the same candidates when they ran as challengers (93% of blacks supported them on average).

is by no means universal, a number of largely black cities that had long-term black leadership have begun to return whites to the mayor's office. In 1995, for example, Gary, a city whose population is nearly 90 percent black, elected a white man, Scott King, to the mayoralty. King captured 83 percent of the citywide vote in the general election, and in subsequent electoral bids he handily won reelection. Similarly, in 1998, after twenty-one years of black mayoral leadership, Jerry Brown took over as mayor of Oakland, a city that is only 24 percent white. Baltimore, another majority black city, also opted to elect a white candidate over a black candidate in 1999 following over a decade of black mayoral leadership: Martin O'Malley garnered one in three black votes on his way to victory over two black candidates (Shields and Penn 1999). All told, almost half of the large majority black cities have replaced long-serving black mayors with white mayors.

And there are other signs of growing division in the black vote, perhaps indications of growing frustration in the black community. In many cities, what were once united black voting blocs have grown more divided. The intra-group divide in cities such as Philadelphia and Memphis has often centered on class lines (Adams 1994; Keiser 1997). In other cities, a range of issues seems to have reduced black unity (Pohlman and Kirby 1996; Wildstrom 1998). But in most cases, these divisions appear to have begun with concerns over the ineffectual nature of black leadership.

Combined, these patterns in the black vote suggest that race, or at least the race of candidates for political office, has lost some of its significance in certain urban arenas. According to many political observers, rather than focus on race, African Americans have begun to focus more on local economic conditions and the quality of basic public services. David Bositis, a researcher at the Joint Center for Political and Economic Studies, has concluded that "Black voters have become more interested in getting results than anything else" (Minzesheimer 1995). Newspaper reports focusing on elections in largely black cities have also tended to conclude that race is becoming less important: "Blacks in cities across America have reached a frustration level and are looking for politicians that can change their living conditions, regardless of color" (Ethnic News Watch 1995).

This sentiment has been echoed by at least some black voters. One black voter in Gary expressed it this way: "My trash isn't collected and there's been a giant pothole outside my door for two years. Do you think I care about the color of the mayor's skin?" (Tyson 1995). Another remarked: "It's not a white world. It's not a black world. If you poke Scott King [the white candidate], he'll bleed the same color I do" (Minzesheimer 1995).

Finally, a Black Panther in Cleveland admitted, "We can't vote based on skin color, but based on what's in our self-interest" (Gaither 1998).

Learning in both the white and black communities has arguably led to elections in which race is peripheral – or at least more peripheral than it once was. An account of recent mayoral politics in Cleveland, for example, concluded that "while race remains a factor . . . voters nevertheless appear more willing to elect candidates of another race than at any time in the last 30 years" (Vickers 1997). A report from a 1995 election in Gary found that "the city's voters have mostly disregarded race in this campaign" (Tyson 1995). And in Baltimore, high crossover voting among both whites and blacks has led many to maintain that race is losing its significance in urban politics (Samuel 1999; Texeira 1999). Cleveland's City Council president described the trend as well as anyone else: "There are layers of issues in any election, and while race is still an issue, it's not the definitive issue" (Vickers 1997).

Certainly, there are many cities and elections where candidates' race continues to play a critical role and where African Americans continue to expect great change from black elected officials. But in other places around the country, there appears to have been a real change in the black community and in black political behavior. In these cities, blacks have begun to realize that black leadership in and of itself cannot solve America's racial problems. The letdown was probably inevitable. Many African Americans had expectations that could never be fulfilled by black incumbents. This is, in essence, white racial learning in reverse. Experience under black leaders provided information that forced African Americans to recognize the limitations of black leadership. Although whites and African Americans differ in many ways, they both appear to be open to at least some change.

LATINO AND ASIAN AMERICAN LEADERS

Another important case to consider in the context of American racial politics is learning under Latino and Asian American incumbents. Demographic changes over recent decades have increasingly placed Latinos and Asian Americans at the forefront of American politics: the number of Latinos in office has more than doubled in the last two decades, so that today there are over 4,500 Latino elected officials nationwide, Latinos occupy twenty-four seats in Congress, and one state has a Latino governor (NALEO 2005). Asian American representation is also growing rapidly, though from a much smaller population base. As one recent article put it,

"Asian American representation in the hallways of power has gone from barely noticeable to modestly influential" (Ratnesar 1998).[10] Between 1996 and 2000 alone, the number of Asian Americans holding office increased by 10 percent nationwide (APALC 2001). In short, the growing presence of these two groups is hard to ignore.

Should we expect the arrival of these new minority leaders to mark the beginning of another learning process for white Americans? In many ways, the context surrounding the arrival of Asian American and Latino leaders mirrors the context surrounding the first African American elected officials. Most white Americans have had relatively limited contact with members of either group, and few have witnessed either Asian Americans or Latinos in positions of authority over the white community. There is also evidence of fairly widespread and fairly negative stereotyping of both groups. Whites are, for example, quite likely to believe that Latinos are unintelligent, welfare prone, hard to get along with, and violent (Bobo and Johnson 2000). Asian Americans, by contrast, tend to be viewed as foreign and mysterious (Kim 1999; Lee 2000).[11] Whites are also as likely to admit feeling threatened by Latinos and Asian Americans as by African Americans (Bobo and Johnson 2000). In particular, in places where either group comprises a rapidly expanding or relatively large portion of the population, whites have singled them out and acted as if they posed a real threat (Hero 1998; Alvarez and Butterfield 2000; Hajnal, Gerber, and Louch 2002). This suggests that many whites may have exaggerated perceptions about what might happen under Latino or Asian American leadership.

Anecdotal evidence points in this same direction. In response to minority challenges, some white campaigns have warned of "an impending [Latino] takeover" and, at least according to political observers, some contests have "centered on the possibility of [Latino] political dominance" (Rosales 2000: 94; Stuart 1983b). In other cases, the white community has mobilized to try to prevent Latino or Asian American victory. In San Antonio, for example, a Latino bid to gain control of the city council led to two years of what has been described as "ethnic turmoil" (Stevens 1981). And in Miami, when Cuban control of the County Commission became a possibility, other groups rallied in a series of highly charged elections to try to

---

[10] Today there are over 600 Asian Americans at the federal, state, or local level, including two senators and four members of the House of Representatives (APALC 2005).

[11] Of all minority groups, it is Asian Americans with whom whites feel they have least in common (Lee 2000).

prevent a Cuban takeover (Stuart 1983a). Another sign that whites have
real concerns about Latino and Asian American leadership is the fact that
Latino and Asian American campaigns often try to address those fears by
downplaying their race and ethnicity in a similar fashion to some African
American candidates. A range of successful Latino and Asian American
candidates have made claims similar to those of Jay C. Kim, who declared
to white voters: "I don't have a special agenda for Asian Americans. They
should not expect anything special from me" (Mydans 1993). According
to many observers, Henry Cisneros "assiduously tried to build bridges"
in his effort to become the first Latino mayor of San Antonio (Stevens
1981). During his campaign for mayor in Denver, Cisneros often stated,
"the issue was not to elect a Hispanic candidate but to elect a candidate with a vision, with ideas for the city" (Schmidt 1983). Accounts of
Michael Woo's bid for the mayoralty in Los Angeles also suggested that
he took pains not to identify too closely with Asian Americans or their
political interests (Clifford 1993). In order to win white votes, these new
minority candidates have, in the views of some, "become in effect ethnic
neutral" politicians (Mydans 1993).

And, as is the case with black leadership, the tenures of Latino and
Asian American leaders seem to have provided the white community with
positive or anti-stereotypical information. Since Latinos and Asian Americans have entered office only recently in most cases, we do not have
extensive information regarding the substantive impact of either Latino
or Asian American representation. But what we do have suggests that
Latino and Asian American elected officials effect little change in the relative fortunes of whites and non-whites and at best deliver small gains to
some segments of the minority community. Fairly broad studies of Latino
representation in Congress and of Latino mayors and council members, in
particular, have revealed "few major departures from existing policy."[12]

---

[12] The quote is from Hero (1992: 152). Hero and Tolbert (1995) have found that the policy choices of Latinos in Congress were no different from those of whites of the same
party who represented similar districts. Similarly, Kerr and Mladenka (1994) could find
no real change in minority employment patterns under Latino mayors and council members. Mladenka (1989) did, however, show some marginal changes in Latino employment
in places with greater Latino representation on the city council. More detailed analysis
of individual cases suggests that Latino leaders, just like their African American counterparts, have often tried to enact policies that appease local businesses and middle-class
interests (Munoz and Henry 1997). Accounts of Henry Cisneros's mayoralty are typical. Observers in San Antonio claimed that "Cisneros promoted neither his Mexican
American identity nor the specific interests of that community. He acted as a mayor who
happened to be Mexican American" (Munoz 1994: 112). One of the toughest critics
referred to Latino representation in San Antonio as the "illusion of inclusion" (Rosales
2000).

No systematic assessment of the policy effects of Asian American elected officials has been undertaken, but anecdotal evidence from a number of Asian American officeholders reveals little in the way of dramatic change. Thus, there are reasons to expect that learning will occur under Latino and Asian American incumbents.

At the same time, there are important differences between the black context and the Asian American and Latino contexts that should alter the information equation somewhat. Specifically, at least two factors make Latino and Asian American leadership less threatening than black leadership. First, Asian Americans and Latinos generally run for office after whites have experienced black leadership or at least have heard about black incumbents elsewhere in the country. The learning that has occurred under black leaders should help to reduce fears about Latino and Asian American challengers. Second, the policy divide between white Americans and the Latino and Asian American populations is not nearly as sharp as the divide between white and black America (Kinder and Sander 1996; Uhlaner 2000; Hajnal and Baldassare 2001; Hochschild and Rogers 1999). The threat from Asian Americans could be particularly small for at least three other reasons. The Asian American population is itself more divided on most policy questions than either the Latino or African American communities (Tam 1995; Garcia 1997; Warren, Corbett, and Stack 1997; Hero 1998; Espiritu 1992). Asian Americans also have a socio-economic status more similar to that of whites than have the other two minority groups. And finally, whites tend to hold some distinctively positive views of Asian Americans – namely, that they are intelligent, hard-working, and high achieving (Bobo and Johnson 2000; Lee 2000). Thus, while I would expect the information model to apply to white Americans experiencing Latino and Asian American leadership, I would also expect learning and changes in white political behavior to be more muted.

Has experience with Latino and Asian American incumbents changed white perceptions and white political behavior? Is there any evidence of learning under Latino and Asian American incumbents? The answer to both of these questions is a provisional yes. Although Latino and Asian American officeholding is very much a work in progress and the data are limited, at first glance there does appear to be a pattern of changing white behavior in response to experience with Latino elected officials. The evidence is clearer for whites who experience Latino leadership than it is for whites who live under Asian American incumbents but in both cases there are signs that white Americans are learning.

To mirror as best as possible the tests for change under African American leadership, I assembled data on white voting patterns in Latino challenger and Latino incumbent mayoral elections.[13] Just as I did with African Americans, I focused on the first Latino to win the mayoralty in major American cities. As before, I compared white support for the Latino challenger to white support for the same Latino running for the first time as an incumbent. The number of cases here is small. There are only four major cities that have elected Latinos who have then gone on to run for reelection (Miami, San Antonio, Denver, and San Jose). The results, however, are fairly clear. In three out of the four cases, when the same candidate ran for reelection, white support increased appreciably. The seven-point gain in white support (from 52 to 59 percent) that occurred in San Jose was typical.[14] Only Federico Pena in Denver faced as much white opposition when he ran as an incumbent as he had when he ran as a challenger. And even here, analysis of the white vote suggests that the role of race diminished in Pena's reelection bid; according to Hero (1992), party and ideology played a more central role in that election. Latino incumbents' success has not been confined to first reelection bids: the four incumbents have won reelection in 13 out of 14 attempts; the loss occurred in Miami, where Maurice Ferre lost not to a white challenger but to another Latino, Xavier Suarez. We can also see evidence of declining turnout in these elections. San Antonio experienced one of the most

---

[13] Estimates of the white vote come from newspaper accounts and published case studies of these elections and are based on either exit polls or ward- or precinct-level analysis (*New York Times* 1973; Munoz 1994; Hero and Beatty 1989; Gerston 1998; Scheibal 2003).

[14] Interestingly, if the white vote in these cases is at all representative, it appears that white voters are much more willing to support Latino mayoral challengers than they were to support black mayoral challengers. The 52% average white support for Latino challengers stands in fairly sharp contrast to the comparable figure for black challengers: 30% white support. Asian American challengers, by almost all accounts, have been even more successful at garnering white support. One study of California, for example, concluded that Asian Americans "have been the most successful of minority candidates in winning white votes" (Ratnesar 1998). The fact that the majority of Asian American elected officials outside of Hawaii have won office in places where white voters predominate attests to the ability of Asian American candidates to obtain fairly broad white support. In California, the state with the largest Asian American population, Cain and Kiewiet found that 73% of Asian American elected officials represented areas that were less than 10% Asian American (1986). Gary Locke's successful bid to become the mainland's first Asian American governor in a state that was only 5% Asian American, and Norman Mineta's victory in a congressional district that was only 2.5% Asian American are just two of the more famous examples. The fact that party identification and political ideology mattered as much or more than race/ethnicity in many of these challenger contests lends further support to the notion that whites were less threatened by Latino and Asian American candidates (Hero 1992). It may be that race and ethnicity are less of a hurdle for Latino and Asian Americans than they are for African American challengers facing white voters.

severe drops when turnout fell to 17 percent in 1983. But almost across the board, interest in mayoral elections has declined as residents gained more experience with Latino mayors (*New York Times* 1983b; Kaufman 1998).

It is difficult to tell whether these trends are spreading to other cities. More Latino candidates seem to be winning office in minority Latino places. Recent victories by Gus Garcia in Austin, Eddie Perez in Hartford, and Judith Valles in San Bernardino – all minority Latino cities – are suggestive of a trend. Antonio Villaraigosa's victory in racially diverse Los Angeles could represent another important turning point.[15] There is also some indication that over time whites are increasingly willing to support Hispanic candidates. Studies of certain states have found that "the number of crossovers is increasing" (Suro 1991). Although some highly racialized elections continue to occur, the overall pattern may point to a lessening of white racial concerns and declining white opposition to Latino candidates.[16]

The data on Asian American incumbents are more limited. In large part, this is because of the small number of cases of Asian American leadership in major offices. Asian Americans have, for example, won the mayoralty of only two cities with populations of over 200,000, and estimates suggest that not much more than a handful of Asian Americans have been directly elected to mayoral offices around the country (APALC 2003). Nevertheless, it is clear that Asian American incumbents who win office in primarily white areas tend to do extremely well when they run for reelection. Analyzing available data on Asian American candidates, I found that across the country, 98 percent of Asian American incumbents who ran for reelection at the city council level or higher between 2000 and 2003 won their reelection bids.[17] And at least at the congressional level, growing victory margins imply that over time Asian American incumbents are winning with an increasing greater amount of white support.[18]

---

[15] In 2005, there were 21 Latinos who were serving as mayors of cities with a population over 100,000 (NALEO 2005).

[16] One of the most prominent recent cases of polarized voting was in San Antonio, where Maria Berriozabal lost a mayoral bid with 95% of the Mexican vote and only 20% of the white vote (Munoz 1994).

[17] These results are derived from election results reported by the Asian Pacific American Institute for Congressional Studies. The data set is far from complete (especially for offices below the level of the state legislature), but it does show that of 60 Asian American incumbents who sought reelection over this time period, 59 were successful.

[18] With few exceptions, congressional election returns since the 1990s indicate that Asian American candidates have generally garnered more and more support as their time in

Moreover, few of these reelection bids appear to stimulate much in the way of a debate over race. Gary Locke, for example, "cruised to a second term" as governor of Washington state in a campaign that featured little attention to race. In a pattern similar to that of black incumbents, Locke simply ran on his record (Pierce 2000). Finally, although Asian Americans have almost always had to win over non-Asian American voters in order to get elected, the number of Asian Americans who are able to do so successfully is clearly growing over time. Much of the growth in Asian American representation can be directly attributed to the growing Asian American population, but white voters also appear to be playing an increasingly important role.

None of these trends provides direct evidence of white learning under Asian American or Latino incumbents. But the available evidence is both interesting and suggestive. The patterns that we see in the vote and in the nature of Latino and Asian American incumbent campaigns hint at growing white acceptance of Latino and Asian American leadership. Clearly, a plausible reading of the data is that white Americans are learning from their experiences under Latino and Asian American incumbents. If true, this suggests that the information model can be applied across a fairly wide range of cases. It also suggests that Latino and Asian American leadership may be another important learning tool that could lead to positive change in inter-group dynamics.

TRANSITIONS AROUND THE WORLD

The patterns that we see across all of these different cases raise questions about the applicability of the information model to a wider range of political contexts around the world. The transition to democracy and majority black rule in South Africa, for example, seems to fit many of the criteria of the model. White fears were widespread in South Africa before the election of the African National Congress, and the transition to black control did not lead to a wholesale redistribution of resources or the downfall of the white community. Thus, the possibility of white learning in South Africa certainly exists.[19]

---

office increased. Since most of the Asian American incumbents are running in primarily white districts, this rules out a white backlash explanation and implies that whites are becoming more supportive over time.

[19] Although there is little evidence of a dramatic shift in white attitudes in response to black leadership in South Africa, the results of the most recent national elections in 2004 did seem to demonstrate a slight reduction in racial divisions (Ferree 2005).

There may be other contexts beyond the arena of race and ethnicity, moreover, where the information model is applicable. There is nothing in the information model itself that requires a racial divide or racial stereotypes. All that is required is a lack of information about one particular group and fear about what that group will do once in power. Thus, the information model can be seen as a model for understanding transitions of power from once-dominant groups to underrepresented minority groups. One could apply such a model to the cases of religion or gender. Did the election of John F. Kennedy as the first Catholic president lead to a change in attitudes toward Catholic candidates? Certainly, one could make a reasonable claim that America's experience under Kennedy reduced the significance voters accorded to the Catholicism of candidates. The concerns about a Catholic president that were expressed when Kennedy ran for office seem not to have played an obvious role in subsequent elections involving Catholic candidates around the country.

Whether gender transitions provide the same information and have the same effect on attitudes and voting behavior is less clear. Interactions between men and women are generally much more extensive than interactions between different religious or racial groups. As a result, lack of information may not be as great a problem when female candidates run for office for the first time. Although existing studies do suggest that men hold stereotypes about female candidates, researchers have found that these stereotypes are not universally negative. Moreover, it is not clear that stereotypes and expectations surrounding female candidates always reduce the level of support that female candidates receive (Huddy and Terkildsen 1993; McDermott 1997). My suspicion is that learning, to the extent it occurs under women in office, is so muted that it would be difficult to register using the blunt measures available to researchers. On the other hand, it is not inconceivable that there was at least a slight adjustment to gender stereotypes in the wake of Margaret Thatcher's strong-willed leadership as the first female prime minister of England. Thus, in exceptional cases, electing women to office might spark real change.

In many of the cases that I have highlighted, and in a range of other political transitions around the world, the main barrier to one group ceding power to another group is thought to be historical enmities and irreconcilable differences over race, religion, or ideology. But these same conflicts can just as easily be viewed as being driven by uncertainty and a lack of information. This may give us a very different perspective on political transitions. For groups losing power, it may not be ideological divides, racial hatreds, or religious antagonisms that really drive their actions and ultimately lead to mobilization and violence. Instead, from the perspective of the information model, the root of the problem may be a lack of information. Perhaps it is impossible to provide information to reassure formerly dominant groups. Indeed, transitions, when allowed, sometimes have the very consequences that members of formerly dominant groups fear. But when both groups have essentially the same interests – the maintenance of the economic health of the larger community and the continued vitality of the country or region – there may be room for information to play a role. In these cases, if the right information can be provided, it may help to overcome fears driven by religious, ideological, or racial differences. At the very least, it seems worthwhile to ask deeper questions about the role of information and of uncertainty in conflicts around the world.

Conclusion

A Tale of Caution and Hope

For years, African Americans fought for access to the vote and the ability to choose their own leaders. When that opportunity finally arrived, many in the African American community were justifiably jubilant. Over the ensuing years, black elected officials have tried to live up to the hopes and expectations of the black community. In many cases, they have tried valiantly to improve conditions in the black community, and frequently their efforts have been rewarded. According to a range of studies, black representation has made a difference. Nevertheless, to many if not most observers of American politics, the victory seems somewhat hollow, as black elected officials simply have not been able to alleviate basic problems facing the African American community. Poverty, poor educational achievement, crime, racial segregation, and other fundamental racial inequalities remain largely unchanged despite years and in some cases decades of black leadership. In light of the ongoing problems plaguing the African American community, some critics now claim that black leadership is "largely irrelevant."[1]

One of the goals of this book has been to show that this view represents only part of the story of black representation. Existing studies have failed to uncover one of the most important consequences of black representation because they have largely focused on the effects of black leadership on the black community. By examining the effects of black leadership on the

---

[1] The quote is from a book entitled *We Have No Leaders* in which Robert Smith lambasts the conservative policies of African American leadership. Other critics, such as Adolph Reed, have argued that black leadership often "doesn't really amount to a transition to local black rule" (1989: 44).

white community, I have shown that black officeholding has an important impact on the attitudes and actions of white Americans. The tests that I have discussed here reveal change on a number of fronts. Under black mayors, there is a measurable shift in white voting patterns and in the racial sentiments expressed by a portion of the white population. Black representation appears to diminish the role of race in the vote, to boost white support for black candidates, relax racial tension, and foster more positive white attitudes toward both black leadership and the black community. All of this could have long-term consequences for race relations in this country. If black representation continues to expand and white Americans continue to grow more sympathetic to the plight of the black community as a result, it may be possible in the future to enact large-scale reforms that reduce basic racial inequalities. Contrary to what many have argued, then, black representation does matter.

This book is not simply a story about black representation. It is also a story about white Americans. What white Americans do or do not do in response to black empowerment tells us a lot about how race works in the minds of white Americans. The pattern of white behavior detailed in this book leads to two critical conclusions about the white community. First, it is clear that race still matters in the American political arena. The fear that whites express, the intense mobilization of the white vote, and the almost overwhelming opposition that most black challengers face from white voters all express whites' strong aversion to black challengers and suggest that many white Americans continue to be quite threatened by the prospects of black empowerment.[2] This fear has declined over time, but even today, under a range of circumstances, racial threat and racial competition continue to shape white political behavior. Moreover, judging by the negative attitudes of some whites toward the black community and the imperviousness of those attitudes to change, there is also evidence that at least a segment of the white community remains prejudiced. It is not clear that anything will change that.

But the second and far more important insight about white Americans that emerges from this book is that for many others change is possible. The alteration of the white vote under black incumbents and the shifting views of many white residents under black mayors strongly suggest that

---

[2] The pattern of reactions across different contexts reinforces this point. The fact that white opposition to black challengers varies systematically with the size of the local black population and is greater in areas with a larger black population also suggests that race is critically important for many white Americans.

some whites can learn from their experiences. All white Americans are not equally open to the information that they get from black Americans and some resist change altogether, but some do change. Many white Americans are not blind and resolute on matters of race. The critical point is that positive change can and does occur.

This point is well worth highlighting. In the past, black gains have usually been met with white resistance, which has often led to a reversal of many of those gains (Klinkner and Smith 1999). The successful effort of white Southerners to eliminate or reduce African American political rights in the aftermath of the Civil War is one of the sharpest examples of this pattern. The often violent efforts of white Americans to try to reverse the gains of the Civil Rights Movement merely repeated this pattern. Even today, increases in black power tend to spawn white mobilization. Given the apparent reluctance of many white Americans to cede power and resources to the black community and the willingness of the white community to occasionally engage in violent actions to try to undo black gains, it is vitally important that we identify and draw attention to contexts where members of the white community respond more positively to black empowerment. My work suggests that there is at least one context where black gains are often followed by more, rather than less, white support. Black representation certainly cannot solve all or even most of America's racial ills, but if it can begin to reduce racial divisions in the political arena, then it is a goal well worth pursuing.

The positive changes that we see under black incumbents inevitably raise a question. Why is black representation different from other forms of interracial contact? In this book, I have argued that it provides information about blacks and their interests that white voters perceive as credible. Black leadership provides this type of information where other types of interactions do not because black electoral victory represents one of the first times that African Americans have the power to affect the well-being of the white community. Black co-workers can seem reassuring, black neighbors can display counter-stereotypical behavior, and black political candidates vying for office can promise not to enact a pro-black agenda, but the words and actions of members of the black community are generally not accepted by whites as informative. Black leaders, on the other hand, because they have power, are perceived as different from other members of the black community, and their incumbency therefore provides information that is much harder for whites to dismiss. The fact that black leaders can inflict real harm on the white community makes black electoral victory especially threatening but also especially informative. As a result, black leadership represents one of the few contacts between the two races that has positive consequences.

The positive change under black representation also provides an important lesson for how we should study race and interracial dynamics. Much of the mainstream literature on race is locked in an overly simplistic debate. On one side, scholars argue that there has been little, if any, change on matters of race. According to these authors, America is essentially still a racist society, and this fact permeates almost all aspects of the political arena. Pettigrew epitomizes this view when he argues, "Race in America still serves as a political lightning rod that attracts political energy whether the candidates intend it or not" (1988: 32). Some are even willing to argue that "race will *always* be at the center of the American experience" (Omi and Winant 1994: 5). On the other side of the debate are those who believe that the importance of race in the political arena has greatly diminished. As Thernstrom notes, "White voters may reject a black candidate for precisely the same reasons that whites may reject a white. . . . On merits or inadequate electoral appeal" (1987: 216). Some go so far as to claim that racism is largely a phenomenon of the past (D'Souza 1995; Highton 2004). "Being Afro-American," one writer concludes, "is no longer a significant obstacle to participation in the public life of the nation" (Patterson 1997).

As I have said, however, to portray white Americans as simply "racist" or always "race-blind" overlooks the variable nature of race in America. This book shows that the key question is not *if* race is central in the political arena but rather *when* it is central. In order to understand how race works in American politics, we have to try to determine when racist voting is more likely to emerge, when color-blind politics are most often prevalent, and ultimately why these differences occur. In short, we need to understand how context changes the meaning of race.[3]

Finally, the positive change that occurs under black mayors highlights the potential for politics to play a central role in the lives of Americans. There is a widely held perception among scholars of American politics that the political arena is peripheral to the lives of Americans. And in

---

[3] Although some researchers have made this point in the past, most studies of racial politics pay it little heed. Huckfeldt and Kohfeld have argued, for example, that "racial conflict is fundamentally a group phenomenon, subject to environment and structural properties that are variable through time. Thus, the pattern and consequence of racial conflict in electoral politics must be understood in terms of particular groups at particular times in particular places" (1989: 44). Cohen and Dawson (1993), Hero (1998), and Bledsoe et al. (1995) have also in different ways demonstrated the importance of context in understanding racial politics.

many ways surveys back up this perception. Few Americans are actively involved in the political arena and most profess to little interest in political affairs (Verba, Schlozman, and Brady 1995). Moreover, most Americans appear to be unaware of either who their elected leaders are or what they are doing in office (Delli Carpini and Keeter 1996; Campbell et al. 1960; Althaus 2003). But the ability of black mayoral leadership not only to change white voting behavior but also to alter white racial attitudes testifies to the significance of politics. Positive change in the arena of racial politics is hard to come by. The fact that the election of one black candidate to office appears to improve white attitudes toward the African American community suggests not only that white Americans do pay close attention to the political arena under certain circumstances but also that attention to politics can, over the long term, affect inter-group dynamics in important ways.

The main contribution of this book is to show how information garnered from black representation alters the attitudes and actions of white Americans. Knowing that this change occurs is important. What is perhaps just as or even more important is being able to use this new knowledge to improve race relations in America and elsewhere. Fortunately, a number of policy lessons flow directly from the research in this book. The first and most obvious recommendation is to increase the number of black elected officials. Expanded minority representation is unlikely to resolve all of our racial struggles, but if it can foster even slightly better understanding among groups, it is a goal well worth pursuing.

But how do we improve the chances of African Americans gaining office? Since blacks already hold office in most of the majority black localities around the country and the creation of more such districts seems unlikely, the real question is how we can get more white voters to support black challengers. Information might help: if white Americans tend to oppose black challengers because they have little information about the likely consequences of black leadership and fear a reversal of the racial status quo, the key to changing the white vote may be to provide information about the real consequences of black representation – in essence, to show that black leadership poses little threat to white well-being. The easiest way to do this is to make information about past cases of black leadership available to whites who have not seen black leadership in action. If we can show white voters in Boston, for example, that black control in Atlanta, Los Angeles, and other cities has created economic prosperity rather than economic decline, it may be possible to reduce white fears and change white votes. Media campaigns could be an important tool.

Candidates themselves could also offer what are essentially short history lessons. Those who are moderates may do well to provide information about their own histories. On this point, the case of Los Angeles is particularly interesting. Tom Bradley lost his first mayoral bid when Sam Yorty raised white fears by talking about the police force quitting, blacks moving in, and a host of other terrible things that might happen if a black man were elected. Bradley won his next mayoral bid and overcame at least some of these white fears by repeatedly highlighting the details of his record on race-relevant issues. By continuously mentioning his fiscally conservative and racially evenhanded record on the city council and noting his stellar career as a member of the city's police department, Bradley seems to have won over a sizeable portion of the white electorate in Los Angeles. Other black challengers with equally reassuring records in lower offices might do well to highlight their own achievements. These kinds of statements are unlikely to be as credible or convincing as actually living under black leadership, but they could help. There are already signs that whites who have never lived directly under black leadership are learning simply by witnessing black leadership from afar.[4] The more concrete information we can provide about black leadership and its consequences, the less likely whites will be to fear a black takeover, and the more likely it is that black representation will expand around the country.

This book offers other possible prescriptions for black candidates seeking office. Past research has provided mixed advice for those black contenders who seek to expand their white support. Some scholars have maintained that black candidates can garner white support by deracializing their campaigns, but other studies have found that even when they attempt to do so they are faced with widespread white resistance (Perry 1991; Nichols 1990; C. Hamilton 1977; Wright 1996; Starks 1991). Unfortunately, few of these studies have controlled for other aspects of the campaign, and none has assessed outcomes in more than a handful of elections. As a result, it has been hard to tell if deracialization really works. The results in Chapter 2 and Chapter 4 indicate that deracialization is in fact an effective strategy for garnering white support. When black candidates move from a racially explicit campaign to a less racially focused campaign, they are able to attract greater white support. In particular, black challengers who advocate fewer race-specific policies, who avoid racially inflammatory comments, and who take care to address white audiences as

---

[4] The growing willingness of white Americans to vote for black *challengers* over time suggests that whites in areas without black leadership may be changing their views.

often or more often than they address black audiences tend to win more white support. Of course, there are dangers associated with this strategy. Promises of racial evenhandedness could lead to fewer pro-black policy changes. And it is possible that deracialized campaigns could negatively affect black turnout and black support.[5] In short, black candidates may have to walk a fine line between trying to garner white support and trying to serve the black community.

We may also be able to expand black representation by keeping black incumbents in office longer. Black incumbents may have a tool – albeit a difficult one – to help them stay in office. Knowing that the vote of large segments of the white community is dependent on an incumbent's record in office gives black incumbents a strong incentive to work toward policies that expand the economy, reduce crime, and generally improve conditions in the city. Especially, in cities where whites make up a large share of the voting population, black mayors should now know that if they can improve local conditions, they have an excellent chance of winning reelection. Of course, figuring out how to maintain a robust local economy and improving one's overall policy record is no easy task for black incumbents, who often serve in economically depressed areas.

Finally, the results of my research suggest that we should begin to reconsider how we draw political boundaries. Many scholars and activists have championed the creation of racially mixed districts both because black candidates have a good chance of winning office in these districts and because racially mixed districts may maximize black substantive representation (Grofman and Handley 1989; Lublin 1997; Cameron, Epstein, and Halloran 1996). The pattern of responses to black mayoral candidates outlined in this book suggests, however, that racial balance may create problems of its own for black candidates. At least at the mayoral level, the limited information provided by black incumbency and the ongoing fear that blacks will take control of the local political arena means that whites tend to remain particularly fearful and highly mobilized in racially balanced localities. Thus, the creation of more racially balanced districts could actually lead to an increase in racial tension and racial conflict. In addition, as a consequence of this ongoing racial conflict, black incumbents also have a more difficult time getting reelected in these places. Further investigation beyond the mayoralty is certainly necessary before

---

[5] It is, however, worth noting that for the black challengers examined in this book, black support was almost universally high and black turnout almost always extraordinary – regardless of the campaign platform.

any concrete recommendation is made, but my results suggest that actors who are interested in redistricting should begin to include two new criteria that they have previously ignored: reelection rates and the level of racial conflict associated with different racial demographics. If results at the mayoral level are repeated for other offices, both of these criteria may force us to reconsider the creation of more racially balanced districts.

THE FUTURE OF RACE RELATIONS IN AMERICA

The overarching message of this book is one of caution and hope. We should not overestimate the effect of black representation. Information matters, but there are real limits to its effects in the racial arena. The information that black representation provides can reduce racial conflict within the confines of mayoral politics, but it does little to reduce conflict in other arenas. Despite years of black mayoral leadership, whites and blacks in many of the cities examined in this book continue to clash over issues such as police procedures, public school policy, affirmative action, and development priorities. Moreover, full-scale violence has occurred with or without the presence of minority leadership. In cases where the interests of the black and white communities truly are in opposition, there may be little that black representation can do to ensure that the two groups do not collide. It is also apparent from the pattern of change under black leadership that not everyone learns from their experiences with black incumbents. White Republicans, in particular, are generally less affected by the presence of black leaders than are white Democrats. Similarly, it is apparent that even in black incumbent elections race is still important. As Chapter 2 demonstrated, when white voters face black incumbents, the size of the black population and the racialization of the black candidate's campaign strongly shape the white vote. And in the end, despite learning, white support for black leadership is far from unanimous. It is rare for more than a slim majority of white voters to support black leaders. In part because of this uneven learning and the ongoing effects of race, African Americans are still greatly underrepresented nationwide. Despite real progress, black representation is not a cure for all of America's racial dilemmas.

In this discouraging context, it helps to remember that change can and does occur. Each new black leader provides additional information to the white community – information that tends to reduce white fears and racial tension. Everyone does not learn, and differences of opinion over policy may remain intact, but racial divides *are* often diminished under black leadership. Black representation represents a small step, perhaps, but it could be an important one. Over time, changes effected by black leaders should filter into other arenas of racial politics. The future of race relations in America may depend in no small part on the presence and expansion of African American political representation.

STATISTICAL APPENDIXES

A

Appendix to Chapter 2

BLACK CHALLENGER/BLACK INCUMBENT DATA SET

Selection of Cases

I singled out the first black mayor of every city with a population over 100,000 by searching the Joint Center for Political and Economic Studies data set, in which there is a database of all black officials in the country elected over the past three decades. I then used newspaper reports and other secondary accounts to single out those cities with biracial (black-white) electoral contests in the general or run-off election for both the election in which the black candidate won to become the first black mayor of the city and the election immediately following in which the black candidate ran as an incumbent for the first time.

Variables

White Vote

The dependent variable in each election is the percentage of white voters who supported the black candidate. Estimates of the white vote come from a number of different sources. For Chicago, Dallas, Houston, Los Angeles, and New York, the vote by race and ethnicity was taken directly from exit polls. If more than one exit poll was available for a given election, an average of all of the exit polls was used. In several other cities (Birmingham, Cleveland, Flint, Gary, Memphis, Newark, New Orleans, and Philadelphia), I used estimates from existing studies that had estimated the vote by race using regression analysis at the precinct or ward level. In one city, San Francisco, estimates of racial voting preferences came from ecological inference. The ecological inference procedure is described by King (1997). If exit polls were unavailable and data were insufficient to perform ecological inference (Atlantic City, Baltimore, Durham, Hartford, Kansas City, Oakland, New Haven, Minneapolis, Rockford, and Seattle), I used estimates derived from homogeneous precinct analysis – more specifically, the complementary percentages method outlined by Loewen and Grofman (1989: 602–3). This method involves a two-stage process. First, I arrived at a preliminary estimate of the vote by race by using the vote in all of the precincts that are predominantly of one race. In the second stage, I estimated the total vote of the nonpredominant groups for each candidate in each of the key precincts using these preliminary estimates. I then subtracted out the votes of the nonpredominant groups in each precinct, and the remainder of the vote in each set of key precincts was used to arrive at a final estimate of the vote of the predominant group. Whenever possible, I obtained multiple estimates of white voting behavior for the same election. Most estimates vary by only a few percentage points. In each city, the data for the two elections were compiled in the same manner (that is, I used exit polls conducted by the same firm or analyzed the same precincts). Data on the black vote were compiled in the same manner using the same data sources.

Racial Demographics (Percentage Black, Change in White Population)
Data on the racial makeup of each city come from the relevant census publications (Bureau of the Census 2002, 1994, 1990, 1978). When not published by the census, data for intercensal years were interpolated.

Racial Focus of the Campaign
To code black campaigns, I focused on three factors: the policy platform, the presence or absence of racial rhetoric, and the extent to which the candidate disproportionately addressed black audiences. I divided campaigns into three categories: campaigns that had any sort of explicit, pro-black focus, campaigns that addressed the black community implicitly through a generally pro-black policy agenda or by actively mobilizing black voters and speaking before black audiences, and campaigns that never mentioned black interests and were fairly race neutral. Coding was based primarily

on local newspaper accounts of the campaign, although secondary sources were also consulted in a number of cases.

Candidate Quality

Candidate quality is a measure of the political experience of the white opponent in each election. In line with Krasno and Green (1988) and other past research, candidate quality was measured on the following four-point scale: (4) candidates with current or past citywide or statewide positions; (3) candidates who had been city council members or state representatives; (2) candidates who had served in other local elected offices; (1) candidates who had served in local appointed offices or were otherwise well-known figures; and (0) candidates with no elected experience. Also, since others have argued for a simpler measure (Krebs 1998), in alternate tests I included a dummy variable that simply indicated whether or not a candidate had previously held an elected office. Finally, to gauge the overall impact of incumbency, I included a dummy variable measuring whether or not the white opponent in the black challenger election was the incumbent mayor.

Campaign Spending

To assess the role of campaign spending, I collected data on the total general election campaign spending of both the black candidate and the major white candidate in each election. I also created a measure of the campaign spending advantage/deficit of the black candidate over the white candidate. In alternate models, each of these three measures as well as logged versions of the three measures was tested. Unfortunately, spending data are available for only about two-thirds of the cases, and this measure was not included in the final model. Spending data are taken either directly from the local election board or from election board figures cited in local newspapers.

Endorsements (Democratic Party, Local Newspaper)

For each election, I noted whether or not the local Democratic Party endorsed the black candidate and whether or not the major local daily newspaper endorsed the black candidate in each contest. Half of the cities are nonpartisan, but in 25 of 26 cases the black candidate was mostly closely aligned with the Democratic Party or with Democratic voters. The support or opposition of the Democratic Party was almost always seen as an important factor in the progress of the election campaign.

If there was no formal endorsement by the Democratic Party, I determined whether there was active opposition, mixed support, or active support of the black candidate from leaders of and workers for the local Democratic Party. Both variables are dummy variables coded (0) endorse opponent, (0.5) no endorsement/mixed support, and (1) endorse black candidate.

Change in Per Capita Income

The basic measure is change in per capita income in the metropolitan area relative to the median change for the entire metropolitan USA. The variable measures how well a metropolitan area has done economically relative to the rest of the country. I used change in per capita income without controlling for national trends. This latter measure was less strongly related to white voter behavior.

Redistributive Spending

This variable assesses the degree to which each local government shifts spending away from developmental spending (highways, airports, and streets) and onto redistributional functions (social services, housing, and education) over the course of the black incumbent's first term. It is measured as a percentage of total government expenditures. Data on local government spending are from the annual local government finances report of the census.

Voter Turnout

The basic measure of turnout is the percentage of registered voters who voted in a given election. I use overall turnout rather than white turnout because turnout by race is not available for all of the cities. Figures for voter turnout come primarily from the Race and Urban Politics dataset (see Lublin and Tate 1995). In other cases, registration and turnout data were gathered from the local registrar or local newspaper reports. Supplementary data on turnout by race/ethnicity were gathered largely from secondary accounts and newspaper reports. Aggregate white, black, and overall turnout are extremely highly correlated in these elections (r > 0.9).

Sources

Unless otherwise indicated, most of the data points for most of the measures were obtained from local newspaper accounts of the campaigns in each city. Missing data were filled in using secondary accounts by

TABLE A.1 *A List of Black Challenger/Incumbent Elections*

City	Candidate	Year 1	Whites Voting Black (%)	Year 2	Whites Voting Black (%)
Atlantic City	James Usry	1984	15	1986	11
Baltimore	Kurt Schmoke	1987	42	1991	35
Birmingham	Richard Arrington	1979	19	1983	20
Charlotte	Harvey Gantt	1983	36	1985	46
Chicago	Harold Washington	1983	20	1987	15
Cleveland	Carl Stokes	1967	19	1969	23
Dallas	Ron Kirk	1995	42	1999	60
Durham	Chester Jenkins	1989	31	1991	21
Flint	James Sharp	1983	18	1987	10
Gary	Richard Hatcher	1967	15	1971	22
Hartford	Thirman Milner	1981	37	1983	–
Houston	Lee Brown	1997	26	1999	49
Kansas City	Emanuel Cleaver	1991	38	1995	46
Los Angeles	Tom Bradley	1973	44	1977	53
Memphis	Willie Herenton	1991	3	1995	39
Minneapolis	Sharon Belton	1993	46	1997	47
New Haven	John Daniels	1989	52	1991	36
New Orleans	Ernest Morial	1978	20	1982	15
New York	David Dinkins	1989	28	1993	22
Newark	Kenneth Gibson	1970	10	1974	23
Oakland	Lionel Wilson	1977	23	1981	62
Philadelphia	Wilson Goode	1983	23	1987	20
Rockford	Charles Box	1989	59	1993	66
San Francisco	Willie Brown	1995	50	1999	48
Seattle	Norm Rice	1989	54	1993	63
Trenton	Douglas Palmer	1990	12	1994	48

academic scholars or by directly contacting city, county, and state offices (primarily local elections boards).

MAYORAL INCUMBENT ELECTIONS DATA SET

This data set includes the outcome of every reelection bid for every black mayor in cities with over 50,000 residents. Black incumbents were identified through the Joint Center for Political and Economic Studies, which has maintained a database of all black elected officials in the country for the past three decades. In addition, data on the race of the opponents and the racial demographics of the city were obtained from the Mayoral

TABLE A.2 *Descriptive Statistics for Black Challenger/Black Incumbent Elections*

Variable	Mean	Std. Dev.	Min.	Max.
Percent White Vote for Black Challenger	29.7	15.6	2.6	58.6
Percent White Vote for Black Incumbent	35.8	17.7	10.4	66.5
Change in White Vote for Black Candidate	6.4	14.7	−16	39
Newspaper Endorsement 1	0.65	0.44	0	1
Newspaper Endorsement 2	0.92	0.18	0.5	1
Party Endorsement 1	0.73	0.41	0	1
Party Endorsement 2	0.85	0.27	0	1
Percent Black	36.2	15.2	6	58
Change in Redistributive Spending	0.88	3.5	−4.6	9.4
Incumbent 1	0.27	0.45	0	1
Quality White Opponent 1	2.5	1.4	0	4
Quality Black Challenger	2.4	1.2	0	4
Quality White Opponent 2	2.5	1.6	0	4
Racial Focus of Black Candidates Campaign 1	0.30	0.32	0	1
Racial Focus of Black Candidates Campaign 2	0.17	0.28	0	1
Percent Turnout 1	55.2	15.9	20	82
Percent Turnout 2	48.2	18.8	5	75.5
Change in White Population	−1.9	1.9	−6	3
Change in Per Capita Income	1.6	5.2	−7	20

Careers Dataset for the period 1970–1985. For a description of the data set, see Wolman, Strate, and Melchior (1996) and Wolman, Page, and Reavely (1990). For more recent elections, data on opponents and election results come primarily from local newspaper reports and in some cases from secondary accounts of the elections.

B

Appendix to Chapter 3

In order to perform the two-stage least-squares analysis, I first devised a treatment or first-stage equation modeling the presence of a black mayor in the city. The first stage included five exogenous variables that served as instrumental variables (per capita black income in the city, the percentage of black adults with a college degree in the city, the percentage of the city that voted Republican in the 1988 presidential election, the median income in the city in 1989, and the percentage of adults in the city with a college degree in 1990). These instrumental variables fit the criteria proposed by Bartels (1991): First, according to Karnig and Welch (1980), they are among the strongest predictors of black mayoral presence (aside from the proportion of a city's population that is black, which is clearly related to white attitudes). In the present data set, they explain an additional 4 percent of the variation in the first stage. Second, they are, at least to a certain extent, exogenous. None of the instrumental variables is highly correlated with individual white racial attitudes in the survey (r < 0.15), and omitted variable Hausman tests suggest that the instrumental variables are, with one exception, not significantly related to white racial attitudes in the second-stage equation. It is also important to note that there is little theoretical reason to expect that the five instrumental variables have a direct impact on white racial attitudes. Given that I control for income, education, partisanship, and political ideology at the individual level, it seems unlikely that citywide measures of income, education, and partisanship would have any additional effect on white racial attitudes. The results of the overall two-stage least-squares analysis are presented in Table B.1. The first stage is presented in Table B.2.

TABLE B.1 *The Impact of Black Representation on White Racial Attitudes (Two-Stage Least-Squares Regression)*

	Views of Black Leadership	Views of the Black Community	
	Blacks Pushing Too Hard	Anti-black Affect	Racial Resentment
Black Mayor (1 = yes 0 = no)	−0.15 (0.06)***	−0.06 (0.02)***	−0.09 (0.04)**
Education	−0.20 (0.02)***	−0.04 (0.01)***	−0.25 (0.02)***
Income	−0.02 (0.03)	−0.00 (0.01)	0.02 (0.02)
Age	0.15 (0.03)***	0.06 (0.01)***	−0.00 (0.03)
Gender (1 = male)	0.03 (0.01)**	0.00 (0.00)	0.03 (0.01)**
Ideology (1 = liberal)	−0.28 (0.03)***	−0.05 (0.01)***	−0.23 (0.03)***
Party ID (1 = Democrat)	−0.09 (0.02)***	−0.00 (0.01)	−0.07 (0.02)***
Employment Status (1 = unemployed)	−0.08 (0.04)**	−0.01 (0.01)	−0.01 (0.03)
Years Living in City	−0.01 (0.02)	−0.00 (0.01)	0.02 (0.02)
Percent Black in City	0.26 (0.08)***	0.09 (0.02)***	0.22 (0.06)***
Level of Urbanism	0.01 (0.02)	−0.02 (0.01)**	−0.06 (0.02)***
South (1 = yes)	0.03 (0.02)*	0.02 (0.00)***	0.02 (0.01)
1986	0.01 (0.02)		
1988	−0.02 (0.02)	0.02 (0.01)***	0.05 (0.02)***
1990	−0.00 (0.00)		−0.02 (0.02)
1992	−0.03 (0.02)	−0.00 (0.01)	0.02 (0.01)*
First Year of Black Mayoralty (1 = yes)	0.06 (0.05)	0.04 (0.01)**	0.04 (0.04)
Constant	0.79 (0.04)***	0.42 (0.01)***	−0.17 (0.03)***
Adj. R^2	0.14	0.06	0.22
N	2181	2280	1911

Note: Figures are unstandardized coefficients with their standard errors.

** $p < 0.01$

* $p < 0.05$

CODING AND DESCRIPTIVE STATISTICS

Independent Variables

1. *Education.* Coded as a 6-category variable: 0 = completed less than 9th grade; 0.2 = 9–12 years; 0.4 = high school diploma; 0.6 = 1–3 years college; 0.8 = bachelor's degree; 1.0 = graduate degree. Mean = 0.61 Std Dev = 0.31.

2. *Age.* Age in years normalized to 0–1. Mean = 0.34. Std Dev = 22.0

TABLE B.2 *Predicting a Black Mayoralty: The First Stage of the Two-Stage Least-Squares Regression*

	Black Mayor 1 = Black Mayor, 0 = No Black Mayor
Education	0.02 (0.03)
Income	0.01 (0.03)
Age	−0.01 (0.02)
Gender (1 = male)	0.01 (0.01)
Ideology (1 = liberal)	0.04 (0.03)
Party ID (1 = Democrat)	−0.03 (0.02)
Employment Status (1 = unemployed)	0.01 (0.03)
Years Living in City	−0.00 (0.02)
Percent Black in City	1.4 (0.04)***
Level of Urbanism	−0.01 (0.03)
South (1 = yes)	−0.06 (0.02)***
Per Capita Black Income in the City[1]	0.06 (0.01)***
Percent of Blacks with College Degree[1]	−0.01 (0.01)
Median Income in City[1]	−0.07 (0.02)***
Percent with College Degree in City[1]	0.04 (0.01)***
Republican Vote in 1988 in City[1]	−0.22 (0.08)***
Constant	−0.00 (0.00)
N	4353
Adj R^2	0.4

Note: Figures in parentheses are standard errors.

[1] Exogenous variables not included in the second stage.

*** $p < 0.01$

** $p < 0.05$

* $p < 0.10$

3. *Gender.* Coded as 1 = male. Mean = 0.46. Std Dev = 0.50.
4. *Employment.* Coded as 1 = unemployed, 0 otherwise. Mean = 0.04. Std Dev = 19.
5. *Ideology.* Coded as a 7-category variable: 0 = very conservative; 0.17 = conservative; 0.33 = somewhat conservative; 0.50 = moderate; 0.67 = somewhat liberal; 0.83 = liberal; 1 = very liberal. Mean = 0.46. Std Dev = 0.22.
6. *Partisan identification.* Coded as a 7-category variable: 0 = strong Republican; 0.17 = weak Republican; 0.33 = independent/Republican; 0.50 = independent; 0.67 = independent/Democrat; 0.83 = weak Democrat; 1.0 = strong Democrat. Mean = 0.51. Std Dev = 0.34.

TABLE B.3 *The Impact of Black Representation on White Racial Attitudes –
Confined to Cities with Black Mayors at Some Point in Their History*

	Views of Black Leadership	Views of the Black Community	
	Blacks Pushing Too Hard	Anti-black Affect	Racial Resentment
Black Mayor (1 = yes 0 = no)	−0.11 (0.15)	−0.01(0.00)*	−.05 (0.02)***
Education	−1.5 (0.23)***	−0.07 (0.01)***	−0.24 (0.03)***
Income	0.08 (0.25)	−0.01 (0.01)	0.02 (0.03)
Age	1.6 (0.32)***	0.03 (0.01)**	−0.00 (0.04)
Gender (1 = male)	0.21 (0.12)*	−0.00 (0.01)	0.01 (0.01)
Ideology (1 = liberal)	−2.2 (0.32)***	−0.06 (0.01)***	−0.25 (0.04)***
Party ID (1 = Democrat)	−0.59 (0.21)***	−0.01 (0.01)	−0.06 (0.02)**
Employment Status (1 = unemployed)	−0.37 (0.36)	−0.00 (0.01)	−0.01 (0.04)
Years Living in City	0.05 (0.21)	0.01 (0.01)	0.05 (0.02)*
Percent Black in City	0.71 (0.40)*	0.04 (0.02)*	0.00 (0.00)
Level of Urbanism	0.06 (0.26)	0.01 (0.01)	−0.08 (0.03)***
South (1 = yes)	0.34 (0.16)**	0.01 (0.01)	0.02 (0.02)
1986	−0.30 (0.22)	−0.00 (0.01)	0.01 (0.02)
1988	−0.59 (0.21)***	0.02 (0.01)***	0.05 (0.02)***
1990	−0.60 (0.25)***		−0.01 (0.02)
1992	−0.87 (0.20)***	−0.02 (0.001)***	
First Year of Black Mayoralty (1 = yes)	−0.08 (0.20)	0.00 (0.01)	0.01 (0.02)
Constant		0.41(0.01)	13 (0.04)
Intercept 1	−4.2 (0.37)***		
Intercept 2	−0.79 (0.34)**		
Adj. R^2/pseudo R^2	0.19	0.09	0.24
χ^2	250		
N	1177	1196	1039

Note: Figures are unstandardized coefficients with their standard errors.

** $p < 0.01$

* $p < 0.05$

7. *Years living in city.* Years of residence in municipality normalized. Mean = 0.29. Std Dev = 0.31.

8. *Percent black in city.* Percent black normalized. Mean = 0.26. Std Dev = 0.19.

9. *South*. Coded as 1 = south; 0 = otherwise. Mean = 0.26. Std Dev = 0.44.

10. *Urbanism Coded*. as 3-category variable: 0 = central city of 50 largest metropolitan areas; 0.50 = central city of other metro areas; 1.0 = suburb of metropolitan area. Mean = 0.61. Std Dev = 0.28.

C

Appendix to Chapter 5

My primary goal in including case studies of individual cities was to illustrate the *process* of racial learning and to demonstrate as clearly as possible how information from the actions of incumbent black mayors and changes in local conditions under black mayors did or did not translate into changes in white attitudes and behavior. As such, I wanted to include at least one city where there was a marked change in white views and votes over time and one city where little change in white political behavior was evident. By looking at both cities, I could answer two critical questions. First, what is it about experiencing black mayoral leadership that leads to greater acceptance of black representation? And, second, why, in some cases, do whites continue to resist black leadership?

Choosing the specific cities was then fairly straightforward. Obviously, I had to choose cities that had experienced a transition from a white to a black mayoralty. Across the United States, there are only thirty-three cities with a population over 100,000 that have experienced a transition from an elected white mayor to an elected black mayor. In order to gauge changes in white support for black leadership, it was also critical to have a series of biracial elections. Thus, I limited the choice set to the 26 cities where a black challenger won against a white opponent and then ran for reelection against a white challenger. Choosing between these cities depended more than anything else on data considerations. Practically speaking, to follow the process of learning and to assess the roles of racial views and the incumbent's performance over time, I needed a fairly extensive empirical record of white attitudes and white political choices. Very few cities in

America have regular or even semi-regular polls that include questions about local leaders, racial concerns, and local conditions.

Only three cities, Los Angeles, Chicago, and New York, fit these data considerations well.[1] Fortunately, these three cities included one city, Los Angeles, where there was a clear, positive change in white behavior over the course of black leadership and two other cities, Chicago and New York, where there was little change in white behavior under the black mayoralty. Given that the empirical record in Chicago is slightly more extensive than the record in New York and that Chicago is probably the most notorious case of white opposition to black leadership, I chose to focus on Chicago rather than New York. Much of the evidence that I could gather on New York is, however, highlighted in Chapter 4 or included at various points throughout the book. Happily, Los Angeles and Chicago also represented two cities with very different racial demographics. Thus, using these two cities, I could compare the dynamics of a minority white city with the patterns found in a racially balanced city.[2] The fact that Los Angeles and Chicago are two of the largest cities in the nation meant that they fit one more criteria: people care about what goes on in these cities. Both are well-known cities that spark greater than average interest.

Given potentially important regional differences in white reactions to black leadership, I also considered adding a case study from the South. There were, however, two main barriers to including a Southern case. The first is finding cities with biracial elections. In most of the cities in the South that have elected black mayors, mayoral elections after the first black mayoral victory generally pit a black incumbent against a second black candidate. This makes it difficult to assess changes in white support for black representation over time. The second problem, as already noted, is finding local polls that include questions about racial views and mayoral politics over time. Data of this kind are by no means necessary to do a case study, but they are one of the few ways to obtain a fairly definitive test of how the role of race has changed over time in a particular city. These two issues left me with four flawed possibilities. Houston and Dallas have some limited polling data but have only recently elected black mayors.

---

[1] Other cities have a range of relevant data – not the least of which are voting records. Data points from the cities not included in the case studies are extremely helpful and whenever possible are used to illustrate different points throughout the book.

[2] I also considered including a case study of a minority white city. Unfortunately, no minority white city fit my criteria. Most of these cities did not have a biracial black incumbent election and of those that did none had a sufficient empirical record with enough survey data measuring white racial concerns and voting preferences to warrant an extended case study.

There is not much time over which to assess changes in white attitudes and voting behavior in these two cities.[3] Birmingham and Memphis have a longer history of black mayoral representation but much less in the way of polling data and certainly nothing like the repeated exit polls that are available in Los Angeles and Chicago. In the end, it was clear that any southern case study would be too thin. In lieu of an extended case study from a Southern city, I included as much of the relevant data from these Southern cities as possible in different chapters of the book. These data suggest that the pattern in Southern cities is not appreciably different from the pattern in non-Southern cities.

1969 SURVEY: CODING AND DESCRIPTIVE STATISTICS

The National Opinion Research Center conducted face-to-face interviews of 198 adults from the 1st and 12th council districts in the city of Los Angeles. The two districts cover the northern half of the San Fernando Valley. These districts were almost exclusively white. Within the districts, neighborhoods were chosen with probabilities proportional to their population. At the time, the valley was the largest "bedroom suburb" of the city, with a population of nearly 1 million. It tends to be more conservative than Los Angeles as a whole, and thus the results of the survey cannot be taken as representative of the city as a whole (see Kinder and Sears 1981 for more details on the survey instrument).

Dependent Variable

Vote

1. "Suppose the election were today between Mayor Yorty and Thomas Bradley. Which one would you vote for?" Coded as 1 = intend to vote for Bradley; 0 = Yorty. Mean = 0.45. Std Dev = 0.49.

Independent Variables

Racial Concerns

1. *Bradley will favor black interests.* "If elected Mayor Thomas Bradley would show more favoritism to his supporters than most other mayors." Coded as 1 = strongly disagree; 2 = somewhat disagree; 3 = don't know; 4 = somewhat agree; 5 = strongly agree. Mean = 3.3. Std Dev = 0.97.

---

[3] In addition, Stein, Ulbig, and Post (2005) have already provided a detailed analysis of changes in white voting patterns using the data available in Houston.

2. *Concerned about black gains*. Scale made up of responses to the following three statements: (A) "Negroes shouldn't push themselves where they're not wanted." (B) "Over the past few years, Negroes have got more than they deserve." (C) "Hard working people like me have not done as well as Negroes over the past few years." Reliability of scale: alpha = 0.60. Mean = 0.59. Std Dev = 0.18.

Incumbent's Record

1. *Satisfied with city services*. "How satisfied are you with some of the public services the city is supposed to provide for your neighborhood?" Scale made up of responses to "Public Schools and Neighborhoods?", "Parks and playgrounds?", Garbage Collection?", and "Police Protection." Reliability of scale: alpha = 0.65. Mean = 0.38. Std Dev = 0.28.

2. *Satisfied with economic gains*. "In general, would you say that you are very satisfied, somewhat satisfied, somewhat dissatisfied, or very dissatisfied with your economic gains over the past five years?" Mean = 2.3. Std Dev = .92.

Political Ideology

1. *Liberal/conservative ideology*. Self-placement, coded as 1 = liberal; 2 = conservative. Mean = 1.5. Std Dev = 0.50.

2. *Party identification*. Coded as 1 = strong Democrat; 2 = moderate Democrat; 3 = Independent/other party; 4 = weak Republican; 5 = strong Republican. Mean = 3.4. Std Dev = 1.3.

White Racial Prejudice

1. *Stereotypes*. Scale made up of responses to the following two statements: (A) "Negroes are just as intelligent as whites." (B) "If a Negro family with about the same income and education as you moved next door, would you mind it?" (C) "How strongly would you object if a member of your family wanted to bring a Negro friend home to dinner?" Reliability of scale: alpha = 0.60. Mean = 2.2. Std Dev = 0.85.

Demographics

1. *Age*. Coded as 1 = 18–29; 2 = 30–44; 3 = 45–64; 4 = 65 and over. Mean = 2.6. Std Dev = 1.4.

2. *Education*. Coded as 1 = seventh grade or less; 2 = grade school graduate; 3 = some high school; 4 = high school graduate;

5 = technical school; 6 = junior college; 7 = some college; 8 = college graduate; 9 = more than college. Mean = 5.2. Std Dev = 2.2.

3. *Income.* Coded as 1 = less than $5,000; 2 = $5–7,500; 3 = $7.5–9,999; 4 = $10–14,999; 5 = $15–19,999; 6 = $20–24,999; 7 = $25–49,999; 8 = over $50,000. Mean = 3.5. Std Dev = 1.7.

4. *Sex.* Coded as 0 = male; 1 = female. Mean = 0.52. Std Dev = 0.59.

1980 SURVEY: QUESTION WORDING, CODING, AND DESCRIPTIVE STATISTICS

The *Los Angeles Times* conducted 1,295 telephone interviews of adult residents of the city of Los Angeles. Of the total respondents 482 were white.

Dependent Variable

Bradley Approval

1. "What is your impression of Los Angeles Mayor Tom Bradley?" Coded as 1 = very unfavorable; 2 = somewhat unfavorable; 3 = somewhat favorable; 4 = very favorable. Mean = 2.9. Std Dev = 0.79.

Independent Variables

Racial Concerns

1. *Concerned about black gains.* Scale made up of three questions: (A) "Do you think the government has paid too much attention to blacks and Mexican-Americans and other minority groups? (B) Do blacks have "too much economic power?" (C) Do blacks have "too much political power?" Reliability of scale: alpha = 0.65 Mean = 1.3. Std Dev = 0.55.

White Racial Prejudice

1. *Prejudice Scale.* Scale made up of responses to the following two statements: (A) "Negroes are just as intelligent as whites." (B) "If a Negro familiy with about the same income and education as you moved next door, would you mind it?" (C) "How strongly would you object if a member of your family wanted to bring a Negro friend home to dinner?" Reliability of scale: alpha = 0.60. Mean = 7.6. Std Dev = 1.4.

TABLE C.1 *The Vote in the 1969 Election*
(Logistic Regression)

	Vote for Bradley
Racial Concerns	
Bradley Will Favor Black Interests	−0.83 (0.19)**
Concerned about Black Gains	−2.5 (1.2)**
White Racial Prejudice	−0.01 (0.22)
Incumbent's Record	
Satisfied with City Services	−0.75 (0.71)
Satisfied with Economic Gains	−0.29 (0.21)
Political Ideology	
Liberal/Conservative Ideology	−0.69 (0.39)
Party Identification	−0.39 (0.14)**
Demographics	
Age	−0.17 (0.14)
Education	0.05 (0.11)
Income	0.08 (0.14)
Female	0.16 (0.36)
Constant	−7.6 (1.7)**
Pseudo R^2	0.26
χ^2	66**
N	188

Note: $^*p < 0.05$
$^{**}p < 0.01$

Incumbent's Record

1. *Satisfied with city.* "How do you feel things are going in Los Angeles these days?" Coded as 1 = very badly; 2 = pretty badly; 3 = pretty well; 4 = very well. Mean = 2.5. Std Dev = 0.77.

2. *Improved race relations.* "Do you think that relations between black people and white people have gotten better since the Watts riot in 1965? "Coded as 1 = gotten worse; 2 = no change 3 = gotten better; Mean = 2.3. Std Dev = 0.56.

Political Ideology

1. *Liberal/conservative ideology.* Self-placement, coded as 1 = Strong Liberal; 2 = Moderate Liberal; 3 = Middle of the Road; 4 = Moderate Conservative; 5 = Strong Conservative. Mean = 2.9. Std Dev = 1.1.

2. *Party identification.* Coded as 1 = registered Democrat; 2 = registered in other party/no party; 3 = registered Republican. Mean = 1.8. Std Dev = 0.92.

TABLE C.2 *Comparing Bradley Approval in 1969 and 1980*

	Support for Bradley	
	As a Challenger[a]	As an Incumbent[b]
Racial Concerns		
Concerned about Black Gains	−2.9 (1.1)**	0.51 (0.32)
Incumbent's Record		
Satisfied with City Services	−0.57 (0.64)	−0.57 (0.12)**
Racial Prejudice		
White Racial Prejudice	−0.07 (0.22)	0.06 (0.07)
Political Ideology		
Liberal/Conservative Ideology	−0.96 (0.37)	−0.25 (0.09)**
Party Identification	−0.30 (0.13)**	−0.02 (0.10)
Demographics		
Age	−0.13 (0.13)	−0.13 (0.09)
Education	0.03 (0.10)	0.07 (0.07)
Income	0.07 (0.13)	−0.02 (0.13)
Female	0.12 (0.34)	0.44 (0.17)*
Constant	−4.2 (1.3)**	–
Cut 1	–	−2.4 (0.93)
Cut 2	–	−1.6 (0.92)
Cut 3	–	0.50 (0.91)
Pseudo R^2	0.18	0.13
χ^2	46**	54**
N	190	194

Note: *$p < 0.05$
**$p < 0.01$
[a] Logistic regression.
[b] Ordered probit.

Demographics

1. *Age.* Coded as 1 = 18–29; 2 = 30–44; 3 = 45–64; 4 = 65 and over. Mean = 2.2. Std Dev = 1.0.
2. *Education.* Coded as 1 = grade school or less; 2 = grade school graduate; 3 = some high school; 4 = high school graduate; 5 = some college; 6 = college graduate; 7 = more than college. Mean = 4.9. Std Dev = 1.3.
3. *Income.* "Yearly income of all the members of your family living at home." Coded as 1 = less than $10,00; 2 = in-between; 3 = more than $25,000. Mean = 2.3. Std Dev = 0.71.
4. *Sex.* Coded as 0 = male; 1 = female. Mean = 0.57. Std Dev = 0.49.

References

Abney, F. Glenn, and John D. Hutcheson. 1981. "Race, Representation, and Trust: Changes in Attitudes After the Election of a Black Mayor." *Public Opinion Quarterly* 45: 91–101.

Achen, Christopher H. 1975. "Mass Political Attitudes and the Survey Response." *American Political Science Review* 69: 1218–31.

Adams, Carolyn T. 1994. "Race and Class in Philadelphia Elections." In *Big City Politics, Governance, and Fiscal Constraints*, edited by G. E. Peterson. Urbana, IL: University of Illinois.

Adorno, Theodore W., Else Frenkel-Brunswick, Daniel J. Levinson, and R. Nevitt Sanford. 1950. *The Authoritarian Personality*. New York: Harper & Row.

Alkalimat, Abdul. 1986. "Mayor Washington's Bid for Re-Election: Will the Democratic Party Survive?" *Black Scholar* 17 (6): 2–13.

Allport, G. W. 1954. *The Nature of Prejudice*. Menlo Park, CA: Addison-Wesley.

Allsop, Dee, and Herbert F. Weisberg. 1988. "Measuring Change in Party Identification in an Election Campaign." *American Journal of Political Science* 32 (4) (Nov.): 996–1017.

Alt, James E. 1994. "The Impact of the Voting Rights Act on Black and White Voter Registration in the South." In *Quiet Revolution in the South: The Impact of the Voting Rights Act, 1965–1990*, edited by C. Davidson and B. Grofman. Princeton, NJ: Princeton University Press.

Althaus, Scott. 2003. *Collective Preferences in Democratic Politics: Opinion Surveys and the Will of the People*. Cambridge: Cambridge University Press.

Alvarez, R. Michael. 1997. *Information and Elections*. Ann Arbor: University of Michigan Press.

Alvarez, R. Michael, and John Brehm. 2002. *Hard Choices, Easy Answers*. Princeton, NJ: Princeton University Press.

Alvarez, R. Michael, and Tara L. Butterfield. 2000. "The Resurgence of Nativism in California? The Case of Proposition 187 and Illegal Immigration." *Social Science Quarterly* 81 (March): 167–80.

Anderson, Susan. 1996. "A City Called Heaven: Black Enchantment and Despair in Los Angeles." In *The City: Los Angeles and Urban Theory at the End of the Twentieth Century*, edited by A. J. Scott and E. W. Sojo. Berkeley: University of California Press.

APALC (Asian Pacific American Legal Consortium). 1978–2005. *National Asian Pacific American Political Almanac*. Los Angeles: Asian American Studies Center, UCLA.

Arian, Asher, Arthur S. Goldberg, John H. Mollenkopf, and Edward T. Rogowsky. 1991. *Changing New York City Politics*. New York: Routledge.

Baker, Stephen C., and Paul Kleppner. 1986. "Race War Chicago Style: The Election of a Black Mayor, 1983." In *Research In Urban Policy*, edited by T. Clark. Greenwich, CT: JAI Press.

Bar-Tal, Daniel. 1997. "Formation and Change of Ethnic and National Stereotypes: An Integrative Model." *International Journal of Intercultural Relations* 21 (4): 491–523.

Bartels, Larry M. 1986. "Issue Voting Under Uncertainty: An Empirical Test." *American Journal of Political Science* 30: 709–28.

Bartels, Larry M. 1991. "Instrumental and 'Quasi-Instrumental' Variables." *American Journal of Political Science* 35 (3): 777–800.

Bartels, Larry M. 1996. "Uninformed Votes: Information Effects in Presidential Elections." *American Journal of Political Science* 40 (1): 194–230.

Beck, Paul Allen, and M. Kent Jennings. 1991. "Family Traditions, Political Periods, and the Development of Partisan Orientations." *Journal of Politics* 53 (3) (Aug): 742–63.

Becker, John F., and Eugene E. Heaton. 1967. "The Election of Senator Edward W. Brooke." *Public Opinion Quarterly* 31 (Fall): 346–58.

Bell, Derrick. 1992. *Faces at the Bottom of the Well: The Permanence of Racism*. New York: Basic Books.

Belsie, Laurent. 1987. "In Chicago Mayoral Primary the Biggest Issue Is Race." *Christian Science Monitor*, February 19: 3.

Bennett, Stephen Earl. 1995 "Comparing Americans' Political Information in 1988 and 1992." *Journal of Politics* 57 (2) (May): 521–32.

Berelson, Bernard R., Paul F. Lazarsfeld, and William N. McPhee. 1954. *Voting*. Chicago: University of Chicago Press.

Bergholz, Richard. 1973a. "Don't Risk Change Yorty Tells Group." *Los Angeles Times*, May 11: A11.

Bergholz, Richard. 1973b. "Yorty Says Hidden Radicals Work in Bradley Campaign." *Los Angeles Times*, May 17: 1, 3.

Bertrand, Marianne, and Sendhil Mullainathan. 2004. "Are Emily and Greg More Employable than Lakisha and Jamal? A Field Experiment on Labor Market Discrimination." *American Economic Review* 94 (4) (Sept): 991–1013.

Black, Earl, and Merle Black. 1973. "The Wallace Vote in Alabama: A Multiple Regression Analysis." *Journal of Politics* 35: 730–6.

Blalock, Hubert M. 1967. *Toward a Theory of Minority-Group Relations*. New York: Wiley.

Blank, Rebecca M. 2001. "An Overview of Trends in Social and Economic Well-Being, By Race." In *America Becoming: Racial Trends and Their Consequences*, edited by N. Smelser, W. J. Wilson, and F. Mitchell. Washington, DC: National Academy Press.

Bledsoe, Timothy, Michael Combs, Lee Sigelman, and Susan Welch. 1995. White Prejudice Toward Blacks: Does Residential Integration Matter? Paper read at Midwest Political Science Association Annual Conference, Chicago.

Bobo, Lawrence. 1983. "Whites' Opposition to Busing: Symbolic Racism or Realistic Group Conflict." *Journal of Personality and Social Psychology* 45 (6): 1196–210.

Bobo, Lawrence, and Franklin D. Gilliam. 1990. "Race, Sociopolitical Participation, and Black Empowerment." *American Political Science Review* 84 (2): 377–93.

Bobo, Lawrence D., and Devon Johnson. 2000. "Racial Attitudes in a Prismatic Metropolis: Mapping Identity, Stereotypes, Competition, and Views on Affirmative Action." In *Prismatic Metropolis: Inequality in Los Angeles*, edited by L. Bobo, M. Oliver, J. Johnson, and A. Valenzuela. New York: Russell Sage Foundation.

Bollens, John C., and Grant B. Geyer. 1973. *Yorty, Politics of a Constant Candidate*. Pacific Palisades: Palisades Publishers.

Bond, Jon R., Gary Covington, and Richard Fleisher. 1985. "Explaining Challenger Quality in Congressional Elections." *Journal of Politics* 41: 510–29.

Borger, Gloria. 1989. "Crossing the Color Line." *U.S. News & World Report*, November 6: 22.

Bosc, Michael. 1987. "Chicago's Mayoral Primary: Racial Lines Are Drawn, But Tempers Are Cooler." *U.S. News & World Report*, February 23: 20.

Bositis, David A. 2002. *Black Elected Officials: A Statistical Summary 2000*. Washington, DC: Joint Center for Political and Economic Studies.

Bowler, Shaun, and Todd Donovan. 1994. "Information and Opinion Change on Ballot Propositions." *Political Behavior* 16: 411–35.

Bowler, Shaun, and Todd Donovan. 1998. *Demanding Choices: Opinion Voting and Democrat Democracies*. Ann Arbor: University of Michigan Press.

Boyarsky, Bill. 1973a. "Yorty and Bradley Slug it Out in First Face-to-Face Debate." *Los Angeles Times*, May 1: A1.

Boyarsky, Bill. 1973b. "Yorty, Bradley Trade Charges of Underworld Ties." *Los Angeles Times*, May 8, A1.

Boyarsky, Bill. 1973c. "Yorty's Last Big Push May Be 1969 Rerun." *Los Angeles Times*, May 20: A3.

Boyarsky, Bill. 1973d. "Yorty Trying to Divide People with Racist Appeal." *Los Angeles Times*, May 25: A2.

Boyarsky, Bill. 1973e. "Mayoralty Race." *Los Angeles Times*, May 27: A24.

Brown, Robert A. 1996. A Tale of the Cities: Urban Fiscal Policy, the Transformation of American Cities, and the Influence of African American Representatives. Ph.D. Dissertation, University of Michigan, Ann Arbor.

Brown, Robert A. 1997. African-American Urban Representation Amid the Urban Transition of the 1970s and 1980s. Paper read at American Political Science Association Annual Meeting, Washington, DC.

Browning, Rufus R., Dale Rogers Marshall, and David H. Tabb. 1984. *Protest Is Not Enough*. Berkeley: University of California Press.

Browning, Rufus P., Dale Rogers Marshall, and David H. Tabb. 1997. *Racial Politics in American Cities, VII.* New York: Longman.

Bullock, Charles S. 1976. Interracial Contact and Student Prejudice. *Youth and Society* 7: 271–309.

Bullock, Charles S. 1984. "Racial Crossover Voting and the Election of Black Officials." *Journal of Politics* 46: 238–51.

Bullock, Charles S., and Bruce A. Campbell. 1984. "Racist or Racial Voting in the 1981 Atlanta Municipal Elections." *Urban Affairs Quarterly* 20 (2): 149–64.

Bullock, Charles S., and Richard E. Dunn. 1997. The Demise of Racial Districting and the Future of Black Representation. Paper read at American Political Science Association Annual Meeting, Washington, DC.

Bullock, Charles S., and Richard E. Dunn. 1999. "The Demise of Racial Districting and the Future of Black Representation." *Emory Law Journal* 48 (4): 1209–53.

Bunch, Lonnie G. 1990. "A Past Not Necessarily Prologue: The Afro-American in Los Angeles Since 1930." In *20th Century Los Angeles: Power, Promotion, and Social Conflict*, edited by N. M. Klein and M. J. Schiesl. Claremont: Regina Book.

Bureau of the Census. 1964–2003. *City Government Finances.* Washington, DC: Bureau of the Census.

Bureau of the Census. *Current Housing Reports–H170.* Bureau of the Census, 1973–2001. [Cited.] Available from http://www.census.gov/prod/www/abs/h170.html.

Bureau of the Census. 1978. *City and County Data Book.* Washington, DC: Bureau of the Census.

Bureau of the Census. 1990. *City and County Data Book.* Washington, DC: Bureau of the Census.

Bureau of the Census. 1994. *City and County Data Book.* Washington, DC: Bureau of the Census.

Bureau of the Census. 2002a. *City and County Data Book.* Washington, DC: Bureau of the Census.

Bureau of the Census. 2002b. *Statistical Abstract of the United States.* Washington, DC: Bureau of the Census.

Bureau of Economic Affairs. *Regional Economic Accounts 2005.* [Cited.] Available from http://www.bea.gov/bea/regional/reis/.

Cain, Bruce E., and Rod Kiewiet. 1986. *Minorities in California.* Pasadena: Seaver Institute.

Cameron, Charles, David Epstein, and Sharyn Halloran. 1996. "Do Majority-Minority Districts Maximize Substantive Black Representation in Congress?" *American Political Science Review* 90 (4): 794–812.

Campbell, Angus, Philip E. Converse, Warren E. Miller, and Donald E. Stokes. 1960. *The American Voter.* Chicago: University of Chicago Press.

Campbell, David, and Joe R. Feagin. 1984. "Black Electoral Victories in the South." *Phylon* 45 (4): 331–45.

Camper, John. 1987. "Small Ethnic Support Still a Boost to Mayor." *Chicago Tribune*, February 18: C1.

Canon, David. 1999. *Race, Redistricting, and Representation:* The *Unintended Consequences of Black Majority Districts.* Chicago: University of Chicago Press.

Cantor, George. 1989. "Mayor Coleman Young: A Mayor Who Cried Racism." *Newsday*, August 15: 56.

Carmines, Edward G., and James A. Stimson. 1989. *Issue Evolution: Race and the Transformation of American Politics.* Princeton, NJ: Princeton University Press.

Carsey, Thomas M. 1995. "The Contextual Effects of Race on White Voter Behavior: The 1989 New York City Mayoral Election." *Journal of Politics* 57 (1): 221–8.

Casmier, Stephen, Bill Lambrecht, Jo Mannies, and Cynthia Todd. 1993. "Black Mayors Expanding Their Ranks." *St. Louis Post-Dispatch*: 1A.

Cho, Yong Hyo. 1974. "City Politics and Racial Polarization: Bloc Voting in Cleveland Elections." *Journal of Black Studies* 4 (4): 396–417.

Citrin, Jack, Donald Philip Green, and David O. Sears. 1990. "White Reactions to Black Candidates: When Does Race Matter?" *Public Opinion Quarterly* 54: 74–96.

Clifford, Frank. 1993. "Woo Tries to Reconcile Pressures of Two Cultures." *Los Angeles Times*, March 30: A1.

Cohen, Cathy, and Michael C. Dawson. 1993. "Neighborhood Poverty and African American Politics." *American Political Science Review* 87 (2): 286–302.

Colburn, David R., and Jeffrey S. Adler, eds. 2003. *African American Mayors: Race, Politics, and the American City.* Urbana, IL: University of Illinois Press.

Cole, Leonard A. 1976. *Blacks in Power: A Comparative Study of Black and White Elected Officials.* Princeton, NJ: Princeton University Press.

Coleman, Milton. 1983a. "Race Clouds Issues for Many Chicago Voters." *Washington Post*, March 28, A1.

Coleman, Milton. 1983b. "Gains Are Solidified Nationwide: Mayors at Focus of Black Power." *Washington Post*, April 24: A1.

Coleman, Milton, and Barry Sussman. 1978. "Mayor's Role Seen as Influential." *Washington Post*, June 13: A1.

Colleau, Sophie M., Kevin Glynn, Steven Lybrand, Richard M. Merelman, Paula Mohan, and James E. Wall. 1990. "Symbolic Racism in Candidate Evaluation: An Experiment." *Political Behavior* 12 (4): 385–402.

Conover, Pamela J., and Stanley Feldman. 1989. "Candidate Perception in an Ambiguous World: Campaigns, Cues and Inference Processes." *American Journal of Political Science* 33: 912–40.

Conover, Pamela Johnston, Stanley Feldman, and Kathleen Knight. 1986. "Judging Inflation and Unemployment: The Origins of Retrospective Evaluations." *Journal of Politics* 48 (3) (Aug): 565–88.

Converse, Philip E. 1964. "The Nature of Belief Systems in Mass Publics." In *Ideology and Discontent*, edited by D. E. Apter. New York: Free Press.

Corzine, Jay, James Creech, and Lin Corzine. 1983. "Black Concentration and Lynchings in the South: Testing Blalock's Power-Threat Hypothesis." *Social Forces* 61: 774–96.

Cox, Gary, and Michael C. Munger. 1989. "Closeness, Expenditures and Turnout in the 1982 House Elections." *American Political Science Review* 83: 217–31.

Crain, L., R. Mahard, and R. Narot. 1982. *Making Desegregation Work: How Schools Create Social Climates*. Cambridge, MA: Ballinger Press.

Curry, Bill. 1979. "First Black Mayor Narrowly Elected In Birmingham." *Washington Post*, October 31.

Davidson, Jean. 1987. "Byrne A Winner In Her Northwest Side." *Chicago Tribune*, January 4: C1.

Davis, Anna. 1995. "Mayor Passes Muster in Poll: Many Give Him Good Grades and See Re-Election." *Commercial Appeal*, July 16: 1A.

Davis, Mike. 1992. *City of Quartz*. New York: Vintage Books.

Dawson, Michael C. 1994. *Behind the Mule: Race and Class in African-American Politics*. Princeton, NJ: Princeton University Press.

Day, Richard, Jeff Andreasen, and Kurt Becker. 1984. "Polling in the 1983 Chicago Mayoral Election." In *The Making of the Mayor, Chicago 1983*, edited by M. G. Holli and P. M. Green. Grand Rapids: William B. Eerdman's Publishing.

Deane, Glenn D. 1990. "Mobility and Adjustments: Paths to the Resolution of Residential Stress." *Demography* 27: 65–79.

Delli Carpini, Michael X., and Scott Keeter. 1996. *What Americans Know about Politics and Why It Matters*. New Haven: Yale University Press.

Devine, Patricia G. 1989. "Stereotypes and Prejudice: Their Automatic and Controlled Components." *Journal of Personality and Social Psychology* 56 (1): 5–18.

Devine, Patricia G., and Andrew J. Elliot. 1995. "Are Racial Stereotypes Really Fading? The Princeton Trilogy Revisited." *Personality and Social Psychology Bulletin* 21: 1139–50.

Donze, Frank. 1998. "Dutch Morial's Historic 1978 Victory Recalled." *Times-Picayune*, May 3: A14.

Dovidio, John F., and Samuel L. Gaertner. 1986. "Prejudice, Discrimination, and Racism: Historical Trends and Contemporary Approaches." In *Prejudice, Discrimination and Racism*, edited by J. F. Dovidio and S. L. Gaertner. Stanford: Stanford University Press.

Dowie, Douglas. 1981. "Bradley Wins 3rd Term in Landslide." *UPI*.

Downs, Anthony. 1957. *An Economic Theory of Democracy*. New York: Harper & Row.

D'souza, Dinesh. 1995. *The End of Racism*. New York: Free Press.

Edds, Margaret. 1987. *Free At Last: What Really Happened When Civil Rights Came to Southern Politics*: Adler & Adler.

Edsall, Thomas Byrne, and Mary D. Edsall. 1991. *Chain Reaction: The Impact of Race, Rights, and Taxes on American Politics*. New York: W. W. Norton.

Eisinger, Peter K. 1980. *Politics and Displacement: Racial and Ethnic Transition in Three American Cities*. Institute for Research on Poverty Monograph Series. New York: Academic Press.

Eisinger, Peter K. 1982. "Black Employment in Municipal Jobs: The Impact of Black Political Power." *American Political Science Review* 76: 380–92.

Eisinger, Peter K. 1983. "Black Mayors and the Politics of Racial Economic Advancement." In *Culture, Ethnicity, and Identity: Current Issues in Research*, edited by W. C. McCready. New York: Academic Press.

Erikson, Robert. 1989. "Economic Conditions and the Presidential Vote." *American Political Science Review* 83: 567.

Espiritu, Yen Le. 1992. *Asian American Panethnicity: Bridging Institutions and Identities*. Philadelphia: Temple University Press.

Ethnic News Watch. 1995. "Black Residents in Indiana Elect New Mayor on Merit, Not for Color of His Skin." *Ethnic News Watch* 112 (90): 6A.

Farley, Reynolds. 1996. *The New American Reality: Who We Are, How We Got Here, Where We Are Going*. New York: Russel Sage Foundation.

Fasenfest, David. 1989. *The Dilemma of Progressive Agendas and Community Develoment: Ward Politics in Chicago under Harold Washington*: North Central Sociological Association.

Fazio, Russel H., Joni R. Jackson, Bridget C. Dunton, and Carol J. Williams. 1995. "Variability in Automatic Activation as an Unobtrusive Measure of Racial Attitudes: A Bona Fide Pipeline?" *Journal of Personality and Social Psychology* 69 (6): 1013–27.

Fears, Daryl. 1998. "Compton Latinos Still on Outside Looking In: Despite Growing Numbers, Black-Run Government Remains Largely Closed to Them." *Los Angeles Times*, April 16: A1.

Federal Bureau of Investigation 1969–2001. *Uniform Crime Reports*. Washington, DC: United States Department of Justice.

Ferree, Karen E. 2005. Explaining South Africa's Racial Census. Unpublished Manuscript.

Fields, Cleo, and A. Leon Higginbotham. 1996. "The Supreme Court's Rejection of Pluralism." *Boston Globe*, June 30: 69.

Fiorina, Morris P. 1981. *Retrospective Voting in American National Elections*. New Haven: Yale University Press.

Fiske, Susan T. 1998. "Stereotyping, Prejudice, and Discrimination." In *The Handbook of Social Psychology*, edited by S. T. F. Daniel Gilbert and Gardner Lindzey. Boston: McGraw-Hill.

Foner, Eric. 1984. *A Short History of Reconstruction*. New York: Harper & Row.

Fossett, Mark A., and K. Jill Kiecolt. 1989. "The Relative Size of Minority Populations and White Racial Attitudes." *Social Science Quarterly* 70 (4): 820–35.

Franklin, Charles H., and John E. Jackson. 1983. "The Dynamics of Party Identification." *American Political Science Review* 77 (4): 957–73.

Franklin, Jimmie Lewis. 1989. *Back to Birmingham: Richard Arrington, Jr., and His Times*. Tuscaloosa: University of Alabama Press.

Fremon, David K. 1988. *Chicago Politics Ward By Ward*. Bloomington: Indiana University Press.

Frey, William H. 1980. "Black In-Migration, White Flight, and the Changing Economic Base of the Central City." *American Journal of Sociology* 85 (6): 1396–417.

Frisby, Michael K. 1991. "The New Black Politician." *Boston Globe*, July 14: 14.

Fulwood, Sam. 1995. "Today's Big City Black Mayors Lead in a Changed Political World." *Los Angeles Times*, September 24: A22.

Gaither, David. 1998. "Black Voters Crossing Racial Lines: A Sign of Weakness or Political Maturity?" *Pacific News Service*, July 10.

Garcia, F. Chris. 1997. *Pursuing Power: Latinos and the Political System*. Notre Dame: University of Notre Dame Press.

Gay, Claudine. 1999. Choosing Sides: Black Electoral Success and Racially Polarized Voting. Paper read at American Political Science Association, September, Atlanta.

Gay, Claudine. 2001. "The Effect of Black Congressional Representation on Political Participation." *American Political Science Review* 95 (3): 603–18.

Gerston, Larry. 1998. "Coming to Power via a Fragile Majority Poses Challenges for Gonzales." *San Jose and Silicon Valley Business Journal*, December 4: 12–13.

Gierzynski, Anthony. 1998. "Money or the Machine: Money and Votes in Chicago Aldermanic Elections." *American Politics Quarterly* 26 (April): 160–73.

Gilens, Martin. 2001. *Why Americans Hate Welfare: Race, Media, and the Politics of Antipoverty Policy*. Chicago: University of Chicago Press.

Giles, Michael W., and Melanie A. Buckner. 1993. "David Duke and Black Threat: An Old Hypothesis Revisited." *Journal of Politics* 55 (3): 702–13.

Giles, Michael W., and Arthur Evans. 1986. "The Power Approach to Intergroup Hostility." *Journal of Conflict Resolution* 30: 469–86.

Giles, Michael W., and Kaenan Hertz. 1994. "Racial Threat and Partisan Identification." *American Political Science Review* 88 (2): 317–26.

Gilliam, Franklin D. 1996. "Exploring Minority Empowerment: Symbolic Politics, Governing Coalitions, and Traces of Political Style in Los Angeles." *American Journal of Political Science* 40 (1): 56–81.

Glaser, James M. 1994. "Back to the Black Belt: Racial Environment and White Racial Attitudes in the South." *Journal of Politics* 56 (1): 21–41.

Goad, Kriste. 1999. "Mayor's Victory Crosses Racial and Party Lines." *Commercial Appeal* October 8: A1.

Goidel, Robert K., and Donald A. Gross. 1994. "A Systems Approach to Campaign Finance in U.S. House Elections." *American Politics Quarterly* 22: 125–153.

Gold, Matea. 2001. "Grass-Roots Politics Hints at Cracks in L.A.'s Ethnic Walls: Fledgling Efforts, Which Are Bridging Some Racial Gaps, May Be Tested in Coming Campaigns." *Los Angeles Times*, Janaury 14: A1.

Graber, Doris. 1984. "Media Magic: Fashioning Characters for the 1983 Mayoral Race." In *The Making of the Mayor, Chicago 1983*, edited by M. G. Holli and P. M. Green. Grand Rapids: William B. Eerdman's Publishing.

Green, Donald P., Bradley Palmquist, Eric Schickler, and Giordano Bruno. 2002. *Partisan Hearts and Minds: Political Parties and the Social Identity of Voters*. New Haven: Yale University Press.

Green, Donald P., Dara Z. Strolovitch, and Janelle S. Wong. 1998. "Defended Neighborhoods, Integration, and Racially Motivated Crime." *American Journal of Sociology* 104 (2): 372–403.

Green, Donald Philip, and Jonathan S. Krasno. 1988. "Salvation for the Spendthrift Incumbent: Reestimating the Effects of Campaign Spending in House Elections." *American Journal of Political Science* 32: 884–907.

Green, Donald Philip, and Bradley Palmquist. 1990. "Of Artifacts and Partisan Instability. *American Journal of Political Science* 34 (3): 872–902.

Grimshaw, William J. 1992. *Bitter Fruit: Black Politics and the Chicago Machine: 1931–1991.* Chicago: University of Chicago Press.

Grofman, Bernard, and Chandler Davidson. 1994. "The Effect of Municipal Election Structure on Black Representation in Eight Southern States." In *Quiet Revolution in the South: The Impact of the Voting Rights Act, 1965–1990,* edited by C. Davidson and B. Grofman. Princeton, NJ: Princeton University Press.

Grofman, Bernard, and Lisa Handley. 1989. "Minority Population Proportion and Black and Hispanic Congressional Success in the 1970s and 1980s." *American Politics Quarterly* 17 (4): 436–45.

Hagstrom, Jerry, and Robert Guskind. 1983. "This Is the Year of the Black Mayor, But Next Year Will Test Black Power." *National Journal*, November 19: 34–6.

Hahn, Harlan, David Klingman, and Harry Pachon. 1976. "Cleavages, Coalitions, and the Black Candidate: The Los Angeles Mayoralty Elections of 1969 and 1973." *Western Political Quarterly* 29: 507–20.

Hajnal, Zoltan L., and Mark Baldassare. 2001. *Finding Common Ground: Racial and Ethnic Attitudes in California.* San Francisco: Public Policy Institute of California.

Hajnal, Zoltan L., Elisabeth R. Gerber, and Hugh Louch. 2002. "Minorities and Direct Legislation: Evidence from California Ballot Proposition Elections." *Journal of Politics* 64 (1): 154–77.

Hajnal, Zoltan L., Paul G. Lewis, and Hugh Louch. 2002. *Municipal Elections in California: Turnout, Timing, and Competition.* San Francisco: Public Policy Institute of California.

Halley, Robert M., Alan C. Acock, and Thomas H. Greene. 1976. "Ethnicity and Social Class: Voting in the 1973 Los Angeles Municipal Elections." *Western Political Quarterly* 29: 520–30.

Hamilton, Charles V. 1977. "De-Racialization: Examination of a Political Strategy." *First World* 1 (2): 3–5.

Hamilton, D. L., ed. 1981. *Cognitive Processes in Stereotyping and Intergroup Behavior.* Hillsdale, NJ: Erlbaum.

Hampton, Gloria J., and Katherine Tate. 1996. Political Participation in Urban Elections: The SES Baseline Model Reexamined. Paper read at Midwest Political Science Association Annual Conference, Chicago.

Handley, Lisa, and Bernard Grofman. 1994. "The Impact of the Voting Rights Act on Minority Representation: Black Officeholding in Southern State Legislatures and Congressional Delegations." In *Quiet Revolution in the South: The Impact of the Voting Rights Act, 1965–1990,* edited by C. Davidson and B. Grofman. Princeton, NJ: Princeton University Press.

Handley, Lisa, Bernard Grofman, and Wayne Arden. 1997. "Electing Minority-Preferred Candidates to Legislative Office: The Relationship between Minority Percentages in Districts and the Election of Minority-Preferred Candidates." In *Race and Redistricting in the 1990s,* edited by B. Grofman. New York: Agathon Press.

Headley, Bernard D. 1985. "Black Political Empowerment and Urban Crime. *Phylon* 46 (3): 193–204.

Hedge, David M., James Button, and Mary Spear. 1992. Black Leadership in the 1990s: A View from the States. Paper read at American Political Science Association Annual Meeting, Chicago.

Henry, Charles P. 1987. "Racial Factors in the 1982 California Gubernatorial Campaign: Why Bradley Lost." In *The New Black Politics: The Search for Political Power*, edited by M. B. Preston, L. J. Henderson, and P. L. Puryear. New York: Longman.

Henry, Charles P. 1992. "Black Leadership and the Deracialization of Politics." *Crisis* 100 (5): 38–42.

Hero, Rodney E. 1992. *Latinos and the U.S. Political System: Two-Tiered Pluralism*. Philadelphia: Temple University Press.

Hero, Rodney. 1998. *Faces of Inequality: Social Diversity in American Politics*. New York: Oxford University Press.

Hero, Rodney E., and Kathleen M. Beatty. 1989. "The Election of Federico Pena as Mayor of Denver: Analysis and Implications." *Social Science Quarterly* 70 (2): 300–10.

Hero, Rodney E., and Caroline J. Tolbert. 1995. "Latinos and Substantive Representation in the U.S. House of Representatives: Direct, Indirect, or Non-Existent?" *American Journal of Political Science* 39 (August): 640–52.

Herring, Mary. 1990. "Legislative Responsiveness to Black Constituents in Three Deep South States." *Journal of Politics* 52 (3): 740–58.

Hicks, Jonathan P. 1993. "Disappointed Black Voters Could Damage Dinkins's Bid." *New York Times*, October 3: A1.

Highton, Benjamin. 2004. "White Voters and African American Candidates for Congress." *Political Behavior* 26 (1): 1–25.

Hobbs, Nate. 1995. "Apathy Rampant as Voters Go to the Polls." *Commercial Appeal*, September 11: 1A.

Hochschild, Jennifer. 1981. *What's Fair? American Beliefs about Distributive Justice*. Cambridge, MA: Harvard University Press.

Hochschild, Jennifer L., and Reuel Rogers. 1999. "Race Relations in a Diversifying Nation." In *New Directions: African Americans in a Diversifying Nation*, edited by J. Jackson. Washington, DC: National Policy Association.

Holbrook, Thomas, and James C. Garand. 1996. "Homo Economus? Economic Information and Economic Voting." *Political Research Quarterly* 49 (2) (June): 351–75.

Holli, Melvin G., and Paul M. Green. 1989. *Bashing Chicago Traditions, Harold Washington's Last Campaign*. Grand Rapids: William B. Eerdman's Publishing.

Holt, Thomas. 1979. "*Black Over White: Negro Political Leadership in South Carolina during Reconstruction*." Urbana, IL: University of Illinois.

Howell, Susan E., and William P. McLean. 2001. "Performance and Race in Evaluating Minority Mayors." *Public Opinion* Quarterly 65 (1) (Feb): 321–43.

Howell, Susan E., and Hugh L. Perry. 2004. "Black Mayors/White Mayors: Explaining Their Approval." *Public Opinion Quarterly* 68 (1) (Feb): 32–56.

Huckfeldt, Robert, and Carol Weitzel Kohfeld. 1989. *Race and the Decline of Class in American Politics*. Urbana, IL: University of Illinois Press.

Huddy, Leonie, and Nayda Terkildsen. 1993. "The Consequences of Gender Stereotypes for Women Candidates at Different Levels and Types of Office." *Political Research Quarterly* 46 (3) (Sept): 503–25.

Hurwitz, Jon, and Mark Peffley, eds. 1998. *Prejudice and Politics: Race and Politics in the United States*. New Haven: Yale University Press.

Hutchings, Vincent. 2003. *Public Opinion and Democratic Accountability: How Citizens Learn about Politics*. Princeton, NJ: Princeton University Press.

Ingwerson, Marshal. 1981. "L.A.'s Tom Bradley: A Nice Guy Who May Finish First." *Christian Science Monitor*, November 20: B1.

Iyengar, Shanto. 1990. "Shortcuts to Political Knowledge: The Role of Selective Attention and Accessibility." In *Information and Democratic Processes*, edited by J. A. Ferejohn and J. H. Kuklinski. Chicago: University of Illinois Press.

Jackman, Mary. 1977. "Prejudice, Tolerance and Attitudes Toward Ethnic Groups." *Social Science Research* 6: 145–69.

Jackman, Mary R., and Marie Crane. 1986. "'Some of My Best Friends Are Black . . .': Interracial Friendship and Whites' Racial Attitudes." *Public Opinion Quarterly* 50: 459–86.

Jackson, Byran O. 1990. "Black Political Power in the City of the Angels: An Analysis of Mayor Tom Bradley's Electoral Success." *National Political Science Review* 2: 169–75.

Jackson, Byran O., and Michael B. Preston. 1994. Race and Ethnicity in Los Angeles Politics. In *Big City Politics, Governance and Fiscal Constraints*, edited by G. E. Peterson. Washington, DC: The Urban Institute Press.

Jacobson, Gary C. 1980. *Money in Congressional Elections*. New Haven: Yale University Press.

Jacobson, Gary C., and Samuel Kernell. 1981. *Strategy and Choice in Congressional Elections*. New Haven: Yale University Press.

Jaynes, Gerald David, and Robin M. Williams, eds. 1989. *A Common Destiny: Blacks and American Society*. Washington, DC: National Academy Press.

JCPS (Joint Center for Political Studies). 1983–2005. *Black Elected Officials: A National Roster*. Washington, DC: Joint Center for Political Studies.

Jeffries, Judson. 1999. "U.S. Senator Edward W. Brooke and Governor L. Douglas Wilder Tell Political Scientists How Blacks Can Win High-Profile Statewide Officed." *PS* September: 583–6.

Jeffries, Vincent, and H. E. Ransford. 1972. "Ideology, Social Structure, and the Yorty-Bradley Mayoral Election." *Social Problems* 19: 358–72.

Joyce, Patrick. 1994. Minority Empowerment, Political Machines and City Jobs: The Dynamics of Black and Latino Public Employment in Chicago and New York City Paper read at American Political Science Association Annual Meeting, New York.

Karnig, Albert K., and Susan Welch. 1980. *Black Representation and Urban Policy*. Chicago: University of Chicago Press.

Kaufman, Karen. 1998. "Racial Conflict and Political Choice: A Study of Mayoral Voting Behavior in Los Angeles and New York." *Urban Affairs Review* 33 (May): 655–85.

Kaufman, Karen. 2004. *The Urban Voter: Group Conflict and Mayoral Voting in American Cities*. Ann Arbor: University of Michigan Press.

Keiser, Richard A. 1997. *Subordination or Empowerment? African-American Leadership and the Struggle for Urban Political Power.* New York: Oxford University Press.

Kendall, Peter. 1995. Chicago *Chicago Tribune.* November 23.

Kerr, Brinck, and Kenneth R. Mladenka. 1994. "Does Politics Matter? A Time-Series Analysis of Minority Employment Patterns." *American Journal of Political Science* 38 (4) (Nov): 918–43.

Key, V. O. 1949. *Southern Politics in State and Nation.* Knoxville, TN: University of Tennessee Press.

Kiewiet, Roderick D. 1983. *Macroecomics and Micropolitics: The Electoral Effects of Economic Issues.* Chicago: University of Chicago Press.

Kim, Claire Jean. 1999. "The Racial Triangulation of Asian Americans." *Politics and Society* 27 (1): 10–138.

Kinder, Donald R. 1986. "The Continuing American Dilemma: White Resistance to Racial Change 40 Years After Myrdal." *Journal of Social Issues* 42 (2): 151–71.

Kinder, Donald, and Tali Mendelberg. 1995. "Cracks in American Apartheid: The Political Impact of Prejudice Among Desegregated Whites." *Journal of Politics* 57 (2): 402–24.

Kinder, Donald R., and Lynn Sanders. 1996. *Divided by Color: Racial Politics and Democratic Ideals.* Chicago: University of Chicago Press.

Kinder, Donald R., and David O. Sears. 1981. "Prejudice and Politics: Symbolic Racism Versus Racial Threats to the Good Life." *Journal of Personality and Social Psychology* 40 (3): 414–31.

King, Gary. 1997. *A Solution to the Ecological Inference Problem.* Princeton, NJ: Princeton University Press.

King, Gary, and Andrew Gelman. 1991. "Systemic Consequences of Incumbency Advantage in US House Elections." *American Journal of Political Science* 35 (1): 110–38.

Kirschenman, Joleen, and Kathryn M. Neckerman. 1991. "'We'd Love to Hire Them, But . . .': The Meaning of Race for Employers." In *The Urban Underclass,* edited by Christopher Jencks and Paul E. Peterson. Washington, DC: The Brookings Institution Press.

Kleppner, Paul. 1985. *Chicago Divided: The Making of a Black Mayor.* DeKalb, IL: Northern Illinois University Press.

Klinkner, Philip A., and Roges M. Smith. 1999. *The Unsteady March: The Rise and Decline of Racial Equality in America.* Chicago: University of Chicago Press.

Kousser, J. Morgan. 1974. *The Shaping of Southern Politics: Suffrage Restriction and the Establishment of the One-Party South, 1880–1910.* New Haven: Yale University Press.

Kousser, J. Morgan. 1992. "The Voting Rights Act and the Two Reconstructions." In *Controversies in Minority Voting: The Voting Rights Act in Perspective,* edited by B. Grofman and C. Davidson. Washington, DC: The Brookings Institution.

Koven, Steven G., and Mack C. Shelley. 1989. "Public Policy Effects on Net Urban Migration." *Policy Studies Journal* 17 (4): 705–18.

Krasno, Jonathan S., and Donald Philip Green. 1988. "Preempting Quality Challengers in House Elections." *Journal of Politics* 50: 920–36.

Krebs, Timothy B. 1998. "The Determinants of Candidates' Vote Share and Advantages of Incumbency in City Council Elections." *American Journal of Political Science* 42 (July): 921–35.

Krosnick, Jon A. 1988. "The Role of Attitude Importance in Social Evaluation: A Study of Policy Preferences, Presidential Candidate Evaluations, and Voting Behavior." *Journal of Personality and Social Psychology* 55: 196–210.

Kuklinski, James H., Paul M. Sniderman, Kathleen Knight, Thomas Piazza, Philip E. Tetlock, Gordon R. Lawrence, and Barbara Mellers. 1997. "Racial Prejudice and Attitudes Toward Affirmative Action." *American Journal of Political Science* 41 (2) (Apr): 402–19.

Kunda, Ziva, and Kathryn C. Oleson. 1997. "When Exceptions Prove the Rule: How Extremity of Deviance Determines the Impact of Deviant Examples on Stereotypes." *Journal of Personality and Social Psychology* 72 (5): 965–79.

Lau, Richard R., and David P. Redlawsk. 1997. "Voting Correctly." *American Political Science Review* 91 (3) (Sept): 585–98.

Lee, Taeku. 2000. "Racial Attitudes and the Color Line(s) at the Close of the Twentieth Century." In *The State of Asian Pacific Americans: Race Relations*, edited by P. Ong. Los Angeles: LEAP.

Levine, Charles H. 1974. *Racial Conflict and the American Mayor*. Lexington, MA: Heath.

Levinson, Florence Hamlish. 1983. *Harold Washington: A Political Biography*. Chicago: Chicago Review Press.

Lewis, James H., D. Garth Taylor, and Paul Kleppner. 1997. *Metro Chicago Political Atlas 97–98*. Springfield: Institute for Public Affairs.

Lewis, William G. 1987. "Toward Representative Bureaucracy: An Assessment of Black Representation in Police Bureaucracies." *Public Administration Review* 49: 257–68.

Lewis-Beck, Michael S. 1988. *Economics and Elections: The Major Western Democracies*. Ann Arbor: University of Michigan Press.

Lieske, Joel. 1989. "The Political Dynamics of Urban Voting Behavior." *American Journal of Political Science* 33: 150–74.

Lieske, Joel, and Jan William Hillard. 1984. "The Racial Factor in Urban Elections." *Western Political Quarterly* 37: 545–63.

Litwin, Susan. 1981. "Inside Tom Bradley: The Making of a Mayor, 1981, and of a Governor, 1982." *New West* 6 (2): 85–9.

Loewen, James. 1990. "Racial Bloc Voting and Political Mobilization in South Carolina." *Review of Black Political Economy* 19: 23–37.

Loewen, James, and Bernard Grofman. 1989. "Recent Developments in Methods Used in Voting Rights Litigation." *Urban Lawyer* 4: 589–604.

Logan, John, and John Mollenkopf. 2003. *People and Politics in America's Big Cities. The Challenges to Urban Democracy*. New York: Drum Major Institute.

Long, L. 1988. *Migration and Residential Mobility in the United States*: Russel Sage Foundation.

Longshore, Douglas. 1988. Racial Control and Intergroup Hostility: A Comparative Analysis. *Research in Race and Ethnic Relations* 5: 47–73.

Los Angeles Times. 1977. "Cheere for Bradley – and the Voters." *Los Angeles Times*, April 7: 2:6.

Los Angeles Times. 1981 "The Good and the Bad." *Los Angeles Times*, April 16: E6.

Los Angeles Times. 1989. "The Poor Get Poorer." *Los Angeles Times*, 21 June: 2: 6.

Los Angeles Times. 1992. "After the Riots: Rebuilding the Community: South Los Angeles's Poverty Rate Worse Than 65." *Los Angeles Times*, August 11: A1.

Lublin, David. 1997. *The Paradox of Representation: Racial Gerrymandering and Minority Interests*. Princeton, NJ: Princeton University Press.

Lublin, David Ian, and Katherine Tate. 1995. "Racial Group Competition in Urban Elections." In *Classifying By Race*, edited by P. E. Peterson. Princeton, NJ: Princeton University Press.

Lupia, Arthur. 1994. "Shortcuts Versus Encyclopedias: Information and Voting Behavior in California Insurance Reform Elections." *American Political Science Review* 88 (1): 63–76.

Lupia, Arthur, and Matthew D. McCubbins. 1998. *The Democratic Dilemma: Can Citizens Learn What They Need To Know?* Cambridge: Cambridge University Press.

MacKuen, Michael B., Robert S. Erikson, and James A. Stimson. 1992. "Peasants or Bankers? The American Electorate and the U.S. Economy." *American Political Science Review* 865: 597–611.

MacManus, Susan A., and Charles S. Bullock. 1993. "Women and Racial/Ethnic Minorities in Mayoral and Council Positions." In *The Municipal Year Book*, edited by I. C. M. Association. Washington, DC: International City Management Association.

Macrae, C. Neil, Miles Hewstone, and Riana G. Griffith. 1993. "Processing Load and Memory for Stereotype-Based Information." *European Journal of Social Psychology* 23 (1): 77–87.

Mansbridge, Jane. 1999. "Should Blacks Represent Blacks and Women Represent Women? A Provisional Yes." *Journal of Politics* 61 (3) (Aug): 628–57.

Marable, Manning. 1992. *The Crisis of Color and Democracy*. Monroe, ME: Common Courage Press.

Massey, Douglas S. 2001. "Residential Segregation and Neighborhood Conditions in U.S. Metropolitan Areas." In *America Becoming: Racial Trends and Their Consequences*, edited by N. Smelser, W. J. Wilson, and F. Mitchell. Washington, DC: National Academy Press.

Massey, Douglas S., and Nancy A. Denton. 1993. *American Apartheid: Segregation and the Making of the Underclass*. Cambridge, MA: Harvard University Press.

Matthews, Donald R., and James W. Prothro. 1963. "Social and Economic Factors in Negro Voter Registration in the South." *American Political Science Review* 57: 24–44.

Maullin, Richard L. 1971. "Los Angeles Liberalism." *Trans-Action* 8 (7): 40–51.

Mayer, Jeremy D. 1996. White Independents, Partisan Defectors, and Black Population Levels: Evidence of White Strategic Voting in the 1988 and 1992

Presidential Elections. Paper read at Midwest Political Science Association Annual Conference, Chicago.

McConahay, John B., Betty B. Hardee, and Valerie Batts. 1981. "Has Racism Declined in America? It Depends on Who Is Asking and What Is Asked." *Journal of Conflict Resolution* 25 (4): 563–79.

McCrary, Peyton. 1990. "Racially Polarized Voting in the South: Quantitative Evidence from the Courtroom." *Social Science History* 14 (4): 507–31.

McDermott, Monika. 1997. "Voting Cues in Low-Information Elections: Candidate Gender as a Social Information Variable in Contemporary United States Elections." *American Journal of Political Science* 41: 270–83.

McHugh, Kevin E. 1985. "Reasons for Migrating or Not." *Sociology and Social Research* 69(4): 585–89.

Mendelberg, Tali. 2001. *The Race Card: Campaign Strategy, Implicit Messages, and the Norm of Equality.* Princeton, NJ: Princeton University Press.

Milbank, Dana. 1993. "Cleveland's Mayors Shuns Black Themes to Court White Votes." *Wall Street Journal,* October 11: A1, A6.

Miller, Alton. 1989. "Harold Washington: In Charge, But Not in Control." *Newsday,* August 18: 74.

Miller, Warren E., and National Election Studies. 1994. *American National Election Studies Cumulative Data File, 1948–2000.* Ann Arbor, MI: University of Michigan, Center for Political Studies.

Minzesheimer, Bob. 1995. *For Black Voters in Gary, IN., 'Getting Results' Is What Counts* (Final Edition) [internet data base – Lexis Nexis]. *USA Today,* 1995 Cited Thursday, November 9.

Mladenka, Kenneth R. 1989. "Barriers to Hispanic Employment Success in 1200 Cities." *Social Science Quarterly* 70 (2): 391–407.

Mladenka, Kenneth R. 1991. "Public Employee Unions, Reformism, and Black Employment in 1,200 American Cities." *Urban Affairs Quarterly* 26 (4): 523–48.

Mollenkopf, John. 1986. "New York: The Great Anomaly." *PS* 19 (3) (Summer): 591–97.

Morganthau, Tom. 1983. "Chicago's Ugly Election." *Newsweek* 101 (15): 18–21.

Munoz, Carlos. 1994. "Mexican Americans and the Promise of Democracy: San Antonio Mayoral Elections." In *Big City Politics, Governance, and Fiscal Constraints,* edited by G. E. Peterson. Urbana, IL: University of Illinois.

Munoz, Carlos, and Charles Henry. 1997. "Coalition Politics in San Antonio and Denver: The Cisneros and Pena Mayoral Campaigns." In *Racial Politics in American Cities,* edited by R. P. Browning, D. R. Marshall and D. H. Tabb. New York: Longman.

Murray, Richard, and Arnold Vedlitz. 1978. "Racial Voting Patterns in the South: An Analysis of Major Elections from 1960 to 1977." *Annals of the American Academy of Political Scientists* 439: 29–39.

Mydans, Seth. 1993. "In Rough World of American Politics Asian-Americans Stand Out as Rare." *New York Times,* June 3: A16.

Nadeau, Richard, and Michael S. Lewis-Beck. 2001. "National Economic Voting in U.S. Presidential Elections." *Journal of Politics* 63 (1) (Feb): 159–81.

NALEO (National Association of Latino Elected Officials). 1990–2005. *National Directory of Latino Elected Officials*. Los Angeles: National Association of Latino Elected Officials.

Neal, Steve. 1986. "Mayor's Poll Lead Puts Byrne to Test." *Chicago Tribune*, December 23: A1.

Nelson, William E., and Philip J. Meranto. 1977. *Electing Black Mayors*. Columbus, OH: Ohio State University Press.

Newton, Jim. 1998. "Ethnic Politics Shape Debate Over Council Size." *Los Angeles Times*, August 24: A1.

New York Times. 1973. "Cubans' Vote Felt in Miami Election." *New York Times*, November 18: 47.

New York Times. 1983a. "Party Versus Race in Chicago." *New York Times*, April 6: A22.

New York Times. 1983b. "San Antonio Mayor Re-elected." *New York Times*, April 3: 23.

Nichols, Bill. 1990. "The New Mainstream, Black Politicians Stress Character, Not Color." *USA Today*, April 4: 1A.

Niemi, Richard G., and Herbert F. Weisberg. 1993. *Controversies in Voting Behavior*. Washington, DC: Congressional Quarterly Press.

Oden, Roger K. 1996. "The Election of Carol Moseley-Braun in the US Senate Race in Illinois." In *Race, Politics, and Governance in the United States*, edited by H. L. Perry. Gainesville, FL: University of Florida Press.

Oliver, Melvin L., James H. Johnson, and Walter C. Farrel. 1993. "Anatomy of a Rebellion: A Political-Economic Analysis." In *Reading Rodney King, Reading Urban Uprising*, edited by R. Gooding-Williams. New York: Routledge.

O'Loughlin, John. 1979. "Black Representation Growth and the Seat-Vote Relationship." *Social Science Quarterly* 60 (1): 72–86.

Olzak, Susan. 1990. "The Political Context of Competition: Lynching and Urban Racial Violence, 1882–1914." *Social Forces* 69: 395–422.

Olzak, Susan. 1992. *The Dynamics of Ethnic Competition and Conflict*. Stanford: Stanford University Press.

Omi, Michael, and Howard Winant. 1994. *Racial Formation in the United States*. New York: Routledge.

Ong, Paul, and Evelyn Blumenberg. 1996. "Income and Racial Inequality in Los Angeles." In *The City: Los Angeles and Urban Theory at the End of the Twentieth Century*, edited by A. J. Scott and E. W. Sojo. Berkeley: University of California Press.

Oreskes, Michael. 1981. "Frustrated by Slow Renewal, Newark Looks for Hope." *New York Times*, October 31: 29.

Paegel, Tom. 1973. "Bradley Denounces Newton's Backing, Hints at Yorty Trick." *Los Angeles Times*, May 21: A3.

Page, Benjamin I., and Robert Y. Shapiro. 1992. *The Rational Public: Fifty Years of Trends in American's Policy Preferences*. Chicago: University of Chicago.

Parent, Wayne, and Wesley Shrum. 1986. "Critical Electoral Success and Black Voter Registration: An Elaboration of the Voter Consent Model." *Social Science Quarterly* 67: 695–703.

Parker, Frank R. 1990. *Black Votes Count: Political Empowerment in Mississippi after 1965*. Chapel Hill: University of North Carolina Press.

Patterson, Orlando. 1997. *The Ordeal of Immigration: Progress and Resentment in America's Racial Crisis*. New York: Civitas.

Payne, Gregory J., and Scott C. Ratzan. 1986a. "The *Los Angeles Times* and Tom Bradley: Did the *Times'* Coverage Cost Bradley the 1982 Election?" *California Journal* 17 (June): 301–3.

Payne, Gregory J., and Scott C. Ratzan. 1986b. *Tom Bradley: The Impossible Dream*. Santa Monica: Roundtable Press.

Peffley, Mark, Jon Hurwitz, and Paul M. Sniderman. 1997. "Racial Stereotypes and Whites' Political Views of Blacks in the Context of Welfare and Crime." *American Journal of Political Science* 41 (1): 30–60.

Perry, Huey L. 1990. "Black Political and Mayoral Leadership in Birmingham and New Orleans." *National Political Science Review* 2: 154–60.

Perry, Huey L. 1991. "Deracialization as an Analytical Construct in American Urban Politics." *Urban Affairs Quarterly* 27 (2): 181–91.

Perry, Huey L., ed. 1996. *Race, Politics and Governance in the United States*. Gainesville, FL: University Press of Florida.

Persons, Georgia A. 1993. "Black Mayoralties and the New Black Politics." In *Dilemmas of Black Politics: Issues of Leadership and Strategy*, edited by G. A. Persons. New York: Harper Collins.

Peterson, Bill. 1983a. "Issue of Race Differs in Two Cities' Elections." *Washington Post*, March 29: A1.

Peterson, Bill. 1983b. "Whites Object Is to Save Status Quo." *Washington Post*, April 10: A1.

Peterson, George E. 1994. "Introduction." In *Big City Politics, Governance, and Fiscal Constraints*, edited by G. E. Peterson. Urbana, IL: University of Illinois.

Peterson, Paul E. 1981. *City Limits*. Chicago: University of Chicago Press.

Pettigrew, T., and E. Q. Campbell. 1960. "Faubus and Segregation." *Public Opinion Quarterly* 24: 436–47.

Pettigrew, Thomas F. 1972. "When a Black Candidate Runs for Mayor: Race and Voting Behavior." In *People and Politics in Urban Society*, edited by H. Hahn. Beverly Hills: Sage.

Pettigrew, Thomas F. 1976. "Black Mayoral Campaigns." In *Urban Governance and Minorities*, edited by H. J. Bryce. New York: Praeger.

Pettigrew, Thomas F. 1988. *Tom Bradley's Campaigns for Governor: The Dilemma of Race and Political Strategies*. Washington, DC: Joint Center for Political Studies.

Pierce, Emily. 2000. "Locke Has Key to Victory in Washington State." *Washington Post*, November 8.

Pinderhughes, Diane. 1994. "Racial and Ethnic Politics in Chicago Mayoral Elections." In *Big City Politics, Governance, and Fiscal Constraints*, edited by G. E. Peterson. Urbana, IL: University of Illinois.

Piven, Frances Fox, and Richard A. Cloward. 1977. *Poor People's Movements: Why They Succeed, How They Fail*. New York: Pantheon Books.

Piven, Frances Fox, and Richard A. Cloward. 1997. The Breaking of the American Social Compact. New York: New Press.

Pohlman, Marcus D., and Michael P. Kirby. 1996. *Racial Politics at the Cross-roads: Memphis Dr. W. W. Herenton.* Knoxville: University of Tennessee Press.

Popkin, Samuel L. 1991. *The Reasoning Voter.* Chicago: University of Chicago Press.

Popkin, Samuel L. 1995. "Information Shortcuts and the Reasoning Voter." In *Information, Participation and Choice: An Economic Theory of Democracy in Perspective*, edited by B. Grofman. Ann Arbor: University of Michigan Press.

Rahn, Wendy M. 1993. "The Role of Partisan Stereotypes in Information Processing about Political Candidates." *American Journal of Political Science* 37 (2): 472–96.

Rahn, Wendy M., John H. Aldrich, Eugene Borgida, and John L. Sullivan. 1990. "A Social-Cognitive Model of Candidate Appraisal." In *Information and Democratic Processes*, edited by J. A. Ferejohn and J. H. Kuklinski. Chicago: University of Illinois Press.

Raines, Howell. 1979. "Abstracts." *New York Times*, October 30: A16.

Ratnesar, Romesh. 1998. "A Place at the Table: Asian American Politicians Come of Age." *Time Magazine*.

Reed, Adolph. 1988. "The Black Urban Regime: Structural Origins and Constraints." In *Power, Community, and the City*, edited by M. P. Smith. New Brunswick: Transaction Press.

Reed, Adolph. 1989. "Atlanta Maynard Jackson: The Deal That Barely Stuck." *Newsday*, August 14: 44.

Reeves, Keith. 1997. *Voting Hopes or Fears? White Voters, Black Candidates, and Racial Politics in America.* New York: Oxford University Press.

Regalado, James A. 1991. "Organized Labor and Los Angeles City Politics." *Urban Affairs Quarterly* 27 (1): 87–108.

Regalado, James A. 1992. "Political Representation, Economic Development, Policymaking, and Social Crisis in Los Angeles, 1973–1992." In *City of Angels*, edited by G. Riposa and C. G. Dersch. Dubuque: Kendall/Hunt Publishing.

Reich, Kenneth. 1973a. "Bradley Leads Yorty, Survey Finds." *Los Angeles Times*, May 1: A3.

Reich, Kenneth. 1973b. "Survey in Key Precincts Shows Bradley Picking Up Strength." *Los Angeles Times*, May 28: A1.

Reich, Kenneth. 1977a. "Bradley Solid Favorite, But Foes Still Hope for Runoff." *Los Angeles Times*, April 3: 1:1.

Reich, Kenneth. 1977b. "Race Banished as Vote Issue, Bradley Says." *Los Angeles Times*, April 6: 1:1.

Rich, Wilbur C. 1987. "Coleman Young and Detroit Politics: 1973–1986." In *The New Black Politics: The Search for Political Power*, edited by M. B. Preston, L. J. Henderson, and P. L. Puryear. New York: Longman.

Rieder, Jonathan. 1985. *Canarsie: The Jews and Italians of Brooklyn against Liberalism.* Cambridge, MA: Harvard University Press.

Rivlin, Gary. 1992. *Fire on the Prairie: Chicago's Harold Washington and the Politics of Race.* New York: Henry Holt and Company.

Robinson, James Lee. 1976. Tom Bradley: Los Angeles's First Black Mayor. Ph.D. Dissertation, UCLA, Los Angeles.

Rosales, Rodolfo. 2000. *The Illusion of Inclusion: The Untold Political Story of San Antonio*. Austin: University of Texas Press.

Rothbart, Myron, and Oliver P. John. 1993. "Intergroup Relations and Stereotype Change: A Social-Cognitive Analysis and Some Longitudinal Findings." In *Prejudice, Politics, and the American Dilemma*, edited by P. M. Sniderman, P. E. Tetlock and E. G. Carmines. Stanford: Stanford University Press.

Russakoff, Dale. 1983. "Birmingham Reelects Black: Once-Split City Unites at Polls." *Washington Post*, October 13: A1.

Sack, Kevin. 1996. "Victory of 5 Redistricted Blacks Recasts Gerrymandering Dispute." *New York Times*, November 23: A1.

Saito, Leland. 1998. *Race and Politics: Asian Americans, Latinos, and Whites in a Los Angeles Suburb*. Urbana, IL: University of Illinois Press.

Saltzstein, Alan L. 1986. "Federal Grants and the City of Los Angeles." *Research in Urban Policy* 2 (A): 55–76.

Samuel, Terence. 1999. "In Two Big City Mayoral Contests, Racial Lines May Be Blurring." *St. Louis Post-Dispatch*, October 17: A12.

Scarberry, Nikki C., Christopher D. Ratcliff, and Charles G. Lord. 1997. "Effects of Individuation Information on the Generalization Part of Allport's Contact Hypothesis." *Personality and Social Psychology Bulletin* 23 (12): 1291–9.

Scheibal, Stephen. 2003. "Garcia Reflects on His Years in Politics." *Austin-American Statesman*, June 15.

Schmidt, William E. 1983. "Denver Election Widens Circle of Hispanic Leaders." *New York Times*, June 23: A16.

Schuman, Howard, Charlotte Steeh, Lawrence Bobo, and Maria Krysan. 1997. *Racial Attitudes in America: Trends and Interpretations*. Revised Edition. Cambridge, MA: Harvard University Press.

Schwada, John. 1989. "The Persistence of Tom Bradley: Despite LA's Woes, Mayor Tom Is About to Win His Fifth Term." *California Journal* 20 (3): 99–102.

Scott, Austin. 1977. "Black Mayors in Atlanta, Detroit Expand Re-election Support. *Washington Post*, October 4: A1.

Sears, David O., and Donald R. Kinder. 1971. "Racial Tensions and Voting in Los Angeles." In *Los Angeles: Viability and Prospects for Metropolitan Leadership*, edited by W. Z. Hirsch. New York: Praeger.

Secter, Bob. 1987. "Segregated City Inflamed: Chicago Election Hinges on Race, Desire for Spoils." *Los Angeles Times*, February 18.

Seidenbaum, Art. 1973. "Side Order of Election." *Los Angeles Times*, May 31: 3:1.

Shaw, M. E. 1973. "Changes in Sociometric Choice Following Forced Integration of an Elementary School." *Journal of Social Issues* 29: 143–57.

Sheffield, James F. Jr., and Charles D. Hadley. 1984. "Racial Voting in a Biracial City: A Reexamination of Some Hypotheses." *American Politics Quarterly* 12 (4): 449–64.

Shields, Gerard, and Ivan Penn. 1999. "O'Malley Tone Set Stage for Crossover." *Baltimore Sun*, 1A.

Shiesl, Martin J. 1990. "Behind the Badge: The Police and Social Discontent in Los Angeles Since 1950." In *20th Century Los Angeles: Power, Promotion, and*

Social Conflict, edited by N. M. Klein and M. J. Schiesl. Claremont: Regina Book.

Sidanius, Jim, Erik Devereux, and Felicia Pratto. 1991. "A Comparison of Symbolic Racism Theory and Social Dominance Theory as Explanations for Racial Policy Attitudes." *Journal of Social Psychology* 132 (3): 377–95.

Sidanius, Jim, Yesilernis Pena, and Mark Sawyer. 2001. "Inclusionary Discrimination: Pigmentocracy and Patriotism in the Dominican Republic." *Political Psychology* 22 (4): 827–50.

Sigelman, Carol K., Lee Sigelman, Barbara J. Walkosz, and Michael Nitz. 1995. "Black Candidates, White Voters: Understanding Racial Bias in Political Perceptions." *American Journal of Political Science* 39 (1): 243–65.

Sigelman, Lee, and Susan Welch. 1993. "The Contact Hypothesis Revisited: Interracial Contact and Positive Racial Attitudes." *Social Forces* 71: 781–95.

Simon, Herbert A. 1945. *Administrative Behavior: A Study of Decision-Making Processes in Administrative Organizations*. New York: Free Press.

Singh, Robert. 1998. *The Congressional Black Caucus: Racial Politics in the U.S. Congress*. Thousand Oaks, CA: Sage Publications.

Sleeper, Jim. 1993. "The End of the Rainbow: America's Changing Urban Politics." *New Republic* 209 (18): 20.

Smith, Robert C. 1996. *We Have No Leaders: African Americans in the Post-Civil Rights Era*. Albany: University of New York Press.

Sniderman, Paul M., and Edward G. Carmines. 1997. *Reaching Beyond Race*. Cambridge, MA: Harvard University Press.

Sniderman, Paul M., and Thomas Piazza. 1993. *The Scar of Race*. London: Belknap Press.

Sniderman, Paul M., Carol M. Swain, and Laurel Elms. 1995. The Dynamics of a Senate Campaign: Incumbency, Ideology, and Race. Paper read at American Political Science Association Annual Meeting, Chicago.

Sonenshein, Raphael J. 1989. "The Los Angeles Brand of Biracial Coalition Politics." *Los Angeles Times*, April 16: 5:4.

Sonenshein, Raphael J. 1990. "Biracial Coalition Politics in Los Angeles." In *Racial Politics in American Cities*, edited by R. P. Browning, Dale Rogers Marshall, and David H. Tabb. New York: Longman.

Sonenshein, Raphael J. 1993. *Politics in Black and White: Race and Power in Los Angeles*. Princeton, NJ: Princeton University Press.

South, Scott J., and Glenn D. Deanne. 1993. "Race and Residential Mobility: Individual Determinants and Structural Constraints." *Social Forces* 72 (1): 147–67.

Span, Paula. 1983. "Newark's Failing Dream." *New York Times*, October 2: 55.

Stahura, John M. 1988. "Black and White Population Change in Small American Suburbs Since World War II: Regional Differences." *Sociological Focus* 21 (4): 317–29.

Stanley, Harold W., and Richard G. Niemi. 1992. *Vital Statistics on American Politics*. 3rd Edition. Washington, DC: CQ Press.

Starks, Robert T. 1991. "A Commentary and Response to Exploring the Meaning and Implication of Deracialization in African-American Urban Politics." *Urban Affairs Quarterly* 27 (2): 216–22.

Stein, Lana, and Arnold Fleischmann. 1987. "Newspaper and Business Endorsements in Municipal Elections: A Test of the Conventional Wisdom." *Journal of Urban Affairs* 9 (4): 325–36.

Stein, Lana, and Carol W. Kohfeld. 1991. "St. Louis's Black-White Elections: Products of Machine Factionalism and Polarization." *Urban Affairs Quarterly* 27 (2): 227–48.

Stein, Robert. M., Stacy G. Ulbig, and Stephanie S. Post. 2005. "Voting for Minority Candidates in Multi-Racial/Ethnic Communities." *Urban Affairs Review* 41 (2) (Nov): 157–81.

Stenner, Karen. 1995. Threat, Authoritarianism and Racial Violence in America, 1960–1989. Paper read at Midwest Political Science Association Annual Conference, Chicago.

Stevens, William K. 1981. "Mayor-Elect of San Antonio Hails Vote as a Victory over the 'Ethnic Factor'." *New York Times*, April 6: A12.

Stokes, Carl B. 1993. "Racial Equality and Appreciation of Diversity in Our Urban Communities: How Far Have We Come?" *Vital Speeches* 59 (12): 357.

Stone, Clarence N. 1997. "Race and Regime in Atlanta." In *Racial Politics in American Cities*, edited by R. P. Browning, D. R. Marshall, and D. H. Tabb. New York: Longman.

Stuart, Reginald. 1983a. "Charges of Racism Mark Miami Runoff Campaign." *New York Times*, November 15: A29.

Stuart, Reginald.1983b. "Mayor's Re-election in Miami Linked to Solid Black Support." *New York Times*, November 17: B11.

Sullivan, Joseph F. 1974. "Contrast Marks Vote in 2 Cities." *New York Times*, 61.

Sun Reporter. 1993. "Black Mayors on the Rise." *Sun Reporter* 56 (38): 1.

Suro, Roberto. 1991. "When Minorities Start Becoming Majorities." *New York Times*, June 23: E5.

Swain, Carol M. 1995. *Black Face, Black Interests: The Representation of African Americans in Congress*. Cambridge, MA: Harvard University Press.

Sylvie, George. 1995. "Black Mayoral Candidates and the Press: Running for Coverage." *Howard Journal of Communications* 6 (1): 89–101.

Tajfel, Henri. 1981. *Human Groups and Social Categories: Studies in Social Psychology*. Cambridge: Cambridge University Press.

Tam, Wendy K. 1995. "Asians – A Monolithic Voting Bloc?" *Political Behavior* 17 (2): 223–49.

Tate, Katherine. 2003. *Black Faces in the Mirror: African Americans and Their Representatives in the U.S. Congress*. Princeton, NJ: Princeton University Press.

Taylor, Marylee C. 1998. "How White Attitudes Vary with the Racial Composition of Local Populations: Numbers Count." *American Sociological Review* 63 (August): 512–35.

Taylor, Paul. 1987. "Don't Fight Em, Hug Em." *Washington Post*, December 20: A2.

Terkildsen, Nayda. 1993. "When White Voters Evaluate Black Candidates: The Processing Implications of Candidate Skin Color, Prejudice, and Self-Monitoring." *American Journal of Political Science* 37 (4): 1032–53.

Texeira, Erin. 1999. "Color Fades from Race for Mayor: Voters, Endorsements Cross Racial Lines in Search of City's Savior." *Baltimore Sun*, September 3: 1A.

Thernstrom, Abigail. 1987. *Whose Votes Count? Affirmative Action and Minority Voting Rights.* Cambridge, MA: Harvard University Press.

Thernstrom, Abigail. 1995. "Racial Gerrymanders Come Before the Court." *Wall Street Journal,* April 12: A15.

Thernstrom, Stephan, and Abigail Thernstrom. 1997. *America in Black and White: One Nation, Indivisible.* New York: Simon and Schuster.

Tufte, Edward R. 1978. *Political Control of the Economy.* Princeton, NJ: Princeton University Press.

Tversky, Amos, and Daniel Kahneman. 1974. "Judgement Under Uncertainty: Heuristics and Biases." *Science* 185: 1124–31.

Tyson, James L. 1995. "Gary Voters Refuse to Play Race Card in City Election." *Christian Science Monitor,* November 6.

Uhlaner, Carole Jean. 2000. "Political Activity and Preferences of African Americans, Latinos, and Asian Americans." In *Immigration and Race: New Challenges for American Democracy,* edited by J. Jaynes. New Haven: Yale University Press.

US News & World Report. 1975. "Is a Black Mayor the Solution? Here's How Six Have Fared." *US News & World Report,* April 7: 34.

Vanderleeuw, James M. 1991. "The Influence of Racial Transition on Incumbency Advantage in Local Elections." *Urban Affairs Quarterly* 27 (1): 36–50.

Verba, Sidney, Kay Lehman Schlozman, and Henry E. Brady. 1995. *Voice and Equality: Civic Voluntarism in American Politics.* Cambridge, MA: Harvard University Press.

Vickers, Robert J. 1997. "Race Now Seems Less of an Issue for Voters in Cleveland." *The Plain Dealer,* October 3: A1.

Voss, D. Stephen, and David Lublin. 2001. "Black Incumbents, White Districts: An Appraisal of the 1996 Congressional Elections." *American Politics Research* 29 (2) (March): 141–82.

Warren, Christopher L., John G. Corbett, and Jr. John F. Stack. 1997. "Hispanic Ascendancy and Tripartite Politics in Miami." In *Racial Politics in American Cities,* edited by R. P. Browning, D. R. Marshall, and D. H. Tabb. New York: Longman.

Washington Post. 1983. The Result in Chicago. *Washington Post,* A22.

Watson, S. M. 1984. "The Second Time Around: A Profile of Black Mayoral Election Campaigns." *Phylon* 45: 165–75.

Weber, Renee, and Jennifer Crocker. 1983. "Cognitive Processes in the Revision of Stereotypic Beliefs." *Journal of Personality and Social Psychology* 45 (5): 961–77.

Welch, Susan, Lee Sigelman, Timothy Bledsoe, and Michael Combs. 2001. *Race and Place: Race Relations in an American City.* Cambridge: Cambridge University Press.

Whitby, Kenny J. 1998. *The Color of Representation: Congressional Behavior and Black Constituents.* Ann Arbor: University of Michigan Press.

Wievel, Tim. 1989. "The Limits of Progressive Municipal Economic Development: Job Creation in Chicago, 1983–1987." *Community Development Journal* 24 (2): 111–19.

Wilder, David A., Andrew F. Simon, and Myles Faith. 1996. "Enhancing the Impact of Counterstereotypic Information: Dispositional Attributes for Deviance." *Journal of Personality and Social Psychology* 71 (2): 276–87.

Wildstrom, Stephen H. 1998. "After the Victory Party, Frustration in the Black Community." *Business Week* 3140 (January 8): 49.

Williams, Linda F. 1990. "White/Black Perceptions of the Electability of Black Political Candidates." *National Black Political Science Review* 2: 45–64.

Wilson, Zaphon. 1993. "Gantt Versus Helms." *In Dilemmas of Black Politics: Issues of Leadership and Strategy*, edited by G. A. Persons. New York: Harper Collins.

Wolman, Harold, Edward Page, and Martha Reavely. 1990. "Mayors and Mayoral Careers." *Urban Affairs Quarterly* 25 (3): 500–15.

Wolman, Harold, John Strate, and Alan Melchior. 1996. "Does Changing Mayors Matter?" *Journal of Politics* 58 (1): 201–23.

Wright, Sharon D. 1996. "The Deracialization Strategy and African American Mayoral Candidates in Memphis Mayoral Elections." In *Race, Politics, and Governance in the United States*, edited by H. L. Perry. Gainesville, FL: University of Florida Press.

Wright, Sharon D. 2000. *Race, Power, and Political Emergence in Memphis*. New York: Garland Series.

Index